THE RAINBOW WAY

We're dedicated to our kids, but can't afford to lose ourselves in the chaos of motherhood. So how do we do it?

This book is the generous answer – and the most important survival guide creative mothers will ever read.

Ariel Gore, founding editor of Hip Mama, author of seven books including *The Mother Trip: Hip Mama's Guide to Staying Sane in the Chaos of Motherhood.*

The Rainbow Way is much more than a practical guide for mothers to stay creative, it is a spiritual and personal journey to understand the essence of one's true self.

It inspired me greatly and I know it will inspire so many others. The best gift of all from this rainbow of ideas is that our creative force as mothers will not only help us grow but it will help our children grow into creative, caring and compassionate human beings.

Mary Trunk, filmmaker, director of *Lost in Living,* a documentary film about creative mothers.

If you're a creative mother, *The Rainbow Way* is the book you've longed for. In these pages, Lucy Pearce does what few others have done: She extends a hand – no, a bear hug – to the tribe of creative mothers who share the particular experience that Lucy articulates so beautifully. Readers will delve deep to uncover their own creative truths – and with those truths, a realm of new possibilities.

Miranda Hersey, writer, creativity coach and host of the blog Studio Mothers.

Lucy's book is a gift of beauty that feels like a waterfall of sweet nectar flowing upon the flower of our soul. With tender warmth, the author takes our hand and invites us on the magical journey of authentic self-expression. Walking beside us each step of the way, she encourages our unfolding dance of creativity with a rainbow of inspirations and ideas.

Guided by Lucy's vibrant support, each woman will traverse her unique path of creative self-discovery... a path that leads us to the exquisitely fulfilling experience of inner communion and outer expression.

Mara Berendt Friedman, celebrated artist of the sacred feminine.

The Rainbow Way: Cultivating Creativity in the Midst of Motherhood is destined to resonate with mothers of all ages. I especially value Lucy Pearce's description of the Rainbow Mother as a lost feminine archetype, one with her own distinct dark side, the Crazy Woman. Having these aspects of our experience as mothers given words makes them real and able to be understood and shared.

The world more than ever needs women who hold the strong vibration of a grounded creativity, one which we also pass to our children to fortify them as they meet the challenges of an accelerated planet. This book is a welcome companion for all mothers navigating the dual, intertwining and sometimes conflicting joys of motherhood and creativity in service to their families and to the world.

Pat B. Allen, author *Art is a Way of Knowing* and *Art is a Spiritual Path.*

Like a new best friend Lucy Pearce offers permission and support for mothers to embark on a creative soul journey. With passionate encouragement and heartfelt advice she dishes up a full gamut of women's wisdom.

As Lucy reminds us "the message of love or beauty or hope

needs to be said by a hundred thousand different voices, written by a hundred thousand different pens, at a hundred thousand different times in history". On each page, as she shares her own labor of love, she enthusiastically invites us all to cultivate our creative expression...in the midst of motherhood.

Jenafer Joy, director of Cosmic Cowgirls LLC – every woman has a story to tell, a song to sing, and a legend to unfold!

The Rainbow Way

Cultivating Creativity
in the Midst of Motherhood

The Rainbow Way

Cultivating Creativity
in the Midst of Motherhood

Lucy H. Pearce

Winchester, UK
Washington, USA

First published by Soul Rocks Books, 2013
Soul Rocks Books is an imprint of John Hunt Publishing Ltd., Laurel House, Station Approach,
Alresford, Hants, SO24 9JH, UK
office1@jhpbooks.net
www.johnhuntpublishing.com
www.soulrocks-books.com

For distributor details and how to order please visit the 'Ordering' section on our website.

ISBN: 978 1 78279 028 0

A CIP catalogue record for this book is available from the British Library.

Design: Lee Nash

Printed and bound by CPI Group (UK) Ltd, Croydon, CR0 4YY

Disclaimer:

The contents of this book are offered as information only and do not
take the place of medical or psychiatric treatment.

We operate a distinctive and ethical publishing philosophy in all
areas of our business, from our global network of authors to
production and worldwide distribution.

CONTENTS

Other titles by Lucy H. Pearce

Moon Time: a guide to celebrating your menstrual cycle

Reaching for the Moon: a girl's guide to her female cycles

Moods of Motherhood

I wish I could speak like music
So that you could hold Truth
Against your body
And dance.
I am trying the best I can
With this crude brush, the tongue,
To cover you with light.
Hafiz

Dedicated to all the creative mothers around the world.
May you shine!

Foreword

I still remember the nights at 2am. Crying in front of the bathroom mirror, my eyes gray and dark from exhaustion, red rimmed from sobbing.

In the morning, when night broke and left, when light streamed through the windows, when yet another day started, I would search for answers. I had tomes of bibles. All the ways I should be parenting. All the hard, hard lessons I needed to know. There is no test greater than this.

How does one ever prepare for the momentous task of becoming a mother? The answer: one cannot. You only go there. And then you sink and swim, sink and swim. But oh, those tomes. Those bibles. I thought it would be easy. Easy if I did it this way.

Baby would sleep peacefully all day in a sling, and I could continue on with normal life. I could keep creating and sitting and living my magical dream-job life. And she'd sleep beside us of course – and that way I wouldn't have to get up all night. I'd barely wake up a bit, you see. And baby and mama would never ever be unhappy, you know…because we'd always be together. Seamless. Unbroken. One organism.

The truth of it is, it wasn't easy. There is nothing that makes the deep, difficult initiation into mamahood easy. It's not supposed to, really. It's the process that crafts you into a warrior, a bear, a courageous woman who creates and sustains new life.

But easy? Oh, no, not easy. Not for me.

Even as my beautiful young baby girl bloomed, even when I knew whole of heart that I was born to have her, I found myself hitting a mud-strewn wall.

I had lists and lists of who I was supposed to be:

A mother who never complained. A mother who never swore. A mother who never cried in front of her children. A mother who sacrificed herself completely for her family. A mother who was always happy. A mother who didn't find anything difficult. A mother who never took time for herself. A mother who never did those things that I truly adored in this world: to sit, and be still. To read. To create. To write. To paint.

It took a tornado of post-partum depression for me to realize that the image of the Perfect Mother wasn't the mother I could ever be. Wasn't the mother I ever even wanted to be.

So I began turning to beloved books to find the answer. It was in Lynn Andrews' and Christiane Northrup's words and stories of being Creative Rainbow Mothers that I found my self, my archetype, my soul's truth, my home.

The truth is, I will never be a perfect mother. I'll never have it all together.

But what I will do is be irrepressibly me. I will create every day. I will make my art. I will sing my song. I will write my words. I will continue to devote time to myself. I will birth the miracles inside me. I will express myself and my emotions. I will not sacrifice myself or my soul. I will not survive motherhood – I will thrive in it.

And my daughter will learn what it looks like for a woman to be in love with herself. To accept herself. To craft the life she needs in order to thrive. She will see it as normal that mothers have lives beyond mothering, have soul purposes that are bigger than just keeping their wee ones alive.

More and more, I am less convinced that one style of parenting will heal all the wrongs in the world. I am less convinced that The Other styles of parenting will result in adults who are irretrievably damaged. It's all just merging into a blur for me. All it truly means – parenting or religion or *anything else in life for that matter* – is **love**.

I know souls who were raised in a rainbow kaleidoscope of ways…and each of them have their own joys, gladness and lessons. Every single person on this planet can be happy, healed and dancing. However their bum was wrapped. However their heart was held. Whatever parenting books their parents read (or not).

My child will grow. I will love her. I will give her what I can. I will be the mama I am.

I will not give myself away in the battle. More importantly, I will not battle. I will open myself to the possibility that love is enough, that healing will part the way – for me, for her, for my love. That we aren't expected to have it all together every moment.

I used to be fixated on The Mother I Would Become. Now I'm choosing to cherish The Mother I Am.

And that's my fondest wish for you too – to accept that you are who you are. To embrace the healing and spiritual powers of creativity in your life. For you to craft a motherhood that sings to your soul.

That's why this book is so important. More than ever before, it is vital for mothers to reclaim their souls and their creativity so that we may mother from our wholeness. In doing so, we will change the destinies of our selves, our families and our world. *The Rainbow Way* is a beautiful guide to shift your mode of living from "Surviving" to "Thriving".

There are seven billion paths up the mountain to God, just as there are seven billion paths to mother.

Make it your own. May it delight you, uplift you, inspire you and give you just what you've been looking for.

Leonie Dawson, Australia
Author of *73 Lessons Every Goddess Must Know*
Business and life mentor, Australia.
www.leoniedawson.com

Acknowledgements

The birth of a book is a labor of love. It requires back rubs, midnight consolations, and reminders to breathe deep and push hard. So whilst this baby bears my name, I want you to meet the doulas, allies, midwives, and those who got me pregnant in the first place!

Tracy Evans, my soul-sister, who has been my chief creative doula on this project, without her it would not have found its final form. To her I owe a depth of gratitude far beyond words.

To Mary, Laura, Paula and Leigh for their feedback throughout the writing process. And Becky Jaine for naming the baby!

These women and so many more gave so generously of their time and insight in sharing their experiences of creative motherhood:

Erin Darcy, Francesca Prior, Isabel Healy, Jools Gilson, Tessa Rubbra, Elizabeth Palmer, Heather Stritzke, Hannah O'Hara, Laura Parrish, Monica, Michelle Millichip, Ola, Amy Vickers Evans, Lorian Beasley Rea, Amber Schmida Green, Karien Van Ditzhuijzen, Grainne McCloskey, the women of The Pebbles Project, Lisa Healy, Caitriona Redmond, Emily Rainsford Ryan, Joanna O'Sullivan, Jill Jordan, Aine Nic Ghabhann-O'Sullivan, Sylda Dwyer, Rachael and Seoinaid. As well as the many other women whose names do not appear, but whose lives have enriched this book through our conversations together.

To Dr Christiane Northrup for granting me permission to quote extensively from her life-changing book: *Women's Bodies, Women's Wisdom* which started this whole adventure.

To Lynn V. Andrews, for spreading the idea of the Creative Rainbow Mother through her books and teaching, and for giving of her time to share her knowledge further with me.

To Leonie Dawson for her wonderful foreword. Her

agreement to open the book is monumental for me, as her influence and spirit have been with me from the first planting of the idea-seed right through the creative process. She is a guiding creative-mama light to me and so many others.

To Pam England, Julie Daley, Indigo Bacal and Jennifer Louden for sharing their words – through interviews and written contributions. I cannot tell you how honored I am to have so many of my real life sheroes be part of this project.

Wendy Cook, Elizabeth Jennings, Marybeth Bonfiglio, Mary Trunk, Sally Reis and Lisa Dieken whose words washed my way on the waves of the world wide web, and who jumped so enthusiastically on board in letting me share them with you.

And other heroines whose work has left an indelible mark on my soul: Adrienne Rich, Julia Cameron, Louise Erdrich, Sylvia Plath, Shiloh Sophia McCloud, Flora Bowley, Meinrad Craighead, Pat Allen, Sue Monk Kidd and Ariel Gore.

To my father, Stephen Pearce, who was writing a book alongside me: his first, my third. Thank you to him and my mother for giving me a childhood bursting with creativity and freedom. And for cheering me every step of the way on this journey.

To my husband, Patrick, who believed in my work and my sanity enough to shift to part-time employment in the midst of a global economic meltdown, so I could have my precious two creative days a week. Thank you for never, ever doubting me.

And finally my three children, Timmy, Merrily and Aisling, without whom I would not be a mama, nor have gotten to dive so deeply into creativity once more. I love you more than you will ever know.

Introduction

All know the way. Few actually walk it.
Bodhidharma

Miracles start to happen when you put as much energy into your dreams as you do into your fears.
Richard Wilkins

Welcome, dearest woman.

If you are creative, and a mother, and are struggling to find balance, welcome home!

If you long to be creative but don't know where to start, let me be your guide.

If you experienced a creative renaissance during pregnancy and motherhood, this book is written for you.

If you feel that life could be richer and more vibrant, and can feel things bubbling inside but can't reach them, then I'm so glad you're here.

If you want to gain a deeper understanding of your unique, female, embodied creative process, then I might just be the woman for you!

This book is an attempt to put language to the reality of being the most fabulous, and misunderstood of creatures: a creative mother. One who answers the callings of her child – and also her creativity. A woman who says: *I cannot, I will not choose. I must mother. I must create.*

Motherhood multiplies all previous challenges to creativity ten-fold, whether you be a stay-at-home, work-at-home or work-out-of-the-home mama. Your life, especially in the "short years" of young children, is almost totally **not** your own. Trying to discover who you are now and fulfil your creative passions is high on the agenda for most mothers – but where is the time and the energy?

I longed and searched for something like this over my early mothering years. I needed a mentor, a guide to show me how to be my creative self **and** a mother without letting either suffer. But there was nothing out there: society it seems either does not see the problem, acknowledge it as important, or think it requires solutions.

But I know that there are a lot of us out there…women like you and me…

Trying to be stay-at-home mothers, and feeling like we're dying inside. Trying to be working women, and feeling like we're dying inside.

Women who are trying to find their way back into their unique creative groove, after the disorientation of early motherhood. After our lives have been turned upside down and inside out. After we have forgotten who we are and found another self.

If you are there now, dearest mama, you will find plenty of gentle guidance within these covers to support you. What I offer is a template. Not of how to be a perfect mother. Nor how to find perfect balance. Both are false holy grails on this journey of motherhood, promised by wishful thinkers and charlatans. I am here to show you a path which balances, as much as possible, your needs for creativity and mothering. Your children's needs for a good, loving, attentive caregiver. And perhaps your needs to make a living.

None of us gets it right all the time. The balance shifts back and forth. But what is important is that your needs, all of them, are in the equation, rather than, as has been so many women's experiences throughout history, ignored, shamed or undervalued.

This book is not about doing more stuff. Lord knows every mother in the world has more than enough to fill every hour of her day twice over. I have not achieved anything if you come away from it beating yourself up for not doing more, for not being good enough, or not being like any of the women in it.

But if you want to make time and space to reclaim yourself, then I am here to support you. After all, though we all have the same 24 hours in a day, we all have differing numbers of children, and children with different needs. We all have different responsibilities to other family members, work commitments, health issues and energy levels. These are an important part of the equation, which also includes how much childcare (paid or unpaid) you have.

After all that, then it's down to time optimization and understanding how the creative process, and you, work, to ensure you get the time you need and use it in the most efficient and rewarding way.

How do you do it?

You ask for a few words of comfort and guidance.
I quickly kneel at your side
Offering you this whole book – as a gift.
Hafiz

The idea for this book stemmed from one question. It is the question that so many women ask me, all the time:

How do you do it? How do you practically make the time for creativity when you have young children?

It isn't something that we are taught in school, nor as adults. We find ourselves as newborn mothers at the deep end with no instructions on how to float our families into the gentler shallows.

After eight years, three children, three books, four blogs, an art exhibition, creative businesses and years of teaching, I consider myself a reasonable expert on the matter, or rather, as expert as one can be at this precarious art of creative motherhood!

Behind the "how" question, which we will focus on in depth, there are more questions:

- Why do some mothers need to create, as a matter of almost life and death?
- What drives her?
- What does she get from creativity?
- What are her specific needs as a woman, as a mother, as a creative?
- How can we empower this sort of woman?
- How can she find support and learn to support herself?
- How has technology changed the playing field for her?
- What are the steps on the path which will transform her from lonely wanderer to fully fledged and fulfilled creative mother?

It is these questions and more that I could not find the answer to myself, as a new mother. It is these questions to which *The Rainbow Way* is my answer, for you.

In the process of writing this book I spoke to painters, potters, doll makers, dancers, illustrators, lots of writers and poets, actors and directors, quilt and jewelry makers, photographers and crafters.

- Mothers of one child and five.
- Women whose children were now grown and mothers still birthing their babies.
- Mothers whose creativity was their main family income and to whom it was a hobby.
- Mothers who home educate and school educate, single mothers and women who are partnered.
- Women who were at the pinnacle of their careers and those who were still figuring out where they wanted to go.

They are women of vision and courage, women who doubt themselves, women who burn with creative fires.

And I asked them those questions. And they answered them from their hard-won experience which has carved their souls to new depths.

I can't wait to introduce you to them over the course of our journey through *The Rainbow Way* (to find out more about them, see the "Contributors" section at the end of the book).

I must confess now, that this book is prejudiced towards mothers who have birthed rather than adopted their babies, although respondents included both adoptive mothers and mothers adopted as children. But my own experience and that of majority of women is that of giving birth to our children, and that is what I have focused on. But, again, here I am prejudiced, and do discuss birth in general in its biologically "normal" experience, which today is certainly not the experience of every woman, and I am very mindful of this. Some of the mothers I spoke to had struggled with infertility. Their birth experiences ranges from home births to C-sections, with everything in between. Some respondents had also had hysterectomies. I feel a desperate need to be sensitive to those whose experience differs, balanced with an urgent need to speak for the biological experience of motherhood: conceiving, gestating and birthing a baby. If your experience was different, please find yourself welcome with open arms, your experience no less valid in any way.

My story

Over the years I have created a new dream for myself: that of the creative mother. Sometimes the balance tipped further towards motherhood, at other times creativity. But both elements have been constants in my life. No matter how tired, how overwhelmed, I was never willing to relinquish either my full-time mothering role, nor my creative work.

I kept comparing myself to other women who seemed really

happy in their role just as mothers, and concluded that I must be doing it wrong. I was happy and recharged when I had my creative time; impatient and mean when I didn't. But this need, this urge, was not a whim, it was an essential for my sanity. And so I learned, little by little, to honor it and build my life around it. At the time I thought I was the only one feeling this way.

I am the mother of three small and very energetic children. As I start the book, I have a five-year-old boy with chicken pox perched on my lap, a three-year-old who will not get her clothes on and a baby who is supposedly eating her lunch, though not much is going into her mouth. The first draft of this book was written in the early mornings before they woke, whilst they watched TV after school, in the evenings when they had finally gone to sleep and in precious two-hour stints on Saturday mornings.

Often I have been cross and frustrated with the process. I have wanted more head-space to write, rather than this constant stopping and starting. The truth of creating as a mother can be very frustrating indeed. I have lost whole chapter ideas when, before I had gotten pen to paper, I had to stop and break up a fight – and whoosh they were gone!

But I have also had constant moments of inspiration, ideas, reflections during my mothering day that I have jotted down and captured: in the car, in cafes, at the kitchen table, before going to sleep, even on the toilet! Ideas that I would never have had if I were alone at my writing desk or in a book-filled library. This, then, is the paradox of creative mothering – it both threatens our creativity, and adds necessity and practical inspiration to our creative fires.

When I was a new mother, I built a life of parenting and work split evenly with my husband. But this diminished as babies two and three were born in quick succession and I became subsumed into full-time mothering. And so I learnt to squirrel away every moment I could and focus my energies more clearly on building my freelance writing career. I began to co-edit a wonderful natural parenting magazine, JUNO, and work on other creative and community projects. Since becoming a mother I have organized arts festivals, made chocolates professionally, taught drama and writing and pregnancy yoga. I have directed plays and made playdough, belly-danced and led craft workshops in friends' kitchens. I have baked cakes for money and forgotten to put the sugar in, and made snowman costumes that fell apart at the seams. I have written articles to great acclaim, and plenty that no one would publish. I have led empowering women's circle ceremonies and drawn disappointing pictures. But I keep on creating because I have to, I need to, and I believe it makes me a better mother to my children than the unfulfilled full-time mother they could have if I didn't.

In a happy turn of events, shortly after I had completed the first draft of this book, my husband had the opportunity to take a part-time job, which meant that I could have two days a week to write. Though we took a massive cut in income, just as the economy was tanking, it was perfect for us on every other level. Once again the balance of creating and mothering had shifted, and I felt I could breathe again. The only thing that is certain is that this will change again, as the children get older and start school I look forward to having five half days a week to do my creative thing!

Through the two years it took me to write *The Rainbow Way*, I went from not having painted in ten years to launching my first solo art exhibition and a range of greetings cards. I went from a freelance feature writer to author of three books. I went from having a newly launched blog to teaching blogging in prestigious places.

This book has transformed my life in the making of it. And I hope it transforms yours in the reading. Wherever you may be on the path, whether starting out or stalled, know that you are not alone.

We're going to take baby steps and giant leaps towards your dreams. Hand in hand. You and me. That's my promise. I know you can do it. How? Because I have, and you are no less creative, no more tired, no less capable than me.

If you're dedicated to reclaiming your creative self, you can create a whole new way of living which honors and supports your rainbow of talents, yearnings and needs – as mother, and a creative woman.

This book is an antidote to inner death. It is full of life, creativity, healing, acceptance, wisdom and transformative practices. Let it be a mirror to help you to see yourself more clearly, your brightness and your shadow, to help you understand your uniqueness. Let it open your eyes to the sisterhood of creative mothers around you. Let it help you to create the life you want for yourself.

You deserve it! And the world needs you to be yourself in all your shining colors.

So here's to our dreams – yours and mine – let us paint them in bright colors and inhabit them as our lives.

PART I

Chapter I

The Rainbow Way

Show not what has been done, but what can be.
How beautiful the world would be if there were a procedure for moving through labyrinths.
Umberto Eco, *The Name of the Rose*

For years the Rainbow Way was nameless to me. Always calling me, navigating my footsteps unseen. My creativity was an unconscious process, hit or miss. But motherhood, and the writing of this book required that I put into words the invisible, indescribable forces which steer the path of the creative mother.

So what, you may be wondering, is the Rainbow Way?

It is my attempt to express the unique creative journey of mothers, through women's experiences, language and symbology, to create for us a native map of the terrain. To make visible and viable that which has previously remained hidden and impossible.

The Rainbow Way...

- Stands in contrast to our culture's monochromatic vision of what is possible or desirable for women, and especially mothers.
- Embraces the many different shades of creative mother. Each woman has her own path to travel, her own soul callings. It is not a "one size fits all" program, but one which provides structure, support and possibility for your own unique journey.
- Shares a lost feminine archetype, the Creative Rainbow Mother, and helps those who identify with her to integrate this new understanding into every area of her life.

- Integrates creative, personal and spiritual development.
- Is a path of color, beauty and transformation, incorporating the sunshine and showers of life.
- Honors a creative mother's dual soul yearnings in a practical way.
- Offers a "road map" to creative motherhood which speaks to body, mind and soul.

But in order to seize this possibility for a more fulfilling life, we have to let go of our old map, which has been handed down to us by well-meaning career counselors, teachers, parents, partners and employers, that which is called "The Only Way" or "The Way Things Are". That is the way that our ancestors and communities have lived, unchanged and unquestioned for generations. When we decide to follow our souls on their creative journey whilst nurturing our mothering hearts, then we are ready to take the first step onto the Rainbow Way.

But it is not enough to just try to change our minds and try to think differently. The Rainbow Way is an embodied process. One which uses our innate creativity to help birth us more fully into our selves. Women's creativity – both artistic and biological – is embodied in our arms, legs, hands, hearts, breasts, wombs and vaginas, in our hormones and cycles of fertility. We cannot enter creativity with our rational brain, in order to enter it we must allow our body, its senses and intuition to lead the way.

The labyrinth

A labyrinth is a symbolic journey . . .but it is a map we can really walk on, blurring the difference between map and world.
Rebecca Solnit, Wanderlust

The Rainbow Way takes the form of a labyrinth. A winding, circuitous path taking us into the center, and out again.

Labyrinths have been used for thousands of years around the world as symbols of the spiritual journey, as meditative tools, and for healing.

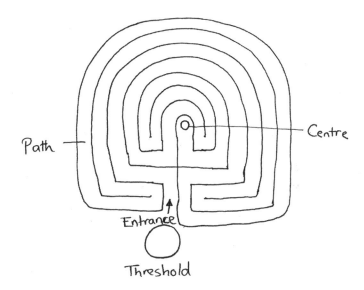

At first glance a labyrinth resembles a maze, as both are made of winding paths. But there is a vital difference. Mazes have dead ends, and wrong turns, whereas a labyrinth has just one path leading into the center and out again. Unlike the maze, which is there to trick us into going the wrong way, all the labyrinth requires of us is trust as we follow the path, step by step, following our intuition. Although walking a labyrinth might feel like we are going round in circles, getting nowhere, in fact, we are always moving on through: we cannot lose our way.

The labyrinth is the perfect symbol of, and guide to, our journey as creative mothers. Though it may be new to you now, it will become familiar over the course of the book. If it is already familiar I guarantee that you will gain new insight into it.

Labyrinths come in many shapes and forms, from the simplest spiral path, to a complex rose-shaped Chartres labyrinth. Though they can have different numbers of paths (circuits) and take different forms, the anatomy of the labyrinth is innately simple. They share the same unique features – one entrance, one path leading in and out, spiraling from the entrance to the center.

When I had finished the first draft of this book, having already named it *The Rainbow Way*, a dear friend who was reading it through asked me: "If you were to create a visual map of the creative journey, what would it look like?"

I puzzled about this all afternoon, desperately trying to logically figure out: *what does the creative journey look like?* And then as I was leaving my studio that evening, my eye fell upon the picture of a seven-circuit labyrinth that I had drawn some months earlier at a workshop I was teaching. Seven spiraling circuits colored red, orange, yellow, green, blue, indigo and violet. One for each of the body's energy chakras. There it was, staring me in the face: the Rainbow Way! Of course! It suddenly all fell into place. This was my map, which had been sitting quietly on my altar of inspiration, waiting to be discovered! This image which I had been drawn to for years. That I had been teaching for years. This symbol which represented the spiritual path. That I had used to teach women about the journey of birth. It had been there all along. Waiting for me!

I could not believe it had never occurred to me before. And later, during my final editing, it was waiting for me again as confirmation that this was indeed the right path. Reading Sue Monk Kidd's life-changing book, *The Dance of the Dissident Daughter,* she discusses in great length the central role of the labyrinth and its myth in women's awakening to themselves.

Please remember...

Whether you identify with the archetype of the Creative Rainbow Mother or not, whether you "get" labyrinths or not makes little difference. They are merely conceptual frameworks for explaining and exploring the intangible concepts of creativity and women's experiences. Please do not get hung up on them. If they work for you, as they have for me, and scores of other women, then I am delighted, if not, then allow your mind to scoot over the terms, rather than block your way. I would ask you to stay open to possibility, to the unknown. Stay curious and receptive to the unfamiliar. That, after all, is the royal road of creativity.

Walking the Way *your* way

Feel yourself being quietly drawn by the deeper pull of what you truly love.
Rumi

This book echoes the creative process it talks about – spiraling in from my personal story, to those of other creative mothers, to those creative heroines, to the archetype of the Creative Rainbow Mother herself and back out again.

It is divided into two parts. The first gives voice to the experience and struggles of being a creative mother. The second focuses on the creative process itself and how you can integrate this into motherhood. Right at the center is a powerful initiation onto the Rainbow Way.

Each step along the way is explained, the voices of other women shared, and exercises – both reflective and creative – allow you to explore the topics and further integrate the lessons into your daily life and creative practice.

They will help you to identify your own blocks, passions, needs and priorities. They should also churn up lots of useful material for further personal creative projects and help you to start getting back into your creative zone, by offering guidelines for simple but meaningful creative projects, which are accessible to you whatever your skill level.

Each chapter should stand alone and give you guidance, inspiration, creative mother's voices and practical tools on the topic you need, when you need it. You can turn to a chapter on getting unstuck or creating with your children, and it can work for you that way.

If you already are an established creative person, I want it to help contribute to your understanding of your own creative process, to help to mesh your roles of mother and creative person more harmoniously, and to take you deeper into your own process.

If you want to learn "how to" be creative then I will teach you real skills in how to approach and access your creativity easily and practically, demystifying the process.

To get the most from its transformational potential, I recommend that you read it from cover to cover and work through the creative exercises and reflections, commit to it like a self-guided creativity course from the comfort of your own home.

Even more powerfully, work through it with a group of other creative mothers (using the chapter on Women Creating Together to help you in setting up a group if you need guidance). Share your responses and insights. You could meet in each other's homes once a week, or create a private group on Facebook. Do the creative activities together or as homework, and use the reflection questions as discussion starters (perhaps using the model of the speaking circle in Chapter 4 to guide you).

Recording your journey

I recommend that you to get yourself a journal or sketch book to use alongside this book. I will be asking you to write and draw a lot in response. Though your responses may turn into later great works, they are initially just for you, and writing and drawing are the two quickest, simplest ways of recording your thoughts, intuitions, memories and feelings.

If you do not consider yourself an artist or writer, please do not let this stop you. Celebrated psychologist James Pennebaker, spent ten years of clinical research studying the effects of writing on healing emotional trauma and has shown that 15 minutes of writing every day for four days, about traumatic or formative events, helps every area of an individual's life, from self-esteem, to productivity and employability. The verbal expression of previously withheld stories helps to reallocate energy from the subconscious to the conscious mind. Drawing helps us to access other parts of our awareness, to express thoughts and feelings which we might not have the words for.

Step one: Find, buy or make yourself a book. You could:
Use a spiral bound sketch book.
Staple a bunch of A4 printer paper together – or tie it with ribbon!
Buy a pretty journal.
Get a folder to keep loose leaves of paper in.
If you will be painting in it or art-journaling, then be sure to use thick paper (140gsm or higher).

Step two: Get some pens or pencils that you like and keep them with the journal. And keep in it a place that you will use it – or take it round with you during the day. Good places include: beside your bed, beside the toilet, in your handbag, on the kitchen counter...

Step three: Fill in the first blank page! Do not be outsmarted by a white sheet of paper! Perhaps fill the first page with your name, a quote that speaks to your heart, an image you love – use a color you like, maybe two, add some doodles, a few stickers that you like, make it feel good.

Step four: If you're feeling really creative why not make a cover for it – choose some nice wrapping paper, perhaps print your own, make it feel like yours.

Congratulations! You've just started your creative journal. May it be a sacred place to rest, reflect, rant, to see yourself more clearly and celebrate your beauty, to work through ideas and birth beautiful dreams. Do not be a stranger to it!

At the end of most sections in this book there are questions for reflection. Be honest, be real, look deeply; answer instinctively as you respond to them. Make a promise not to second-guess yourself. This is a space where the first thing that comes to you is OK: this is the place for raw instinct.

Why not use it as a scrapbook for your creative endeavors? Stick in photographs, write down recipes or your feelings about what you've painted. Jot down ideas of things you'd like to write about, things you'd like to research more, images you love, articles which have caught your interest. Make this full and rich and messy, a real workbook full of you: your thoughts, ideas, reflections, achievements, plans, possible projects.

Let this be the map to your creative journey, an archaeological record of your soul. It will show you where you came from and document your creative development. This is also where you can capture your ideas, to work them up into bigger creations later.

You can take the Rainbow Way as far as you need to – whether you just want to get creatively unblocked or find practical ways of fitting creativity into your mothering journey. Or if, like me, you are open to letting the Way transform your whole life!

Reflections

How have you used journaling in the past?

Do you have any blocks to getting a journal started? Where do these come from?

Are you excited about having a space of your own to reflect and dream? Or does this make you feel anxious?

How does it feel starting afresh, filling that first blank page?

Chapter 2

Creativity

Odd how the creative power at once brings the whole universe to order.
Virginia Woolf

There is a vitality, a life force, a quickening that is translated through you into action, and because there is only one you in all time, this expression is unique… You have to keep open and aware directly to the urges that motivate you. Keep the channel open.
Martha Graham

What is creativity?

What exactly do you mean by creativity, I hear you cry! Creativity is a broad term, intentionally so:

- Creativity is the magic that happens when intention meets matter, the application of human skills on materials which shape it into something new, beautiful, useful or reflective. In grandiose terms it is transformational alchemy.
- At its most basic level creativity is making stuff. Taking one substance, say wool, and turning it into another, in this case, a sweater. Taking flour, butter and sugar and turning it into cake. This takes concentrated effort, defined skills, some degree of imagination and the ability to follow – or create – a recipe or pattern.
- But we can also create intangible things – such as events, workshops, or concepts: we take the germ of an idea and turn it into a reality.
- Creativity is about stepping into the unknown: first with our minds, and then through our actions.

- It also refers to a way of thinking and problem-solving, an imaginative approach to living, a way of "thinking outside the box" and finding innovative solutions.
- Many forms of creativity require that we tap into our imagination, reflecting on and studying our inner or outer worlds in minute detail, translating our inner experience through color, words, sound, movement, touch...
- This imaginative communication can help us, or others, to find healing, joy, beauty or a deeper understanding of ourselves.
- Creativity is all around us, all the time. Trees make leaves, flowers make fruits, spiders make webs, women's bodies grow babies. It is how the world works. We are doing it all the time, whether we think of ourselves as creative or not. Whether we are doing it consciously is a different matter.
- When we become conscious creators, we take the time and intent to focus our energy on what we want to create, or how we want it to look. We are creating the world anew in our own image.

There is a juiciness to creativity, a succulence that comes up from within, a sensuality which both produces and is soothed by the act and product of creativity. Creativity is pleasing to us on a deep level. Be it the feel of clay in our hands, the colors that make us feel alive as we knit or sew, the meaning that we find in the words that we write, the energizing feel of movement as we dance and the music moves through our bodies.

Taking part in creativity helps us to be more fully alive on every level, it asks that we engage with life in a visceral, and interactive way. **Paula,** a home-schooling mother of four, puts it beautifully:

I think that the Holy Spirit that Christians talk of is something that is expressed or channeled through art and creativity – it is an energy that comes of being connected to life rather than hiding from it, although it is also connected to the secret self – there is a balance between the inner and outer world, a relationship, a movement or dance if you like, between the two. Both are needed for really creative magic to happen, for something to really have soul.

Are you creative?

I'm curious, what is your gut response to this question? If you're anything like the majority of women I spoke to in the writing of this book, you will have a hard time thinking of yourself as creative. Let alone calling yourself a Creative Mother.

There seems an innate nervousness to calling ourselves creative – though most of us are. Most of the women I spoke to struggled with defining themselves as creative, let alone "artists". And yet they painted pictures, wrote books, danced, sang or knitted, or sometimes all those things and more! One woman, who had made her living from writing for twenty-five years, wasn't sure if the term really applied to her! Another, who went to art college forty years ago and has sewed and painted almost every day since, shirked the label.

Why is this?

I think that the answer to this block is the first key to unlocking our creative selves, and giving ourselves the time, space and permission to be creative. What we consider creativity to be, and whether or not we "have it" or "are it" is a large part of our self-definition.

The chances are, if you've picked up a book on creativity, some part of you either thinks of yourself as creative, finds joy in creativity or aspires to be creative. Right?

I know all about denying creativity. Let me tell you a story…

Many years ago at the opening of one of my father's painting exhibitions an older woman asked me that very question I just asked you.

No, I answered, in all seriousness, *I'm not creative.*

My father had made his name as a renowned potter, now he was branching into design, sculpture and painting. Whereas I hated making pots and I'd never had a painting exhibition...

And I really meant it, I wasn't just being humble – I didn't value my creativity because I wasn't a money-making Artist.

In that moment I kind of forgot the A Level in art; all the oil ● paintings; the plays I had written, directed, adapted, translated, acted in at school and University; the dance classes I loved; my fervor for cooking; singing in numerous choirs; the instruments; the crafting. Oh yes, and the poetry, novel chapters and journals full of writing stashed away in drawers. It was all hobbies, just silly stuff!

We can be very good at belittling our skills. And it is far more than just modesty. It is something to do with what "art" should look like, what writing "should" be like. Discovering the research of Sally Reis gave me a huge insight into this:

The creative process in women may emerge differently than in males, and in some women, it may have difficulty in emerging. Women's perceptions of the creative process in art as well as other areas have been filtered through male perspectives and the cultural roles developed for women but not by women. Therefore, female writers, artists, scientists and creators in all domains deal with male conceptions of creativity and a creative process that has been accepted as the standard within that domain, but may only be the standard for male creators.

It was then that I realized that I wasn't alone in my lack of creative confidence. It was endemic amongst women – because we were comparing ourselves to something which felt instinctively "not us" – so of course we didn't fit, and couldn't belong. We will explore this in much more detail later in Part I.

Can anyone be creative?

Mary, a mother of two, asks a question I hear a lot from people:

Can you learn to be creative? I feel it is something you have in you, and I don't have it!

I believe that we all have a creative spark in us, but in some it has just never been kindled, and in others it has been prematurely extinguished. Creativity is a process which is innate to humans, and one which we engage with, usually unconsciously on a daily basis.

The creative flow is everywhere. It is the underlying principle of life; we do not need to make it happen. By aligning ourselves with the creative processes arising naturally within us, and in the world, rather than feeling isolated from them, we can begin to co-create. The more aware we become of the process and how it feels in ourselves, the more we can align ourselves with it. The more we can heighten our senses, and refine our skills, the more accomplished the products of our creativity.

However, most people confuse "creative" with "artistic" and associate creativity with its end product – a masterful painting or beautifully iced cake. We are all creative, though not all of us might have raw artistic talent, just like we are all active, but not all of us are naturally athletic. But raw talent is only a part of the equation – the rest comes down to regular practice, learned skills, supportive habits and lifestyle, good teachers and mentors to get the best from us and, most importantly of all, confidence.

I love **Pam England**'s insight on the subject:

Human beings in every place and time have beautified and decorated dwellings, tools, pottery, clothes, ceremonial masks, even their bodies; part of being human is to make art. We imbue our creations with meaning and draw meaning from them. Making art can be a social ritual; sometimes it is a journey into solitude.

Through art we see what we have not seen before, we are surprised, confirmed, and changed by the process of making it, and by our reflections on it.

And yet prevailing attitudes about art-making keep most adults from making art. For example, making art is: reserved for those with special talent; for everyone else, it is frivolous; time would be better spent learning facts. Tapping into old childhood anxiety or messages about not knowing how to draw or color (or sing, dance, or write for that matter) interferes with impulses to create.

So I need to stress here that when I talk about creativity I am not talking about Art. This is not a book about composing opera or making oil paintings, unless, of course, that is your favored form of expression. This is a book about self-expression, making stuff which makes **you** feel good, having fun, making the world a little brighter and enjoying that whilst you have children, including them in the adventure.

Not everyone need dedicate themselves to the life of the artist. As a creative mother, unless your children are much older or you can afford full-time childcare, you are unlikely to be able to. But we can all learn to quiet ourselves, to look outside with open hearts and listen inside with curiosity. We can all develop our senses and practice giving expression to our inner experiences. Every single one of us can learn to express what we truly love, what we find beautiful and multiply this in the world. We can all gain pleasure from seeing our mastery of skills develop and grow in whichever field we are interested in, be it cooking or prop-making, dress-making or ballet. This is the heart of the creative path, and it is open to anyone. I love the way that **Leah**, an artist and mother of two, reflects on the cultural understanding of the term artist in **Pam England**'s book, *Birthing From Within*:

In some cultures there is no word for artist. Everybody has that innate urge to create, everybody is a creative being, that's human.

The Balinese, who have no word for art, say of their art: 'We have no art, we do everything as well as we can.' But in our culture we are constricted and told from a very early age that some people are special – they're artists.

And if you are still not sure if you dare apply the word creative to yourself, let alone "writer" or "artist", I dare you to read these passionate words from my dear cyber friend, **Becky**, and not feel something stir in your soul. I first read them in the early days of learning to call myself a writer, and held them close to my heart as I stepped into their permission to own myself as a creative:

For those among us who grapple with the titles of writer, artist or musician, I offer a reflection on my journey to accepting myself as a writer.

Who do you regard as "writers"? Are they people who write for others? Are they people who write for themselves? Are they people who have achieved status as a writer by selling their work?

For most of my life, to me writers were artists I respected as significant literary contributors – those widely read and praised –those whose words stood the test of time, inspiring their readers by capturing their attention through their words. Writers were people whose works stayed with their readers long after the book was read. Somehow it felt presumptuous to put myself in the similar category with my loves: Emerson, Thoreau, Nin, Shakespeare. I mean, who the heck was I to call myself a "writer"?

Many artists feel the same about the title of artist, as do musicians about being called a musician.

Our society creates, praises, and values creators of art, music, and literary works equating the sale of their art to success – by creating pleasure en masse: the most CDs sold, money exchanged for a painting, selling out a concert hall, book sales etc. Should sales be the barometer of success? Risking cliché: surely beauty is in the eye of the beholder.

Personally, I refuse to define art and artist (works and writers) by society's collective acceptance of talents (vis-à-vis monetary exchange) as the gold standard. I believe these beautiful essential expressive human art forms are dwindling – at risk of extinction – at the hands of a collective definition of art, music and writing.

As creators, it is our silent – most often unpraised, unnoted but most worthy – responsibility to write, make music, and create art first and foremost for ourselves, and to define ourselves as writers, musicians, and artists by our personal satisfaction not society's.

A few years ago, I decided to define "writer" to myself, and created my own definition.

To me, being a writer means finding personal depth and courage to use words to express that which is difficult to put words upon – whether our words are witnessed by others or not. Being a writer to me means taking time to paint with words, to edit, replace, and to painstakingly birth a vision, born of energy, thought, and letters. Being a writer isn't something that was externally dubbed upon me, or a title I earned. Being a writer is sacred work, a responsibility to use my chi (energy), my time, my life experience to select and connect words from my palette (my vocabulary) to capture the essence of intentions, feelings and ideas: the light, dark, good, bad, painful, and joyous.

I write because I must. I am a writer by self-proclamation.

How creativity shuts down

Art is not what you make, it's who you are.
Leonie Dawson

Creativity comes quite naturally to most of us when we are young – we like colors and textures, to scribble and explore. The cool squishy feel of clay in our hands, the splashes of bright color as we paint, the beat of a drum and the emotion of music. We are naturally programmed to immerse ourselves in the creative flow, in the process of doing, totally unaware and unconcerned about the end result.

And then, after the first few years, we learn to watch for responses to our creations. Turning to our mother, *Look mama!* we say, to our first art critic, showing her our creation with great pride and an open heart. And that's when it starts to change – how does she respond? Does it make us truly witnessed and appreciated? Or ashamed that we aren't good enough, chastised that we've made a mess? Or is our work compared to that of an elder sibling?

And then at school we are told to color in, only inside the lines, make things the right color, all make the same art project. Be good, do it right, don't make a mess. Stop! Now start. Write a story, but it has to be one-page long, no longer, or shorter, and about owls. And later again if you carry your creative skills on it becomes about theory, adulation of the great masters and A grades.

Somewhere, quietly, unless we value it deeply, and come from a family that values it, or have a wonderful teacher who sees us truly, our creativity slips out somewhere by the back door, as we get subsumed by grades and earning money, looking right and fitting in.

One of the most powerful exchanges I had on this topic was with writer and dancer **Julie Daley**, a heroine of mine, who oozes creativity in her life and work. To the outside world she is the embodiment of a unique and highly creative spirit. Her response truly floored me, and illustrates just how much impact the judgment of others in our formative years can have:

I have had the hardest time reclaiming the word artist. I have done everything to push that word away. Everything. I'm realizing it because everything as a child pointed to that being my love.

One of my happiest memories was painting in pre-school, in the back yard, they had these big planks of wood on saw horses and they'd bring out a big roll of butcher paper. I remember putting my smock on and running outside, grabbing my paintbrush, and I loved yellow, I would just paint yellow all the time. It didn't have to be anything, I just loved seeing the yellow go on the paper. It's so funny, those little things we do as kids, I didn't care if things were representational, it was just the joy.

As I got older, as a teenager, at art club, the teachers were just like: "This doesn't look right, you need to do this and that." And I remember just feeling so constricted and restricted. And I just stopped painting. So I didn't take art at high school, because I couldn't be sure I'd get an A. I had straight As. Except one B+, in writing, and I was so upset, because the teacher could subjectively say that he didn't think my writing was worth an A. And I swore then that I'd never be a writer. I'd never subject myself to that.

I remember another time, talking to my dad, sharing something with him that I was really excited about, (he was a math major and computer scientist back in the 1950s; he was a very logical man). And he looked at me and said, "But honey that's just not logical!" And I went silent, and thought: "Oh, that's not valued."

And so I ended up being a programmer. That shows how sensitive I was to being judged.

My mother was a painter, her mother was a painter and her mother before her. Three generations back. But I haven't ever really considered what it's like to have three women in my lineage be artists. I know it, I have their paintings in my home, I love it, but it's like I've disassociated from that part of me somehow. There's definitely some healing happening round this still for me. I have only just started painting again in the past year. So recently in this group I'm in, I decided I was just going to say it: "I'm an artist!" And they all started laughing and said: "Of course you are!" They could all see what I couldn't!

Can you see how we begin to lose touch with our own creativity? Our own passions and images, our innate desire to experiment, our grand visions which we share with the world, with faith and trust, are squashed in their vulnerability. And then, at some point, we decide it isn't worth it, we choose not to make ourselves vulnerable again, because it feels unsafe. We feel ashamed that our judgment was so off, that it did not align with the reality of another who we looked up to. And so we stop doing our creative thing every day. Until we don't know how to start again. And so by the time we are fully fledged adults, only professional artists have their creativity intact. Most of us are in denial: too busy, too scared to even try.

Mon's story is all too familiar when she describes what can happen to many of us in the whirlwind of work and life before kids:

After a degree in psychology, I took a Fine Arts degree majoring in photography, but put aside those creative endeavors to travel. I expressed my creativity by writing a lot during that time. Then, once married, I, wrongly, gave up my creative self.

Reflections

How do you define creativity?

Do you think of yourself as creative or artistic?

If not, who do you think fits those descriptions? What are their qualifications? Why don't you have them?

How were you received in your unbridled childish creative enthusiasm?

How were you approved of?

How did you shine?

Where were you judged?

Was there a moment when you lost your voice? Shut down your creativity? What was said to make it happen? Why did you believe it? Was it true? What would it, or did it, take for you to try again?

Why do we create?

Why did she make things? Well, she enjoyed it of course, but it also somehow helped remind her who she was and where she came from.
Pinterest meme

The most unanswerable question for many of us is: Why do I need to create? What is it that I get from creating that I can't get elsewhere? The world doesn't need my art, so why do I need to create it so badly?

I am sure that many of us can identify with the impassioned response of filmmaker and writer, Kristina, when she describes the reason she gives so much of her energy and passion to her art:

Because it's the only thing that makes me feel 100% free, 100% me, 100% like I'm living life fully.

She was just one creative mother featured in Mary Trunk's powerful 2012 film, *Lost in Living*. Merrill, another subject of the film, herself a mother of three and author of more than twenty-five books shares:

In fiction I could take control of the situation, which in real life I could not at all... Because my power is in my pen. I really needed art. And when it was missing there was a gaping hole in my life.

I felt I just had a secret place to go, a place that wasn't just laundry, shopping, diapers, and nursery school. I felt that I was keeping my sanity. I never felt like I would get back to it some time, I needed to get to it every day.

A well-known writer and artist I spoke to referred to painting as her "daily dose of anti-depressants, if I don't paint for a couple of days I start to feel really odd," she shared.

When I pondered the question, I realized that apart from

having focused time to myself, I had a deep need to feel free, to feel fully immersed, to feel in flow, to be part of something bigger than me which I didn't get from my mothering. Creativity was a familiar place to retreat to: a world outside the daily world which I often find too challenging to deal with. I find some sort of relief on every level when I create: physically, emotionally and mentally. It is as though there are things I need to get out, out of my body and my brain. My head is full of ideas, clamoring to be born. The buzz of "just imagine…" and "what if…" is addictive!

My creations enable me to hold onto the fleeting inspiration which comes to me out of the blue – visions of hope, of joy, of color. The creative process helps me to dive more deeply into ideas, to work through these insights in a physical way, learning more about them, and myself, as I do. It gives voice to the deepest part of myself which has no other means of expression.

In truth because so much of the time I feel sad or lonely or unclear, creativity is my way to clarity and sanity, my literal, multicolored life line. In the wise words of **Thomas Merton**: *Art enables us to find ourselves, and lose ourselves, at the same time.*

How creative are you?

So now we've got a clearer idea of what we're talking about, let's see how creative you really are. Grab a few colored pens…photocopy the page if you're precious about books, or it belongs to someone else…

Now, have a look down this list:

- In bright red, circle everything that you have ever done – yes, even if it was only once when you were a child.
- In out-going orange, circle anything which you have taken classes in.
- In gorgeous green, circle anything which you enjoy as an adult as a hobby. I'm not saying you have to be the best painter in the world, but if you do paint, circle it… I dare you!

- In brilliant blue, circle anything which you have earned money from.
- In daring purple, circle anything which you would love to do but haven't quite got around to or had the nerve to try.

TABLE 1

This non-exhaustive list includes...

drawing	gardening	body art
herbalism	prop-building	flower arranging
painting	cake-decorating	dress-making
dancing	set design	interior design
singing	carpentry	Book-binding
playing an instrument	photography	embroidery
soul working	knitting	print-making
weaving	poetry	editing
crafting	spinning	quilting
crochet	ceramics	weaving
jewelry making	design	acting
writing	performing	sculpting

wood-working	story telling	drumming
movement work	scrap-booking	voice work
choreography	puppetry	costume design
making rituals	sewing	baking
henna/ tattoos	blogging	mosaic
event organisation	cooking	composing

Feel free to add anything that I may have missed in the spaces above!

How was that? Chances are you have quite a lot of circles on this page. Have you noticed how many of these creative things we do in our everyday lives as mothers? How many things we could chose to do more creatively if we wanted to without taking up a brand new hobby?

Oh, sure, I hear you, the photographs you take are crap really, your cakes are always burnt – cakes, what cakes, I know, you can't bake! – a three-year-old could play piano better than you, or draw, or sing for that matter... And you love to write but you couldn't support your family with your income...

Some of us earn our livings as creatives, some have our creativity as a hobby and some hide it under the mattress and pretend it's not there. But whatever your level, I guarantee you don't acknowledge the extent of its possibilities... Am I right?

Look again at all those colorful circles. What a lot of talents you have. How many skills you have developed, and can develop further. You have a rainbow of abilities!

Eight stages of creativity

Don't compare your beginning to someone else's middle.
Jon Acuff

One of the main reasons people feel like they're not creative, is that they are comparing their beginning to someone else's middle. Or put another way, they are comparing their process, to someone else's finished product. When we see ourselves in comparison to another, we tend to judge ourselves as more or less creative. And if we come out on the lesser side, we quickly diminish that to "not creative at all".

I have developed a general map of the terrain of creativity: the **eight stages of creativity.** They are not set in stone, but I wanted to find some way to delineate the "stages" so that you can keep your expectations of yourself and your work under control when starting out. Most of us have an impatience when we are starting to learn a new creative art form, or a level of perfectionism that requires everything to be exhibition standard.

Each step is a level of considerable accomplishment, and the truth is that we zigzag backwards and forwards between them, at various stages in our creative lives as we try new forms or media, or have more or less time for our creativity.

Stages 1-4 are usually completely private, 5-6 are entering the public sphere – where both appreciation, praise, criticism, collaboration and money are all acquired. 7-8 are very unusual heights to get to, historically, and still dominated by men.

1. **Paint by numbers** – tracing, coloring in, kit building.

2. **Copying** – following instructions or recipes to the word.

3. **Improvisation** – taking a starting point from another piece of work, or a technique and starting to riff around it.

4. **Composition** – you are starting to develop your own more complex designs and ideas, to plan and create structure for yourself.

5. **Stand-alone work** – you are consistently creating work from your own inner well of ideas, refining your techniques and themes. At this stage you will usually begin selling your work and/ or teaching.

6. **Recognized body of work** – people can clearly recognize your individual style, use of materials and subject matter, you begin to become a respected authority through your work.

7. **Internationally acclaimed** – a world renowned teacher/ creative figure or artist – your work will be widely recognized by large numbers of people outside of your field or niche.

8. **Historical figure** in your art – your work is remembered, celebrated, referenced and valued by many generations after your death.

So many of us dream of jumping from levels one to eight in a flash. Hollywood film-making and reality pop shows make us feel like this is both possible and desirable.

As much as is possible, throughout the course of this book, and in your life beyond, become aware when you start comparing yourself to others – in creativity or mothering. Become aware of where you (and they) are at in the process, and allow that to be.

Each of us is walking our own labyrinths and each is at our own unique place on the path. So by all means, find the threads of experience that unite you with other creative souls. But do not compare, dearest mama, and find yourself lacking. It is the only guaranteed way to make yourself smaller, to shut yourself off from the creative power which courses through us all.

Reflections

What stage am I at now in my creative journey?

What new creative practice is calling me, but I am too scared to be a beginner again?

Chapter 3

Renaissance

What we need is a renaissance. We need to go forward by going backward.
Stanley Crouch

Renaissance: a revival of intellectual or artistic achievement and vigor.
The Free Dictionary

Many women have asked me why I focus on the creative mother, rather than creative women, or even simply creativity?

Apart from the fact that I feel that as a group we are extremely under-supported in our development, it is largely because of a little-spoken-about phenomenon: creative renaissance.

I have discovered, through talking to scores of creative women, that for many women something miraculous happens when they become pregnant or give birth. The vital forces which have been ignited in their bodies through pregnancy also rekindle their creative passion. Their hearts and wombs are fully engaged with nurturing life, and it seems that a woman's body does not differentiate between the biological and artistic acts of creation, they are fuelled by the same fire and cultivated under the same conditions.

I believe that the word renaissance perfectly describes the experience of many mothers. From "re-" meaning again, and "naissance" meaning birth, it speaks of the fact that through pregnancy, birth, and motherhood, women find themselves "born again". For many this is an instantaneous life-altering shift, and felt as a spiritual experience, for others it is a growing sense of realization that "something profound has changed in my life: I am no longer who I once thought I was."

The other understanding of "renaissance" is to do with a revival of artistic achievement and vigor, and so many of the women I spoke to in the writing of this book experienced a personal artistic renaissance when they became mothers.

For years we may have ignored our creative sides. Busy with our career, love-life, travel and friendships it was left to one side. Now, suddenly it is an all-consuming urge. Some inner compulsion has awakened and will not be quieted down: we must give birth to art, writing, knitting, sewing, songs, plays...and do it now, not in twenty years when the children are grown.

It is a secret that we were not told by our mothers or sisters, and certainly not by our careers counselors or teachers: we can gain access to unknown depths when our mother-self is born and if we have a creative temperament, the birth of a child might also include a massive artistic resurgence.

Those who do not understand this renaissance that creative mothers experience try to reassure us and quiet down our fire: *you have all the time in the world to paint or write, babies are only young once. Don't be selfish, you need to focus on your children.*

They do not understand that this way madness and sadness lie. Many think that this is the only way: have babies and abandon your life and dreams until the children have left home. *You are the frame, now,* an older woman counseled me, *your child is the picture. It is all about him now.*

And this has been true for generations of creative women – once her belly has been filled with the life of another, her own is expected to end. Her hand has been stopped from writing, her heart from painting, her voice from speaking. She has been told that a woman's place is in the home, is to be caring for children, her husband or ailing parents. This traditional dialogue has been joined by new expectations: that she has to get a job – any job, a respectable job. Never that she should follow her instincts and her heart. To honor her children's needs for a mother's care, and her need for a meaningful, creative life and work.

The truth of the matter is that the creative mother who is unable to create, will not be a better mother, instead she is unable to mother properly either. For the creative mother, creativity is her life force that makes her bloom. Take that from her and you take her soul.

Flights into sanity

Donald Winnicott, renowned British psychoanalyst and pediatrician stated that during pregnancy a mother develops "a state of heightened sensitivity" which continues for some weeks after the baby's birth. However, when this passes, the mother has what he calls a "flight into sanity" and she begins to be aware of the world which exists outside of her state of "primary maternal preoccupation" with her baby.

For many of the women I spoke to this period of heightened sensitivity was also accompanied by a rebirth of themselves as women and creatives, and the flight of sanity was expressed in a profound rediscovery of their creative energies and ideas.

For me it was writing which called to me, rather than drama which I had trained in and taught for many years before. Laura transitioned from painting to toy-making, specializing in dolls. Hannah found that she was pulled from fiction writing to non-fiction. For many it meant the movement from more abstract forms of expression and "high art" to more practical crafts, or intuitive forms of creativity.

The creative renaissance in new mothers is the result of an incredibly complex, once-in-a-lifetime shift of the woman's hormonal, emotional, physical and psychological states, along with a total shift in her social role, responsibilities and daily routine. She is blasted from her previous existence into an entirely new self, and some of the myriad changes include:

- During pregnancy and early motherhood, a woman's mind is in a near-constant state of relaxed activity (growing a baby, and later producing milk), whilst her body is engaged in repetitive, habitual activity: breastfeeding, nappy changing, rocking, soothing. This is the optimal state for creative flow, as we will see in Part II.

- But this is not the only flow – added blood flow to the womb and vaginal area have been shown in repeated research to activate the corresponding parts of the brain connected to creativity.

- A woman's pregnancy and post-partum period is characterized by heightened sensitivity; powerful emotions; an awakening of forgotten memories and dreams and a greater awareness of and reliance on her intuitive faculties.

- She has an altered wake-sleep cycle and dreaming cycle: her brain cycles more frequently through brainwave patterns which are associated with creativity.

- She experiences a new sense of self and the awakening of a new archetype within her as she perceives herself as "mother" for the first time.

- As a new mother she has increased opportunities for play, being outdoors and in her familiar home environment, and a massive exposure to different people, music, images, stories and educational experiences.

- And perhaps most importantly of all, the changes in her hormonal state during pregnancy, birth, breastfeeding and parenting encounters flood her brain and body with an array of neurochemicals like oxytocin, endorphins, adrenaline and relaxin making her more open and dreamy for months, or even years.

The activated womb

Mon, a photographer, writer and mother of one, touches on another key aspect of the maternal creativity puzzle: the activation of the womb, often seen as a woman's creative center, which we will explore in more depth later in the book:

Having my girl was a catalyst, a whirlwind of self-empowerment, creatively speaking. They say the womb is woman's center of creativity, and having a child opened up what I allowed to lie dormant within me. It flooded out, I could barely keep up. It was a second birthing. Like bringing a child into the world, there is no turning back now.

For many women this is the first time their womb has been "activated". Perhaps a lifetime of unfulfilling sexual encounters, or a sense of disconnection from their menstrual cycle, means that their womb has been a part of their body which has been ignored or even despised. Now, called into life through the act of pregnancy, the latent energies within are activated. Hence the sudden "switching on" of creativity.

For the first time in their adult lives, women's eyes are opened to their ability to nurture life, to create, and their hormones are moving them into the perfect level of consciousness to do just this. Whereas before, getting into this creative state would require willpower and dedication, now her hormones and activated womb magically smooth the way. The pregnant woman finds that she is no longer in control of her own body's processes in a way she previously believed, she is now surrendered to them. Her logical brain, which has been honed by her education, and her body which has previously competed on a male stage, are now flooded with feminine creative powers.

To find pleasure and comfort, to make some sort of sense of these new experiences, a woman who has previously been taught to express herself creatively, will often turn to these skills as a way to express these new feelings, powerful dreams, strange longings and disorienting physical changes that she is experiencing.

For such a common experience, it is incredible that you will find little said about it. It is not a topic which is well-funded, or of great interest to most (male) research scientists. And so each woman in our culture tends to experience this transformation and renaissance by herself, with little guidance or preparation. Then, having had the experience, thinks that she is alone in it and either ignores or dismisses it as she has no frame of reference for it.

As a culture we do not acknowledge what a massive shift becoming a mother is for any woman, let alone explore this creative renaissance that so many women experience. It is my deepest desire to help to prepare and initiate women, because without guidance and support a woman can feel alone, misunderstood, or just plain "wrong" in her experiences, which her doctor, friends and partner have no understanding of.

Experiences of renaissance

It was during the latter stages of my first pregnancy that I touched my own power and creativity for what seemed like the first time in years. I discovered a wonderful book, *Birthing from Within*, which used art therapy techniques as a form of birth preparation.

And so I found myself 38 weeks pregnant, molding clay figurines, hypnotically squeezing the clay through my fingers, allowing my subconscious thoughts to guide me. It was a surrendered state of creativity, the like of which I had not experienced since childhood. A tiger-woman emerged, birthing on all fours, and she was there with me, sharing her animal instincts during my birth. A chubby clay baby reminded me of the final result during the pushing. A watercolor painting of a water lily opening reminded me of the need to mindfully open during the birthing process.

For women who have learnt ways of tapping into their creativity, who know how to tune into this subterranean stream of images and ideas which slip below the radar of the conscious mind, the coupling of increased creative brain activity (increased alpha and theta waves), decreased physical activity and hormonal receptivity, can lead to a natural rise in intuitive creativity, as **Rachael,** a writer and mother of two, found:

Since I became pregnant, I've tended in writing poetry to rely more on gifts than on the process of drafting and drafting and drafting. On occasion I've been able to tap into **something** *– a deeply grounded feeling – and write out of that, usually very quickly, thus bypassing my manipulative monkey mind. For whatever reason, when I was pregnant, that feeling came upon me quite often.*

For **Laura**, a mother of three, her own personal renaissance was like a bolt from the blue:

I knew I was quite creative, I had done and enjoyed art at school and still did the occasional painting and drawing. But I had little motivation to find an artistic path. When I fell pregnant, wham! It hit me and I needed to create. I do think that mothering sparks incredible creativity but there is definitely a flip side to that in that there is so little time to fulfill our creative desires.

I don't relate...

If you do not identify with this idea of renaissance, you are not alone either, in fact a number of creative women I spoke to did not relate to it, and as a result felt that they therefore were less connected to the idea of the Creative Rainbow Mother. But on reflection I noticed that all of them had something in common: they had been professional creatives for a number of years before motherhood, and so their sense of identity was with the "work" aspect of creativity. For them creativity was less a dreamy experience, and rather a more prosaic way that they made their money. The motherhood element did not kick-start it, because they were already following their soul-work. However, all of them experienced a similar level of adjustment, in how to get the time and space they needed for their work. **Jennifer Louden**, bestselling author, shared her experience with me:

Pregnancy was very much a time of enjoying my creativity. I have struggled for much of my life with being driven, whereas the essential experience of pregnancy was surrender. The first two months I felt so awful, I couldn't do anything much. But after that I remember a wonderful sense of a natural rhythm, of trusting my body and letting myself rest.

My writing process was not necessarily deeper, but I was more trusting and accepting when creativity came. I had more trust in what I wanted to say. It definitely was an altered state.

When we become mothers, we experience first-hand a full-bodied surrender to the creativity of life itself. Pregnancy and birth open a woman to the experience of being a vessel for creativity, of being a co-creative force, to the sense of something, physically and psychically, coming through you. This is an experience which artists of both genders throughout history have referred to when speaking of the creative act, and we as mothers, are initiated into it through pregnancy and birth. No wonder many of us experience a visceral renaissance.

Reflections

Did you have a spiritual epiphany or creative awakening during pregnancy and birth?

What form did it take? Were you aware of it at the time or only in retrospect?

What does renaissance mean to you in your life? Write the word down in large letters and all around it write words, or doodle images that you associate with it.

Creative exercise

Grab some pastels or paints – bring this feeling of your creative awakening to mind. How does it make you feel – invigorated, alive, scared, confused, aroused? Are you part of this image – is it external to you, or internal? If embodied, where does it stem from in your body – your head, heart, womb, is it part of your energy field? Or is it coming to you from an external force? What do you consider this force to be? Can you picture it? Are you a passive recipient or a co-creator of this state? Have you ever experienced this sort of feeling before? When and what was it that was similar? How did you feel then?

Delve deep – this is your material. This is the stuff of power. This is where the magic lies!

Chapter 4

Circle of Mothers

In more ways than one, women talk in circles: conversation takes a spiral shape in its subjective exploration of every subject.

Listening, witnessing, role modeling, reacting, deepening, mirroring, laughing, crying, grieving, drawing upon experience, and sharing wisdom of experience, women in circles support each other and discover themselves through talk.

Jean Shinoda Bolen, *The Millionth Circle*

Once I started talking about creative motherhood to other women, the floodgates opened. They were grateful to be asked for their personal experiences, glad to be able to reflect, often for the first time, on something so integral to their lives. And many said that in reflecting they found a deeper understanding of themselves, their own process and where they were stuck. It helped to clarify where they wanted to be right now in their mothering and creative lives.

There was, it seemed, a deep hunger for acknowledgement and support of their complex lives. Mothers were yearning to find more balance, to reflect on their own mothering and creative processes, and find how they might better combine the two.

The women featured in this chapter are creative mothers just like you. Women who are not usually interviewed, who do not get their voices heard, because they are not (yet!) famous. And yet their voices, their feelings, have just as much value, just as much to teach us, as those of their celebrated sisters.

The women I spoke to were reasonably evenly divided into two groups. Those who had had careers which they had chosen to give up in order to follow a more personally fulfilling path of creative motherhood. And those whose path only emerged once motherhood was part of the picture. Very few had jobs which were unrelated to their creativity in some way. But those who did were doing some sort of social or community work. Creative mothers, it seems, are driven to live their ideals and walk their soul paths without compromise.

Some of the women walk a high-paying, professional creative path, others have chosen to focus their energies on being a stay-at-home mother and creativity is a hobby.

Perhaps unsurprisingly, those women who found their creativity satisfied by making things for their homes and families, and whose creativity was child-directed, expressed the greatest sense of well-being and satisfaction. However, many mother's art forms, such as writing and painting, called to them as strongly, or more so, than their children – this then set up trade-offs and feelings of frustration.

All struggled to some degree with finding balance, but not one expressed regret in following her heart in trying to combine their creativity and motherhood. The most common struggles cited were: lack of time and energy, not knowing where to start, feeling blocked when they did have the time, not having space to create, and not feeling creative enough.

For all mothers their over-riding love and commitment to their children shone through their words. Which is why being a creative mother was such a soul battle – they were being pulled between their two absolute priorities.

Most of the women anticipated mothering to be much easier and more rewarding than it is: filled with fun, light and joy. They have also been surprised by the intensity of their love and biological attachment to their children, their desire not to be separated from them.

These women are committed to self and family evaluation, to finding balance for themselves and optimal care for their children and are engaged in consciously creating the sort of family that they want. This conscious creation of family and self shone through, despite physical tiredness from pregnancy, breastfeeding and mothering, husbands working long hours, social structures of isolation, single parenthood, little time to themselves, a lack of confidence or money worries.

The message I heard again and again was the desire not to repeat the self-sacrifice of mothers in generations past, nor to sacrifice precious baby time. All of them were committed to combining creativity and motherhood, not because they were seeking to "have it all", as society seems to demand of modern mothers, but because they are following their soul's desire to be themselves as fully as they can within the limitations which their lives have placed on them.

A virtual women's circle of creative mothers

I have belonged to a women's circle for many years now and one of the most powerful and transformative tools we use is the talking circle, also known as council sharing. All the women are seated in a circle. There is a candle and a Tibetan brass singing bowl in the center. We ring this bowl at the beginning of the circle: its hypnotic sound echoing around the room, getting gradually quieter as we center ourselves.

And then each woman, when she feels called to share, picks up the bowl, and cradling it in her hands, begins to speak whatever is in her heart. Sometimes she may falter at first, or maybe her words come gushing out like a river which has burst its dam. She speaks to the topic at hand, from her soul-depths, uninterrupted until she is finished. When she is done, she replaces the bowl on the table, or passes it to another woman, who takes her turn to speak.

The circle of women holds the space for the speaker as she finds her words and feelings. This profound listening, the holding of another woman's heart without words is a powerful experience, which touches the soul of the listeners. They often cry or smile in recognition, feeling a connection to the soul of the speaking woman: *I thought we were so different*, they think, *but underneath it all we are woven with the same threads.*

This is how I would like to introduce many of the creative mothers to you, through a virtual talking circle: an experience of shared togetherness, of commonality. And I invite you, every time you find their voices throughout the book, to enter the women's circle again and open yourself to their words, let them seep into your cells and soak up their wisdom.

So let us begin, as we always do. I will sound the singing bowl. Hear it echo around. Let it bring you into yourself. Take a deep breath into your belly, feel your feet rooted in the earth, your head soaring up to the heavens, feel your heart begin to open to the stories of others which are about to unfold. Though these words are black ink on the pages of a book, they are also the innermost thoughts and feelings of real women, mothers speaking from their souls. Take a moment to settle in to yourself, so that you can really hear them, and honor their vulnerability in sharing them here with you.

Erin, a painter and writer, starts to speak, her belly rounded with her second babe growing in her womb, her red hair tumbling in curls down over her shoulders:

Do we ever really balance motherhood and creativity? I feel the two simply merge, it becomes a dance, not a balance…as the tides of motherhood shift, with the newborn asleep on my chest, wrapped close, mimicking the full-moon belly, I paint. And then the babe no longer sleeps on my chest, but instead wishes for my arms to simply hold her, and so I put the brush down, and I hold her.

The babe won't nap without a breast near her mouth, and so I lay, and I rest too – a gift… and soon enough again – the babe will paint and play alongside you, or nap for a sweet blissful hour or two, giving you a moment to catch yourself and, should the muse be patient enough, to create.

Sometimes, creating is simply making a cup of tea, and sitting in silence, in my own body – without anyone needing it.

Creating is staring out the window, knowing there are things to be done, but that for this moment, I am sitting, watching the sky…thinking.

Creating, is knowing that I am doing the work that I need – to be living in the moment, fully, not wishing days away or yearning for something in the past. Balance…a dance. An ebb and flow. Creating evolves as and with your child.

Paula, a home-educating mama of four, and a blossoming writer shares her experience:

I am guessing that I am not the only mama who looks around at the rest of the world on her down days and feels lacking. Everyone in blog-land seems so uber-creative: felting, knitting, painting, baking, sewing, making beautiful things of one kind or another. It can feel a bit depressing when I am just about getting through the day making sure the kids are fed, watered and dressed, let alone getting everyone out of the door for outings. These things can, on some days, feel like a major achievement and take every ounce of my energy, patience and mojo.

Some days I look around at my friends, and quietly envy their talents and skills – I'll be honest here, I even envy their children some days. I'm not proud of this. But it's how I really feel.

It gets to me a little that I am neither a fantastic smallholder, keeper of bees, talented quilter, expert gardener, prolific painter, or able to do Swedish massage. The house is getting shabbier and shabbier as I have less and less energy to keep up with the tide of snotty fingers, yogurt drips, felt-tip scribbles, and unidentified stains. The greater part of my garden looks like a mess too, with ground elder and stinging nettles running riot. I feel less than shiny and happy. And I wonder how many of us feel like this sometimes? Surely it can't be just me?

Tessa, a potter, and one of the older women in the circle, takes the bowl. Now in her sixties, she recalls her journey of creative mothering with its twists and turns, from a more circumspect distance:

> I had a couple of false starts when the children were very little. I found making pots was too difficult to combine with small children. I turned my hand to making all our clothes, gardening, and cooking.
>
> When my children were 12 and 10 my mother-in-law died, and the annex to our cottage became vacant. I realized it would make a fabulous workshop and showroom, so that's when I got started properly. It took me two years to get back into making pots good enough to sell, but by having my own space and time, I began to develop. It was the right time in my life to be doing it. The children were growing up, and I had established my own thing, which meant a lot to me (and still does!) after 35 years.

Then, **Tracy**, a performer, drama teacher and mother of one, with eyes the color of the sea and a soft Celtic burr, shares her story:

> I didn't have any models of women who had passed through this experience and had come out the other side. We were all just doing it at the same time. Both of my sisters and my closest friends may have shared many similar experiences and philosophies, but most of them were staying at home with the children, so I found it difficult having to balance work and home life without having people around who were going through the same thing.
>
> What actually helped me through it all was meeting a woman whose workshops I have been attending for the last three years. She inherently urged women to realize that we are more than just one role: we may be mothers, wives, lovers, carers, workers, artists and more. She encouraged me to find my "naked voice", and connecting with this has helped me to be a stronger woman all round.

More recently my challenge has been how to find my own place in the world as a woman, a mother, a wife and an artist. These are sometimes conflicting areas of my life. So how can I find a way of living that allows me to play all of these roles out with maximum "flow"? I am currently trying out alternative paths, such as living apart from my husband, to find what works best. The challenge is that there are no alternative models really available for me in our society, and so it is challenging to have to encounter other people's judgment and projections because I am choosing to live differently.

Artist and mother **Laura P**, addresses how she discovered what really mattered to her in terms of mothering and creativity, a realization which was so different to my own, but vital to her soul needs as a creative mother:

Having children turned everything I thought I knew on its ear! I began to see that being a good mother was the most creative activity I could aspire to. My ideas of what was important "before children" seemed shallow and surface. This kind of creativity went deep, was challenging and filled with frustration and tears and learning and growing for me. The rewards, compared to my earlier idea of reward for creativity, were True and alive. Gold compared to glitter.

Leigh, a stay-at-home mother of three and talented crafter echoes this changing view of her own creativity and its role post-children:

I considered myself "artistic" before having kids. I drew and painted for my own pleasure. But being "creative" took on new meanings for me when I had children. I realized almost everything I did for my kids was a manifestation of my creative side – how I fed them, clothed them, entertained them... Now I express my artistic-ness in creative projects with my kids and in making toys, clothes, presents for them and friends.

Francesca, my own mother and a talented fabric artist, talks about her own experience of growing up as the third child of creative parents:

Artistic temperament was rampant in our house and our wider family – creativity alongside quite a bit of mental instability. It was really quite hard being surrounded by creativity. There was evidence of their creativity all over the house when I was growing up. Architectural plans on Daddy's desk in the sitting room, Mummy on hands and knees cutting out yet another garment. The house was full of pottery made by my sister, chairs upholstered, cushions made, my own clothes sewn and knitted for me, home-grown fruit and veg...

*I think my creativity was sort of fed through the umbilical to me, and I seemed to make it up as I went along, I don't remember doing any projects with my mum or dad. My father was very critical of my creativity, and my mother would finish my unfinished pieces to her own standards, which to my perfectionist nature made it very hard. Her creativity was the **most** important thing in our family. I really struggled to express my creativity, for the criticism was so harsh. Praise, encouragement, understanding and patience did not figure.*

Having children was my greatest challenge. Not knowing how to mother them – as I hadn't had the physical hands-on mother love myself I had to make it up as I went along! Looking back I am proud that I survived. And what I am most proud of is how I have grown as a person in the process, and what truly amazing adults my children have grown into. I hope that one day they can forgive me for all the mistakes I made as a mother, and that I, in turn, am at last able to forgive my own mother, accepting she, too, did the best she could.

Karien, a writer and mother of three explains the constant contradictions of creative motherhood so well:

I find balancing my creative and mothering sides so difficult. They are such a drain on my resources. On the other hand I find that writing lifts me up, motivates me to be a better mother. It is my own thing, something to be proud of. On the other hand those energy-consuming children are what inspires my writing, which closes the cycle. I can do this because and despite of them.

Another of the older women takes her turn, **Isabel** has a lifetime's experience as a professional journalist, and is a budding fiber artist with a growing love of yarn-bombing in provocative places. She is the mother of one:

I was always creative, always inventive, original and excited and fulfilled by creative pursuits, but I didn't think of them as that — I thought it was what everybody did! For me, creativity whether in writing, art, cooking, craft-work, ideas, jewelry-making or embellishment, was a survival necessity as well as an intellectual necessity. I had no idea that my originality, talents and abilities with my hands and word-weaving was a gift. In many ways I just survived. Luckily I had lots and lots of energy, and a mother-tiger attitude towards protecting and doing the best for my daughter, and as creativity was my life, I just did it.

I used to write 1,000 words a day, and then go out and present/research/write for radio or make a television program...or all three combined...as well as keeping child and house and garden, entertaining and taking my responsibilities within the wider family...but that's just what one does as a woman. Men would make a big deal of it, and yes, you're right, we should make a bigger deal of it so that such huge, vital, difficult work be appreciated for what it is...not "I'm just a housewife". Men are never "just" anything.

Elizabeth speaks to the frustrations that she is experiencing at the moment:

Helpful women have often said about having children "how quickly it all passes, enjoy it while you can" – that has been a hard lesson to understand and accept. Patience to accept what is possible now is really hard to achieve. Squeezing in the time – the jumper unfinished, the soft play bag embroidered with stars but not sewn together, folded apron material sitting on top of the machine, the bag of clay that waits...I am proud of just finishing anything!

I think the desire to create will last all my life – I realize that the time for me to be that person has not been available, or should I say right – I have become aware that the young stage of my children's life is passing and there will be more time for me later – it's too easy to be a "want it now" person. But I am so glad that I will have more time very soon.

Without doubt though, as luck would have it, the very best thing I have ever made is my children.

I feel my spirit rise as I listen to Elizabeth's words, and so I reach over and take the bowl...

Before I had children I had a dream. A dream of the sort of mama I wanted to be. One who always had a homemade cake in a pretty tin and a jar of homemade cookies, a stylish handmade home with French-print curtains, a carefully tended cottage garden, lots of time to play together outside and making all our own Christmas presents. Happy children, happy stay-at-home mama and a beautiful life.

I still have that dream in my head. And I do have a beautiful life – but just not quite the one I pictured.

You see, in this maternal fantasy, it was someone else in the picture. Someone always patient and kind, loving and selflessly giving. Someone whose creative expression would be satisfied by domesticity. A tidy someone who oozed order and decorum...

But, and this is a secret just between us, I am not that sort of person. I wasn't before I had children, so why would I suddenly transform into her through the act of giving birth?

I have always been the girl curled up in the corner of her messy room reading a book, or writing in silence. Dreaming, reflecting, researching, drawing, and with a thousand projects on the go at once. In my little fantasy world there was no space for that. I was kind of led to believe that because I wasn't a high-powered career woman, I could happily put my projects aside to be a mothering angel. I had opted into being a stay-at-home mum, so that's what I'd do, right?

My son was just four weeks old when I realized that I need to correct my creative/mother balance. I started to follow The Artist's Way by Julia Cameron. Her morning pages exercise reconnecting me with my old sense of self, which through work, training, pregnancy and now mothering felt like a far-distant land, and one to which I had lost the return ticket.

No one can really warn you just how much energy and patience young children require of you, how much physical and emotional giving, and just how much of a struggle it is if you are not "that sort of mother".

I love my children wholeheartedly. And whilst I feel it is important to be at home with them whilst they are young, for me, mothering is not enough. The energy required of mothering depletes me fast. In my life as a mother I often feel overwhelmed, out of control, full of other people's emotions, other's needs, my head spinning trying to keep all the balls in the air.

But I am remembering. I am changing old patterns that I saw in my mother and my grandmothers. It is not easy, often I feel foolish, indulgent, apologetic. Often I overdo it, forgetting that in the midst of all these hopes and dreams and creative projects lies a human being who gets sick and tired, and needs to rest. And there are three children too, who also need me, often more than I would want, but they do, and that is valid. And my husband too... I am becoming more and more myself every day. As a creative mother, and as a woman, and that fills my heart with joy and gratitude.

Here, take the bowl, it is your turn now. Tell us your story – tell us your dreams, your struggles, your reality. Speak it out loud, write it in your journal, make a video, record your voice speaking it – tell us your truth, dearest woman, we are listening, we long to hear your words.

Reflections

How did it feel listening and contributing to a circle of women?

Do you have a trusted circle in your life with whom you can speak openly?

Do you yearn for one? What do you long to share? How might you begin to share more deeply what is in your heart? Talk to a soul sister, write a blog post, or join or start a women's circle of your own!

Creative exercise

Paint, draw, write a poem or a journal entry on:

"The sort of mother I thought I would be" – paint your dream – you, the family, the home – what is your fantasy?

And then on:

"The mother that I am" – you, the family, the home that you have.

Often we focus on what we don't have, and all the ways things aren't perfect. Let's change perspectives.

Where does your dream vision come from? Whose story is it? Often it is a mish-mash of our own "best bits" of childhood, story books, films, magazines and books.

Can you reflect honestly on the differences?

How is what you have better than you could have anticipated?

How can you bring more of your dream alive in your current life?

Which parts of the dream no longer fit you – how can

you let them go?

What have you learnt about your very real self in between creating that dream and now?

Chapter 5

Heroines

Motherhood is good for the soul. Poetry is good for the soul. The archetype of the selfish male artist tells us that we can't manage all these things at once, that we can't be simultaneously responsible to children, babysitters, self, and art, that we have to sacrifice, to abandon – but we know that's a lie.
Ariel Gore, "Women and Happiness", *Psychology Today*

I was discussing the topic of creative women with my soul-sister Tracy, a writer-director-performer-facilitator and mother of one. We reflected on the hunger that we women have to see ourselves reflected in the eyes and words of others: it is this need which calls us to our female friendships and women's groups, and to devour women's films, books, magazines, blogs and poetry. We wondered aloud why women seem to need to hear other women's stories and experiences in order to strengthen their own resolve and validate their own feelings. And then we wondered some more, why was it that the men we know do not seem to need this?

We came to the conclusion that it is because women's lives, women's feelings, women's creativity have been underground, whereas men's lives and examples are explicitly taught and visible all around. Women's lives have lain unvalued, unspoken, unpainted, undramatized for so long that we begin to doubt their reality.

We live in a man's world. In every art gallery that we go to, the walls are covered with the works of the great masters. In *The Art Book* only 20 of the 500 great artists are women. It is said that it is easier for a woman to appear in the Tate Gallery naked, than it is as an artist. The walls of libraries hold the male classics. In the *Norton Anthology of American Literature 1914 onwards* only 37 of

139 writers are female. The plays we watch are overwhelmingly filled with male characters. Our history lessons were full of the achievements of men. Please do not think I am man-bashing. I am not. Simply verbalizing what passes for normality in our culture.

The reality of mothers in the arts

It is no coincidence that the vast majority of celebrated female creatives throughout history were not mothers: Jane Austen, Charlotte Brontë, Virginia Woolf, Georgia O'Keeffe, Mary Cassett, George Eliot, Anaïs Nin, Marilyn Monroe, Edith Wharton, Janis Joplin, Bridget Riley, Frida Kahlo... These women's chosen primary allegiance was to their art. To be an artist or writer in the past was a role women took on *instead* of motherhood, and often instead of marriage too.

But these are names from the past. We've had the feminist revolution, so surely things are different now. Unfortunately not as much as you would hope. **Tracey Emin,** Turner Prize nominee and Brit-artist, writes in *The Independent* of her active choice not to have children and to choose the life of professional creative:

I'd never have believed that I would say or think this, but as I get older, it's becoming more and more obvious that my children are hanging on the Tate Britain walls.

When I first started becoming successful, I was filled with strange guilt and misunderstanding of myself. I felt that my abortions had somehow been a Faustian pact, and in return for my children's souls, I had been given my success.

Professor and artist **Elizabeth MacKenzie** reflects on this on her blog, *Negotiating Doubt*:

When I went to art school in the late 1970s young women assumed if they wanted to be an artist they shouldn't become mothers. I'm not sure this has changed very much.

But it's not just creative women's embittered personal experiences that tell this story. Research by academics, foundations and film makers back it up too:

- In 2006, research from the American National Endowment for the Arts revealed that: *Only 29 percent of women artists had children under 18, almost six percentage points lower than for women workers in general.*
- The 2008 film documentary, *Who Does She Think She Is?* which chronicled the lives of five artists and their challenges in pursuing their passions while nurturing families, cites the following statistics: *We have 80 percent female students at the School of Visual Arts. But in the real world, we have 70 to 80 percent male artists in galleries and museums.*

Why is it that motherhood and a life of the professional artist are in such conflict? In an essay entitled *Where Are All the Famous Women Artists?* written in the form of an open letter, Shelley Essack speaks with passion and insight:

> *Art is fabulous; one of the most rewarding endeavors a human being can pursue. But (and this is huge), you burn with it. Art consumes the artist deliciously, but it is a harsh discipline in terms of time and concentration. To create it spectacularly a person needs to eat, sleep and breathe art – which means a lot of other things must be neglected (temporarily or totally) by default.*
>
> *Facts are, Ladies, it's us who bear the live young, and usually us who keep them alive. Raising children, in case you're wondering, takes a phenomenal amount of physical labor and attention. Parenting is important, rewarding work in its own right, but it doesn't leave a ton of free time, let alone free time during which the brain is bursting with creativity.*

Above and beyond Essack's point that women put in the majority of physical energy in bearing and raising the young, a further crippling reality for most women who might want to be a professional creative, is that in order to work outside the home, her work has got to cover the cost of the childcare. Many artists, especially starting out, do not earn enough to do this, and therefore, where it was morality which in the past stopped a creative mother from creating anything beyond the domestic sphere, in the modern era economics has added its disabling clout.

Permission givers

For those of us who walk the path of the creative mother, we look for beacons of hope, for women who shine their light and say – yes it is possible, to be a mother and an artist, these were my struggles, this was how I managed it, this is why I did it.

I first found my sheroes in the pages of books. Sylvia Plath, Louise Erdrich and Adrienne Rich spoke deeply to my experience, before the era of blogs and Facebook, where I began to encounter more real-life permission givers.

These women shared my intense soul-struggle of balancing creating with mothering. They all deeply desired to have families, only to discover that the reality of mothering (and often being a wife) was stifling and suffocating.

In a *Salon* interview with Robert Spillman, writer and poet, **Louise Erdrich**, discusses a creative mothering icon of hers, Toni Morrison, the Pulitzer prize-winning novelist and mother of two:

Toni Morrison talks about finding a writer who gives one "permission" to write, someone who breaks down the barriers and allows you the self-confidence to write.

Who gives you permission to live your life fully as a creative mother – either by living an inspired life, by sharing their wisdom or by simply talking about the challenges they face?

Sylvia Plath, was a heroine of mine in my late teen years. An academic and poet herself, she married another poet, Ted Hughes, whose mind was just as brilliant and whose career had previously been almost parallel to her own. However, when children arrived she watched in barely concealed fury as he seemed to fly in freedom, whilst she was required to put her poetic skills to one side in order to mother their children. As a teen I thought that her suicide was simply the act of a woman consumed by her art, but as a creative mother myself, I recognize in her words and desperate actions, the voice of the Crazy Woman, the dark side of the Creative Mother, whom I will discuss in the next chapters. In her I see a sister, wrestling against the expectations of domesticity and motherhood. She speaks of her competing longings in her diary:

> *I would live a life of conflict, of balancing children, sonnets, love and dirty dishes; and banging an affirmation of life out on pianos and ski slopes and in bed, in bed, in bed!*

I am always very grateful when creative mothers address the mundane, domestic arrangements of their lives and lift the curtain to show how they practically balance their creative time with mothering. In her diary **Plath** shares:

> *I am up at five, in my study, with coffee, writing like mad – have managed a poem a day before breakfast... Terrific stuff...as though domesticity had choked me.*

Louise Erdrich is one of America's most talented writers and mother of six: three adopted and three birthed children. Married to another writer, they seem to have carved out an incredible working relationship and childcare strategy in the 1980s and 1990s which honored both of their creative needs and their children's needs for hands-on parenting. She documents it in part in her spellbinding book, *The Blue Jay's Dance: A Childbirth Year*:

I write poems during the late nights up until the week of birth, and fiction by day. I suppose one could say, pulling in the obviously metaphors, that my work is hormone driven, inscribed in mother's milk, pregnant with itself. I do begin to think that I am in touch with something larger than me. I feel that I am transcribing verbatim from a flow of language running through the room, an ink current into which I dip the pen. It is a dark stream, swift running, a twisting flow that never doubles back. The amazement is that I need only enter the room at those strange hours to be drawn back into the language. The frustration is that I cannot be there all the time.

Choices

These women's reflections on the fullness of motherhood, both light and dark, are refreshing and reassuring. They honestly speak about what it has prevented for them, the limitations it has caused in their personal lives and careers, as well as the richness, groundedness and insight into their own characters and those of others, that their children's presence has brought. This is a refreshing contrast to the saccharine tracts of others which tell us how wonderful and fulfilling every aspect of motherhood is.

Adrienne Rich, a mother of three boys, poet and writer, mothering in the 1950s and 60s shares the constant balancing act required of her:

My children cause me the most exquisite suffering of which I have any experience. It is in the suffering of ambivalence: the murderous alternation between bitter resentment and raw-edged nerves, and blissful gratification and tenderness. Sometimes I seem to myself, in my feelings toward these tiny, guiltless beings, a monster of selfishness and intolerance. Their voices wear away at my nerves, their constant needs, above all their need for simplicity and patience, fill me with despair at my own failures, despair too at my fate, which is to serve a function for which I was not fitted.

My needs were always balanced against those of a child, and always losing. For me, poetry was where I lived as no-one's mother, where I existed as myself.

I adore the way **Louise Erdrich** expresses the trade-offs of creative motherhood in this memorable segment in an interview entitled *The Art of Fiction*, in *The Paris Review:*

By having children, I've both sabotaged and saved myself as a writer. With a child you certainly can't be a Bruce Chatwin or a Hemingway, living the adventurer-writer life. No running with the bulls at Pamplona. [...] Without my children, I'd have written with less fervor; I wouldn't understand life in the same way. I'd probably have become obsessively self-absorbed, or slacked off. Maybe I'd have become an alcoholic. Many of the writers I love most were alcoholics. I've made my choice, I sometimes think: wonderful children instead of hard liquor.

The ultimate expression for me of a creative mother's impossible choices is this excerpt from **Sylvia Plath**'s book, *The Bell Jar*. The image of the tree with its branches speaks deep to my soul.

I saw my life branching out before me like the green fig-tree in the story.

From the tip of every branch, like a fat purple fig, a wonderful future beckoned and winked. One fig was a husband and a happy home and children, and another fig was a famous poet, another fig was a brilliant professor, and another fig was Europe and Africa and South America, and another fig was a pack of lovers with queer names and off-beat professions [...] and beyond and above these figs were many more figs I couldn't quite make out.

I saw myself sitting in the crotch of this fig-tree, starving to death, just because I couldn't make up my mind which of the figs I would choose. I wanted each and every one of them, but choosing one meant losing all the rest, and, as I sat there, the figs began to wrinkle and go black, and, one by one, they plopped to the ground at my feet.

Another of my heroines I was lucky enough to interview for this book, **Jennifer Louden**, the bestselling author of many books on women's self-care, was so touching in her openness:

A lot of my problem with caring for my daughter was feeling that I had to do it all. That I couldn't ask. That was my story for a long time. I'd hire people for a few hours. Friends had full-time nannies. But I couldn't. I wanted to look after her myself.

The second wave of feminism wouldn't allow that you wanted both – to be a mother and to work, and that you had a kid and you wanted to stay home to take care of them. I felt really alone. No one was talking about any of this. I used to think: "I'm just trying to be human as I do this thing, and I'm going to fail at something." But this isn't a mommy problem. And I used to get really mad when people would ask me about it in interviews. It's a conversation our whole society needs to have.

Mentors

I was extremely surprised that almost none of the women that I spoke with had had creative mother mentors in their lives. **Hannah** speaks for many when she says:

I've always had mentors so feel sad I don't have any right now on this complex path.

I found this fascinating, because women tend to be social creatures who come into their own power in groups, and who find their truths through sharing their experiences with others. If this is not happening on a large scale, no wonder creative mothers are struggling.

As creative mothers we need all the mentors we can find: living or dead, celebrated artists and family members. We need to collect, study and cherish each creative woman who has had the courage to create a life in her own image, not, I must add, to copy her, but rather, as someone who gives you permission – to dream big, to take risks, to live brightly, to follow your intuition. Throughout the ages male artists would serve apprenticeships under master artists or craftsmen. And women used to learn to mother whilst watching their mother or aunts tend to an extended family, as well as helping to care for the children of sisters and cousins. So whilst women artists have always been on the back foot in terms of mentoring and role models, now women are entering motherhood with little experience either.

No wonder the creative mother feels at such a loss entering this new land with no guides, no maps, no external acknowledgement of the reality she now finds herself in. It is very much at the forefront of my intention and ambition that this book, and the women that you discover through it, take that place for you, so that you no longer feel lost, alone or unsupported in your journey.

Reflections

Who are your creative mother heroines?

Have you heard them discuss their struggles and insights?

Seek out as many as you can and find out as much as you can about their experiences, to inform your own.

Make a collage of their most inspiring quotations or works of art to inspire and support you on your journey.

Chapter 6

Discovering the Creative Rainbow Mother

We don't need someone to show us the ropes. We are the ones we have been waiting for. Deep inside us we know the feeling we need to guide us. Our task is to learn to trust our inner knowing.
Sonia Johnson, *Going out of our Minds*

After a particularly bad day as a failed maternal angel and domestic goddess, I felt totally despondent. I knew that I just wasn't cut out for this mothering lark.

I curled up in bed with one of my favorite books, **Christiane Northrup**'s *Women's Bodies, Women's Wisdom*. I turned to the section on mothering and what I read was nothing short of a revelation to me, and I'm just hoping that it might be to you too:

The author Lynn Andrews once wrote that there are two types of mother: Earth Mothers and Creative Rainbow Mothers.

Earth Mothers nurture their children and feed them – and they thrive on this. Our society rewards this kind of woman as the "good mother."

Creative Rainbow Mothers, on the other hand, inspire their children without necessarily having meals on the table on time.

I know that, beyond a doubt, I'm a Creative Rainbow Mother.

I once read the cookery book Laurel's Kitchen and fantasized about how wonderful it would be to bake bread daily and relish being what Laurel calls "The Keeper of the Keys" – and to create that ever-important nurturing home space. But this is not who I am – and to try to be something I'm not would ultimately do my children and I a great disservice.

I love to be alone. I love to read. I love quiet and music and writing. My soul is fed by long hours of unbroken creative time.

Young children require a much different type of energy – a type of energy I don't have in abundance.

The penny dropped. I too am a Creative Rainbow Mother, but I had been comparing myself to Earth Mothers, and finding myself failing. I had never had a word for myself before. And I had been doubly confused, because people often referred to me as an Earth Mother. And I can see why: I love to bake, I'm a very affectionate person, have lots of children and wear floaty hippy skirts. But I didn't feel it fitted me. It didn't come naturally. In order to be that person, I need a lot of my own creative time.

I cannot express the degree of relief I felt at discovering the Creative Rainbow Mother archetype: it was a paradigm-changing "a-ha" moment of self-realization and acceptance for me. One perhaps that you share. I was deeply comforted, inspired and reassured to find myself writ large. I was neither alone nor wrong. Nor was I a bad mother.

Despite thinking that the term Creative Rainbow Mother was a little "out there", OK, quite a lot out there if truth be told (it's OK, it's not just you!) and that my readers might think I'd completely lost the plot, I ran to my computer, despite it being well past bedtime, and shared the above passage and my very tired thoughts on the subject on my blog, *Dreaming Aloud*.

Overnight the comments came flying in thick and fast, from women around the world, both regular readers and new voices. So many other mothers identified themselves with this too. They felt completely "seen" in this description, like they no longer had to try to be something they were not. The communal sense of relief was palpable. And each time I have shared the idea with new women, the response is the same: an audible release of tension. They finally felt they had permission to be who they were: there was nothing "wrong" with them.

This was a framework which made sense to lots of mothers out there. This was an idea which needed to be talked about. I wanted to know more. I was hungry for it. But I was amazed, and disappointed, there was very little information out there about Creative Rainbow Mothers.

It was in my incessant searches for more about the archetype online that I discovered the wonderful work of Leonie Dawson, who had discovered the archetype through the words of Christiane Northrup too, and resonated strongly with it. And also the work of Lynn V. Andrews who had first introduced the concept through her book, *Jaguar Woman*, and with whom I was lucky enough to speak in the writing of this book. But after that the trail went cold. What follows, therefore, is a careful piecing together of what facts exist, expanded and supported by my own intuitive understanding and observation.

A new maternal archetype

Traditional psychology is often spare or entirely silent about deeper issues important to women: the archetypal, the intuitive, the sexual and cyclical, a woman's way, a woman's knowing, her creative fire.
Clarissa Pinkola Estes, *Women Who Run With The Wolves*

Why have we not heard about the Creative Rainbow Mother before?

For hundreds of years her secret has been guarded by a group of wise women: The Sisterhood of the Shields. She is rooted in Mayan tradition, and loosely connected to the Mayan Rainbow goddess Ix Chel. For centuries the Sisterhood has initiated women during their first pregnancy in *La Ultima Madre* – the initiation of the "Final Mother".

La Ultima Madre teaches that there are two types of mothers: the Creative Rainbow Woman and Nurturing Earth Mother.

Lynn V. Andrews, celebrated author and shaman, introduced the idea of the Creative Rainbow Woman to Western women in her third book, *Jaguar Woman*, published in 1985 and elucidated the concept further in a 2005 article in The Meta Arts magazine.

Andrews, who identifies herself with the Creative Rainbow Woman archetype, refers to the two mothering archetypes as the "Ecstatic Rainbow Mother" and the "Nurturing Earth Mother". Each of these has her shadow side or opposite face, like a yin and yang. These are described as four energy hoops or archetypes, which can be imagined as two double-headed arrows overlapping to make a cross. Rainbow Mother's dark side is "Crazy Woman" and Earth Mother's is "Death Mother".

The Rainbow Mother is often perceived, either in her own mind, or those of others, as a misfit. A dreamer and creatrix, she is always fluttering like a butterfly from one project to another, always trying new things. She regularly needs to descend into her creative depths, bringing visions between the physical world and the dream-time.

The ecstatic Rainbow Mother is the energy of the poet, the dancer, the weaver and the Seer. Artists are intimate with Rainbow Mother, for she is their muse. And she is completely misunderstood in our society, a world that does not support its artists, its writers and thinkers. She wants to dream and inspire people to health and well-being, and routine wilts her.

Lynn Andrews, *The Meta Arts magazine*

A Creative Rainbow Mother's home, despite her often being a real home-body, tends to reflect her abundant yet chaotic approach to life – with half-finished projects, creative materials and inspiration, and mess, all around her. She does not prioritize housework over soul work! Not for her the routines of the Earth Mother, nor the consistency which society tells her she must provide for her children in order to be a good mother.

Whilst the Nurturing Mother finds immense comfort, safety and satisfaction in marriage, domesticity, growing food and children, and enjoys order around her, the Creative Rainbow Mother regularly feels the need to fly free. And the truth is that she is a divided soul. Her home and family, despite her great love for them, usually come second in her heart. Her spirit follows a different calling, often her art, but sometimes another career, which is, if she is honest with herself, the most important thing in her life. But she needs her home, her partner and children to help her to ground her energy and keep her in this world – and so there is a constant tension built into her relationships.

Of course I hate labels and stereotypes as much as the next creative individual. I am sure that each woman has a degree of Earth and Rainbow mother in her, just as I am sure that there must be other mother 'types' omitted from this dichotomy. After all, none of us is a one-dimensional being. We all hold many archetypes, or energy patterns associated with different characters, within us: Mother, Lover, Virgin, Fool, Wise Woman, Student, Teacher, Artist...which can teach us more about the aspects of our personalities that we need insight and guidance in. When we use archetypes as a tool in this way, often the patterns of our character and unconscious behavior which previously baffled us fall into relief. This is the gift of archetypes: to allow us momentary detachment from our individuality, in order to see ourselves more clearly.

Creative exercise

What archetypes can you see in your life?

Make a list of all the characters you are aware of within you.

Now choose just one that you feel drawn to working with. Flick through a number of magazines, picking out images and colors which you associate with this archetype. Create a collage in your journal, or on a deck of index cards to represent this archetype.

For more guidance on this process see Seena B. Frost's book *SoulCollage*.

Understanding the energy of Creative Rainbow Women

The energy of the Creative Rainbow Mother is to conceive, gestate and birth, over and over. Whereas that of the Earth Mother is to nurture the existent: she deals with what is with great devotion, where the Creative Rainbow Woman is always after what will be, trying to unravel the red thread of creation a little faster, in the constant urge to co-create, rather than accept. The Creative Rainbow Woman needs to cultivate a certain set of skills (not those usually taught to women, whose training has previously only been that of the Earth Mother, the homemaker and nurturer). These skills include:

- An understanding of erotic and ecstatic states, in order to seduce the muse and open ourselves to becoming pregnant with creations.
- Knowing how to ensure that our bodies and souls are as fertile as possible.
- Caring for ourselves during creative gestation.
- Understanding the stages of creative birth and how to navigate them: when to push and when to surrender.
- Knowing how to find a creative doula, midwife or birth partner who supports our vision.
- Learning how to support others in their process.

If we understand our dominant energy force we can learn to work with, rather than against, ourselves.

When envisaging the difference between the Earth and Creative Rainbow Mother archetypes I like to think of them in terms of energy. The Earth Mother is encircling, embracing, she holds a space with calmness and strength. She is the Venus fertility image, an earth goddess: sturdy, reliable, consistent, patient. A strong but gentle flow of constant energy comes from her heart, her arms embracing firmly to comfort, to hold on, and sometimes to hold back. The Creative Rainbow Mother is more like a whirling dance of colors, with sparks of energy flying out like fireworks – grab hold of one and you can take a journey to the stars, but you might also get your fingers burned. Hers is an expressive, expulsive energy, dynamic, shifting, uncertain. Think of the power of a volcano, or explosion: a big bright light, and then silence. Whilst the Earth Mother pulls towards her, the Rainbow Mama pushes away. The Earth Mother is magnetic when we need to be calmed and soothed, the Rainbow Mother is hypnotic and exciting when we want to learn, explore and play.

Earth Mothers tend to recharge their energies through giving and interaction, order and routine. The energy pattern of an Earth Mother is a straight line, like the horizon – it might rise and fall, but slowly.

Creative Rainbow Mothers tend to recharge through solitude and creative activity. The energy pattern of a Creative Rainbow is high peaks and low troughs, like a heart-rate monitor, rising and falling in quick succession: her energy pulsates. The high energy of a Creative Rainbow is not sustainable. It is necessarily followed by periods of reflection, lethargy and a sense of emptiness. The key to managing her creative energy is primarily not to let the highs and lows become too exaggerated. This is done mainly by taking care of physical needs and keeping her biological self in balance – eating, sleeping, resting, both when feeling creative and when feeling low.

We need to recognize the cyclical nature of our patterns, to know that neither lasts forever, that a low is just that and that soon the energy will swing up once more. If it goes unchecked, or is overblown, then these swings can turn into full-blown depressive episodes which are disabling not only for the mother, but for the whole family which orbits her energies. We need to learn to surf these energy changes rather than be swept away or dragged under by them. Knowing when you need to retreat and recharge and how to do this in small spurts is a vital skill for all mothers, especially creatives. All of this will be explored in more detail in Part II.

Children always need energy, they cannot turn this need off, though as they get older they can learn what part of the cycle you are in and become more self-reliant in some areas or accept deferred gratification of their needs. Younger children cannot be expected to do this. This is why parenting young children is so draining for the creative mother. Just at the moment that she feels she has not an ounce more energy to give, and that she needs to retreat into herself, the child, sensing this withdrawal, draws closer and sticks to her like super glue, pulling her fully back into this world.

In traditional societies, Creative Rainbow Mothers would be honored for their unique talents and abilities, and Earth Mothers for theirs. In our own, the Creative Rainbow Mother is expected to be an Earth Mother too. And all mothers are supposed to be able to do it alone. Whereas in reality we evolved to live in a tribal society when raising children, and most mothers I speak to mourn the lack of this, and feel it as a deep hole in their mothering experience.

I found it interesting to note in my research for this book, that a larger than average number of Creative Rainbow Mothers had one child. As a mother of three, this seems like a wise move from women who know that they must prioritize their creative energies: they know that with one they can give of their best to their child and their work. Those of us who only realized our Creative Rainbow Mama tendencies in midst procreation, are those who struggle most with energy issues and keeping our mental health on keel.

The Creative Rainbow Mother...

- *Has the energy of the poet, seeker, dreamer and artist.*
- *Inspires and celebrates her children in her own way.*
- *Seeks to understand her own unique energy and work with it, honoring her own cycles above those of clock and calendar.*

- *Acknowledges that her creativity is embodied within her uniquely beautiful female body.*
- *Needs to discover, make space for and honor her own creativity and find satisfying outlets for it which will recharge her energy.*
- *Journeys to the dream-time and regularly immerses herself in ecstasy.*
- *Finds a way to make a home in a way that does not suck her energy.*
- *Honors the Crazy Woman and seeks balance and healing in her life.*
- *Weaves a web of beauty around her.*

Creative exercise

Take a moment to create an image of a Creative Rainbow Mother. Draw, paint or collage her. How is she colorful? Does she have multicolor clothes or aura, rainbow makeup on her eyes and nails, does everything she touches turn to color?

She who lives between the worlds

Each woman has potential access to Rio Abajo Rio, this river beneath the river. She arrives there through deep meditation, dance, writing, painting, prayer-making, singing, drumming, active imagination, or any activity which requires an intense altered consciousness. A woman arrives in this world-between-worlds through yearning and by seeking something she can see just out of the corner of her eye. She arrives there by deeply creative acts, through intentional solitude, and by the practice of any of the arts.
Clarissa Pinkola Estes, *Women Who Run with the Wolves*

The creative urge takes us "between the worlds", between (in philosophical terminology) the nouminal (that which we can only imagine) and the phenomenal (that which we can touch), between the real and the ideal, between the conscious and subconscious, and in terms of our brain waves, between the creative, relaxed, dreamy alpha state and the more active, alert, go-go-go beta waves. It is my theory that in Creative Rainbow Mothers this need to change between the two states is more pronounced, more frequent, and the dissonance which emerges when the frequent shifts between the two is blocked, causes physical and emotional ill-health and the emergence of the Crazy Woman.

The Creative Rainbow Woman who understands and uses her creative, artistic powers as tools, to help her switch between these two states, ensures optimal health for herself and stability for her family. Rather than resist or resent this, she understands that her path constantly takes her between the inner and the outer, dreams and the material world, darkness and light. Her path is the Rainbow Way, the spiraling labyrinth, the *Rio abajo Rio*.

The Way has two guardians – Creative Rainbow Mother, and the Crazy Woman. The creative mother cannot ignore either.

Crazy Woman lives in the darkness, in the center of the labyrinth. Guardian of the womb space, the dark unseen places of life and creativity. She emerges if we try to spend all our time out in the world, turned on, serving others. She starts to walk out of the labyrinth to find us. For she knows we are not on the Rainbow Way, we are not walking the spiral path which is our soul's avowed journey, we are trying to be that which we are not. Out she comes towards us. The longer we have been away from our depths, the louder she shouts and screams to find us. But if we have forgotten her wisdom, forgotten the Rainbow Way, she has to use more and more force until we follow her. And still we resist her, thinking she is mad and bad and wrong. Thinking we are crazy, irresponsible, lazy...

The Creative Rainbow Woman is the other handmaiden of our creative feminine lives. She who comes with her colors, ideas, poems and songs, her dreams dripping from her fingers like jewels. She draws us out of our centers, if we have been there too long, she finds her path blocked. If we can't follow her, then her energy can heal our stuckness, she brings color to our darkness. She leads us out of depression, grayness, and loneliness with art, music and dance. Her ways offer healing. If we will only follow them, they will lead us out of the labyrinth and back into the world, to community, to beauty, freedom and love.

As children we lived between the worlds naturally, and when adulthood beckoned, we found our way there through alcohol, drugs, orgasm, experiences in nature, meditation, and half-waking states. But motherhood usually makes this sense of being "between the worlds" a regular occurrence rather than a rarity.

Ecstasy (from the root, ex-stasis, meaning outside of the normal realm), or being between the worlds, is not simply confined to irregular peak experiences. It also arises when we are pre-menstrual and menstrual, breastfeeding and deep in a creative project. During pregnancy, birth and the early days of mothering, our hormones can often put us into this state for weeks on end – some call it fuzzy brain or mama brain. But if, rather than resist it or dismiss it, we can immerse ourselves in gentle surrender into this state like a lovely warm bath, this feeling of being between the worlds usually produces a feeling of headiness, spaciness, euphoria, relaxation, flow, release, a sense of oneness with all things. This place is where our creative self lies, outside of logic, this is the soup of images, of poetry and paintings, where the colors of patchwork dance.

It is wonderful, but it is also addictive and leaves us perpetually wanting more of these feel-good chemicals, rather than the fast-paced beta waves and adrenaline that daily life requires of modern humans.

This is a big downside of motherhood in today's world: ecstatic states do not mesh well with the hyper-alert vigilance that babies and young children require in a nuclear family situation full of sharp corners, stairs, electrical sockets and speeding cars. This sets up a tension between our desire to drift between the worlds, and our need to be present in our domestic duties as mother.

Our children's need for us as sole caregivers to be present, engaged and responsive can be deeply challenging. Often in the midst of a creative project I find that even though I am at home on parenting duty, my mind is ticking over, half-focused on the project, problem solving and creating. This can lead to (added) impatience and frustration at their demands, which compete with my need to be between the worlds.

But what is also true is that children also live between the worlds a lot themselves. When they are babies it means that we can live at their pace without resistance – we can snuggle and drift and nurse and simply be together.

With pre-schoolers they need us to be able to access this place to enter creative play with them. However, they need us to be able to access this state within their own imaginary worlds rather than imposing our own on them. This is one reason why allowing ourselves time and space for our own creative projects, and strengthening our own creativity, is of such benefit to our children.

Reflections

What meaning do you find in the Creative Rainbow Mother archetype?

What resonated with you about the archetype?

What did not ring true?

Do the same again with the Earth Mother archetype.

What feelings do you have towards identifying with the Creative Rainbow archetype? Do you hanker to be an Earth Mother?

How do you sabotage or not support yourself in being a Creative Rainbow?

Creative exercise

Self-portrait of myself as mother

Open to a clean page in your journal. Paint it a lovely color, perhaps even rainbow colors. Fill the whole page with color. There is no way you can do it "wrong".

Take a photo of you that you love. Stick it onto the page of your journal. Now write around it lots of positive traits of yourself as a mother: affectionate, loving, interested, devoted, funny, patient – you don't have to be them all the time. But if you do it regularly, then put it down. See it and really feel it.

Chapter 7

The Crazy Woman

There have been times in my life when I haven't had time to do art and I go crazy.
Janis Mars Wunderlich, sculptor

For each of us as women, there is a deep place within, where hidden and growing our true spirit rises… Within these deep places, each one holds an incredible reserve of creativity and power, of unexamined and unrecorded emotion and feeling. The woman's place of power within each of us is neither white nor surface; it is dark, it is ancient, and it is deep.
Audrey Lorde

I have mentioned the Crazy Woman many times now, in passing, teasingly, I have dropped her name on the wind. For so many women she has remained nameless the whole of their lives. Unnamed, unacknowledged, unwelcome. But felt. Deeply felt.

But she is no new invention. The Crazy Woman has been depicted in ancient goddesses around the world: Kali, Medea, Hecate, Durga…only here and now it seems, she remains unnamed, in the hope that she would un-exist.

I have found that the Crazy Woman is the crux of my work for many women: the unspoken, unspeakable archetype with which almost every Creative Rainbow Woman instinctively identifies. Time and again women have found that she is the key to their own personal unlocking. This is where their power is held, in darkness and anger. We are taught to fear her domain, and avoid it. Cover her up with gentleness, niceness, meekness and silence. Prettify her with cosmetics. Bite your tongue. Swallow your words. Be grateful. Do not, whatever you do, make a fuss. Be a good girl and smile. Don't ask questions. Don't complain. Shhhh, don't shout! This is what our culture teaches.

What have you learnt about the Crazy Woman so far in your life – from your mother, grandmother, aunts, teachers, female friends? Was she acceptable or locked away? Was she papered over with niceness and face powder? Was she medicated with anti-depressants or alcohol? Did she emerge in screaming fits or suicide attempts? In physical abuse or shaming? In divorce or hospitalization?

And more importantly how have you learnt to deal with her? What role has she played in your life to date?

Many of us simply try to deny she is even there. I remember once, in all honesty, claiming that I never felt angry! But denying our shadow side does not mean it is not there, it just hides it further, makes it stronger and deeper as it grows in the darkness of our denial and rejection, causing more suffering when it finally emerges through the layers of our psyches. Warns **Lynn Andrews** in *Jaguar Woman*:

> *As in all things there is great danger. If you don't honor Crazy Woman, she might destroy you.*

The Crazy Woman has been locked away: the mad woman in our attic, who could, we are sure, do untold damage if let loose. She is deeply threatening to society. We dare not admit to her for fear of our children being taken from us, of being hospitalized in a mental institution, of being deemed "unable to cope", of bringing shame to our families and ourselves. And so our Crazy Woman side is further denied, pushed further away, or medicated with anti-depressants, self-harm, eating disorders or alcohol.

When you're tired and drained and you have given every drop of energy, love, patience; when your kids have been crawling all over you for days and weeks; when you need a break, some head space, some body space and just can't get it, you start to truly feel like you are going crazy, dying inside, and this can lead to us wanting to die, or kill, or at least to hurt – to be done with it all.

What we need to remember in these moments is that we are experiencing the emergence of the Crazy Woman who trails death in smoke around her. She senses the psychic suffocation of our creative selves, when we are so subsumed by mothering and external demands, when we do not have time to tend our creative fires, and emerges to strike away the barriers that are keeping us from ourselves. She comes to destroy, so that new life can emerge. But all we can sense is the death and destruction that she threatens, not the renaissance beyond.

> *Crazy Woman does not really wish to kill you. She wishes to maim your talents and paralyze your ability; she wishes to strip you of all your sacredness. She pulls your sanity and tests you, trying to lure you away from your center.*
>
> **Lynn Andrews,** *The Meta Arts magazine*

Crazy Woman's power and fury are truly terrifying, her force overwhelming, to us, our partners and children. It is as though a demon has been unleashed. This is how another Creative Rainbow Mother describes her:

> *I struggle so much with anger – it scares the crap out of me. The household I grew up in was defined by anger, and I feel that out-of-control rage in myself (sometimes at the silliest things).*

I know her. You know her. She lives within us all. Like a fish out of water, the Creative Rainbow Mother needs to create just as she needs to breathe. As **Hannah** describes:

> *It's harder not to create and write. I become resentful and petty and feel my soul shrinking. Writing feeds me more than anything else.*

It sounds so odd I'm sure to those who do not have that drive within them, but the Creative Rainbow Mama will understand the deep impetus, the unstoppable, unrelenting engine of creativity which drives her. **Michelle**, a creative mother of two based in Australia shares her experience:

> I tried just waiting [until the children were older to be creative], but it was sending me slowly insane. I felt frustrated, trapped and resentful of my husband who continued to pursue his interests. It wasn't good for me or for my family. But I had to let go of my preferred methods of being creative (leaving half-finished projects lying on the dining table, working with chemicals and tools) and find a new way to be creative in the middle of life. If I'm not creating something I get a bit "twitchy" – I feel out of balance, easily angered, my husband would probably add – grumpy!

Most Creative Rainbow Women feel ensnared by the needs of others, by their obligations: they are exquisitely aware of how close they walk to potential failure. The harder they try to keep up the appearance of coping, of serving everyone else first, the more of their energy they squander and the more depleted they become. Closer and closer draws the Crazy Woman, as **Mon** shares:

> As my daughter became more mobile, I struggled with time. It has been a process of many downs – feeling frustration, anger, fear at losing time. I'm Zen about it, but it's a daily work. Many days I scream inside, for time, for space. But we only have influence over one thing – our perspective.

But these words are all very well. The Crazy Woman does not deal in words, only lived wisdom. I had reached this point in the book, the part on the Crazy Woman, and so, with the deep irony and synchronicity inherent in living a creative life, she decided to visit me with her full force, to illustrate what she looked like, how she felt: *I am Crazy Woman hear me roar!* All hell broke loose in my house! Chicken pox hit, knocking down one child at a time, disrupting sleep and leaving us at breaking point as a family. For three weeks I didn't have a moment to write a concentrated sentence and yet ideas were coming to me thick and fast. There was always a whining child – or three – wanting to be on my lap: hot, cranky and uncomfortable in their skins. Our fifteen-month-old, rather than weaning, became almost totally breastfed again. Bed times went out the window, nights blended into days. I was getting no head space, no writing time, no physical space. My husband's work commitments were keeping him out of the house. I screamed, I smacked, I cried and yelled and slammed doors, and wrote angry blog posts, and cried, and wrote, and suddenly she was gone. So please know that you are not alone in being a Crazy Woman, in fact you're in great company!

The domesticated wild woman

My creative spirit calls me. I try to keep my heart with my kiddies, not to burn too many bridges. But the call is loud and strong. And I am aware that I am kindling the flames of mother-hate within them, flames that will be fanned by the winds of age and independence.

The voice of the wild calls. I want to be free. The louder it calls, the more I feel my weakness as a partner, a mother: my gaping lack of ability. I want to run away, to fly to a far distant land, to be free of my captivity, my drudgery, from this life I have so willingly chosen for myself, from this domestic bliss I have so carefully constructed, piece by piece. It feels like shackles to my soul. It chafes and confines. I long to be free. Just me. Pure, and free. Me and the wind and the moon and the trees, and my trusty pen. Free.

How that word sings. I long for freedom. Can taste it like the memory of ice cream eaten on an exotic beach. Everything about my life as a mother is far from free. My day is wound carefully around the needs of others.

I feel like a domesticated wild woman. I don't belong here pairing socks and making pancakes, wiping bottoms and lulling fractious children to sleep. I want to have no one to answer to, to be nice, polite to, to make a nutritious meal, carefully cut up for. I wish to wake when I want, and sleep when I want. Alone.

I want to write all day, then to sit and watch the fire and eat chocolate and drink too much wine, then walk in the woods by moonlight, before curling up alone in a warm bed with a book that makes my soul soar before going to sleep for a night full of uninterrupted sleep.

Lucy Pearce, www.dreamingaloud.net

Expressing the Crazy Woman

How can we find safe expression for the Crazy Woman? How can we be true to her and ourselves? How can we find balance in our lives so that she need not emerge too often or destructively?

Think back over her last few visits to you – why did she come? What invited her into your life? How did she express herself? What did she want? What was her message?

She is you. Your shadow side with lessons to teach you about what you choose to hide away. She calls your deepest soul attention to that which you refuse to shine your light on. She may terrify you, embarrass you, mess up your carefully made plans and your carefully done mascara, but she is your soul sister, your twin self. She has been scorned, shamed, silenced, rejected and demonized throughout history. Open your arms and your heart to her and her lessons.

Drop everything and drink tea with her. Take her to bed and ravish her with sleep, let her guide you into other realms of your consciousness. Draw her, mold her from clay and place the image of her in an honored place in your home or studio. Trust her rather than refuse her. Let her lead you by the hand and thank her for her presence, her power, her message.

Listen to her, really listen, what is she trying to say? Her voice is not gentle, her gestures pure violence, she does not mince her words and does not care for the hurt feelings of others. She is power-full. Feel her words in your gut, then move them gently into your heart. When you take away the anger, the tired, the hurt what is the kernel of truth she is wanting you to hear? Heed it, live it out, or she will bring it more fiercely next time.

Next time she visits, try and dance to her wild tune a different way. Instead of attacking yourself, or those you love, stop, listen to the words that are racing round your head, the voice that is screaming out loud. Copy them down in your journal and heed them well.

If you find asking for what you need take what you need anyway. Lovingly, clearly, take what you need, be your own best friend – tap into the Crazy Woman's power to help you!

Reflections

Take a moment, dear mama, to reflect:
What meaning do you find in the Crazy Woman archetype?
How do you honor this archetype in your life?
How do you sabotage or deny her?
What role does the Crazy Woman play in your life?
What images does it create in your mind?

Creative exercise

Dare you bring the Crazy Woman to life?
One day when she's roaming strong will you find her voice and allow her to live through you?
Can you paint her, write a poem in her voice, find an image of her which speaks to you? Dare you dance in her body, sing her song?
What do her eyes look like, what does she hold in her hands? What is that in her mouth? What is she doing with her feet?

Chapter 8

Unblocking, Releasing, Letting Go

Before a woman of our time can realize her creative powers, she must participate in the down-going. She must gather herself together.
Betty Meador, *Uncursing the Dark*

And so with the energy of the Crazy Woman pulsing through our veins, we look for release of all that is dark, heavy and painful for us.

In the next chapter, you will have the opportunity to be initiated into the Creative Rainbow Mother archetype. Just as with any ritual, it is important that we take time beforehand to let go of the old, so that we do not take our negative emotions and confusions into the alchemical process of ritual. I know that many of you will be wanting to race ahead with getting creative rather than do some self-help, I know you! By all means do – but be aware that this is also a form of resistance: when we don't look at where we are stuck, we stay stuck. This soul searching and sifting through the past, frees up lots of energy – and powerful material – to fuel your creative process.

As we stand on the threshold of the Rainbow Way, we need to unblock the entrance, shifting any rubble and debris that may have accumulated there which is blocking our way onto our creative path, and prevents us finding flow and ease in our creativity. Like pruning the dead wood from a plant in winter so that it can grow stronger new growth in spring, so we let go of the old, leaving space for new life and creativity to rise up. As **Caron Kent** puts it in *Puzzled Body*:

The more the unconscious is relieved of restrictive pressure, the more spontaneous activity of the unconscious is released on the bodily and imaginative levels.

Extensive academic research with creative women has demonstrated that:

> *Internal personal barriers often exist in the process of completing creative work. The way women have been raised and the cultural messages they encounter seem to result in these internal barriers and failure to develop the belief in self necessary for a commitment to highly creative work.*

Sally Reis

This is why I feel this process of clearing old beliefs is so important. We will be concentrating on the three main blocks that most women experience:

- Your inherited values, beliefs and stories about creativity and yourself.
- Your feelings about motherhood.
- Your sense of power as a woman.

A creative block is literally that: something blocking the natural flow of creative energy which exists everywhere. Since the creative flow happens on a subconscious level, so too do our blocks. So our job is to identify the block, and help to shift this. Often just naming it, bringing it into consciousness is enough, by speaking it aloud or writing it in a journal, giving voice to what has previously been unspeakable. Visualization helps. Painting, drawing, dramatization, expressive movement…all these techniques help too.

Our blocks are truly the only thing that holds us back from following our dreams, creating the lives and the art we long to. Our unbridled creative spirits are always there, shimmering, beautiful, quixotic, flighty as a butterfly, infinite in possibility, a fractal encompassing every color and note and idea and word and pattern. It is just how many layers of false beliefs, hurts, denials, rejections, and misinterpretations lie between us and them.

Please know that this is not a one-time thing! Both creativity and motherhood have vast legacies of negativity to be shifted, and they are always accumulating a fresh patina of dust from the world, new parts are always bubbling up into awareness from the huge desolate wastelands of the subconscious. This is where we act from and until it is made conscious, transformed and healed, this part of ourselves will sabotage us, meaning that we act unconsciously, rather than co-creating from a sense of love and possibility.

Embracing our legacy, releasing our negative inheritance

Nothing has a stronger influence psychologically on their environment and especially on their children than the unlived life of the parent.
C.G. Jung

Vast tracts of failures, real and imagined, go back down the generations. Beliefs which were transmitted in our blood and the bread we broke together around the family table. Shame which is passed on from generation to generation from the day we are born.

We receive these gifts, these negative messages, and unwrap them, thinking that they must be for us, because we were given them by our loved ones. And we accept them as ours. These stories become the reality that we inhabit, the thing we call life. Not knowing, not realizing that we do not need to accept these gifts of shame, self-loathing, fear, inadequacy, martyrdom, just because they were given to us by people who we love and trust: because they were given from one unconscious being to another.

As adults we have the opportunity to go through our family inheritance, to bring it into our conscious awareness and sort through it carefully. *This I choose to inherit, this love of color, this desire to make the world a better place, this passion for the natural* world, *this eye for design... I will embrace it and it will connect me to my ancestors and our shared love. It runs strong in my blood, and I am grateful for it. But this, this self-effacement, this abuse, this anxiety, thank you but this is no longer needed here. It does not fit. And I will not pass it on to the next generation. I will love it and find ways to heal it, to lay it down, to let it go.*

People Like Us

In our families we learn who we "are" and who we are "supposed" to be. Whether we are "artistic" or not, "good", "messy", "in the way" all these things and more we drink up.

Some women I spoke to recalled how creativity was not what "people like us" did. **Mary**, who now considers herself "not creative" recalls how creativity was not discussed, let alone encouraged or supported when she was growing up:

> *I don't think [my parents] ever thought about [creativity] or thought it existed. Growing up in a very working class home it just wasn't in our lives. They would have been scared of stuff like art or theater that might perhaps have inspired creativity. I know in some working class homes it might be valued but I think in the majority it's something to be feared (if it's even thought about in the first place!)*

Paula was determined not to waste her creative talents as she had seen her own parents do:

> *My parents are both actually very creative but have frustratingly squandered their gifts. You know the phrase "Don't hide your lamp under a bushel". Well this is what they have basically done. My mum could have easily had a career as an artist but has always been too shy to project herself beyond the walls of her own home or the safety of our family circle. She never had the confidence to put herself out there. So projecting myself has actually not come that easily to me, and I need a lot of bravado to do it, followed by a lot of*

self-doubt and angst, but I push myself anyway. I just don't ever want to end up having lived my life so timidly, feeling frustrated and misunderstood and alone. So part of my creativeness is about me trying to break free of that claustrophobic unfulfilled upbringing.

Michelle shares the impact of her family's beliefs about the value of creativity on her own creative development:

My parents never considered any of my – or their – creative interests as something to make a living from. My mum never even attempted to make money from all the beautiful things she made. So trying to now build a home-based business for myself has required a lot of internal dialogue about whether it's a good idea or a waste of time.

We often talk about the family influences of important public figures. Have you ever considered your lineage? Not just the names of the people in your family, but what you have inherited from them, either genetically, unconsciously, or through conscious teaching. Take some time to work back through your family tree, reflecting on your family inheritance.

Once you have done this think of your creative lineage which has shaped you into the creatrix you now are. Move through your life from early childhood, to mid-childhood years, through your teens, twenties and thirties. For each period make a list: who were your most influential living teachers of that time, your mentors, which books, art and films impacted you most, which historical and public figures inspired you? Every teacher, artist, musician, mentor – all these are your personal lineage, everyone adds to the unique creative voice which is yours alone.

Reflections

How was creativity perceived in your family of origin?
Were you considered creative by your family? How did
you feel about that? Did it impact the way you view

yourself as creative now?

Did you have a sense of yourself as creative as a child?

Who was allowed to be creative? Was there any sort of competition between family members for attention?

What value does your partner or close friends place on creativity now? How does that impact your self-image?

Mothers

We think back through our mothers if we are women.

Virginia Woolf

For a little girl her mother is her primary evidence of what it means to be a woman in the world. For some she is a goddess, for others a demon. But for most women the mother-daughter relationship is fraught with the unspoken and unspeakable, with private hurts, and silenced treasures of love, pain, and long-held wishes never to be fulfilled which we hold to our hearts and croon softly to.

To behold our mothers is to see ourselves in a cracked mirror: *same-same but different*, as they say in Thailand. We are ourselves, but even in adulthood we are never truly separate. Our mother holds a key to us, one that we often wish we could steal away so that we might be whole unto ourselves. So in understanding our creative drives, our mothering vision for ourselves, we must examine our maternal relationship with honesty. We need to see how it was, not what we wish it might have been: to shine the positives to a glimmer, patch in the gaping holes and lay to rest old ghosts.

For some of the women I spoke to, their mothers were shining beacons of creativity, such as **Laura's**:

My mother was a massive influence in my life, she still is. I don't think I had a conscious picture of myself as a mother, but the picture of "mother" in my head is that of my mum. She is incredibly creative and home-making is her specialty.

And for some, such as **Becky**, their mothers' lives highlighted to them the importance of honoring the vision of the Creative Rainbow Mother in their own lives:

My dear mother inspired me to want to be both a successful professional and a successful mother.

My mum is an amazing woman, but I see her career and private loves of writing and music trumped and diminished by her responsibilities to raising my brother and I. She left her career and became a mother, and while I am eternally grateful, I can't help but wonder if she recovered from this personal sacrifice. Her example has always made me eager to accomplish successes on both fronts: securing a way to make money and make a difference in the world, and raising happy and conscientious children. I'm still figuring out how to do both, and have clean clothes, floors and toilet bowls!

For other women there was only space for one creative in the house and that place was already taken by her mother. Take **Heather's** story:

My mother was a professional pianist and I grew up around artists of all types, but she has never really understood why creativity was so important to me. I don't know that they meant to, but my parents often made my creative pursuits seem less important than other things by always making it more of a postscript to whatever else they were talking about.

Reflections

What do you really love about your mother? What makes her special to you?

What can you not forgive your mother for? What are you

still angry about?

What did you need from your mother that she could not give you?

What was your mother's story of creativity and motherhood? What was her mother's story?

How has this influenced you and your beliefs about your own creativity, your role as a mother? What do you try to emulate, what have you sworn not to repeat?

What are you willing to let go of – on your own part, on your fore-mothers' behalves?

What do you wish for your own daughters/daughters in law/nieces/granddaughters?

How can you help to model this in your own life?

What changes can you help to bring about in the way you talk, live, act, in your choices, even political changes you might help to bring about, to inspire and help the next generation of creative mothers coming through?

Creative exercise

I tell you, there are a great line of women stretching behind you into the past, and you have to seek them out and find them in yourself and be conscious of them.
Doris Lessing

Take some time to sketch your maternal lineage. Start with yourself, and underneath write your name, and then "daughter of..." and your mother's full name, then draw your mother, with "daughter of", and your grandmother's full name. Go back as far as you can. For many of us our knowledge of our ancestors gets hazy after the third generation. Keep going back with any details you know: a name, where they lived, how many children they had, the sort of clothes that women in that era would have worn.

Use old family photos or portraits to help you. Go back another three generations or more. If they are blank, so be it, just add guesstimated dates so you can imagine the historical era she lived in, and what her life might have been like.

And then around each woman, write her defining qualities, her passions, her character...

What similarities do you share with your foremothers and where do you diverge?

How much do you know about your foremothers? How important is this to you?

How could you find out more?

What context does this put your life, aspirations and achievements into?

Fathers

As girls we grow up in a patriarchal culture, built on masculine values of competition, confidence and aggression, with feminine values of nurturing, sensuality and creativity for its own pleasure devalued. Our fathers can be guides or competitors. They might demand that we assert ourselves and achieve, or that we be good women, wives and mothers in a traditional sense, and live up to prescribed nurturing female roles. If we are lucky, we learn what it means to be fully loved and accepted by a man who embraces our creativity and our unique character.

Many of the creative women I spoke to were glowing in their memories of their fathers. It seems as though their father's love and approval lit a flame of self-belief in them. Take **Emily**, for instance:

My dad is a painter, and some of my earliest memories are of smelling the linseed oil and turpentine late at night and creeping downstairs to see what he was painting... Sometimes (depending the mood and lateness!) my mother would make us toast, and when I now paint that smell gives me such joy.

My parents were hugely encouraging, and brought us to exhibitions all over the country. They had friends who were artists and sculptors, so we were immersed in that. It definitely made me believe in myself as a painter and creative person, and gave me "permission" to do things outside the norm.

A father's approval and love means the world to even a grown mama, as **Lisa** shares:

My father taught me that being creative and making something worthwhile takes patience and love. And he always encouraged me in anything creative I was working on.

Others who lost their fathers in early adulthood, remember their father's creativity with fondness, and wish that he had been able to witness their creative blooming. **Sylda's** recollections of her father are perhaps the greatest testament a daughter could give to her father:

My father has been the single most positive influence on my life and my creativity. He nurtured and supported every whimsy and outlandish fantasy I had as a child and there were many! When he died when I was 20 I was all at sea for a long time but the memory of his gentle spirit still encourages me now.

For me the journey has been more complicated. It has been one of desperately searching for approval: a need to be accepted on my own terms, which were, at first glance, very different to those of my father. It was only when that battle was over, in the past year, and a mutual acceptance and respect found, each for the other's work and process, that we have seen how much we share. We now relish our mutuality and respect each other's differences. I feel at peace, no longer yearning for approval, and this has been a key to my own creative flowering. I found that when I laid down my battles and need for permission and approval from my outer males (my husband and my father) the inner voice of my critic (which is also male) quieted too. When I claimed my feminine creative territory and my own authority, love and creativity blossomed inside and out.

Reflections

What expectations did your father have of you as a little girl and a woman?

What influence has your father had on your emerging creative self?

To what extent do you crave his approval or permission – as an artist, as a woman?

What creative interests do you share? If he is still alive how do you, or can you, enjoy these together today?

The fear of being a bad mother

Any mother is the bad mother if she is tired enough. Isn't this allowed? She is a frightening vision of the mother as unfed, the empty trying to give.
Pat Allen, *Art is a Way of Knowing*

As a culture we worship at the feet of the good mother. We idolize her. And we live in terror of being, or being seen to be, the bad mother.

A good mother, according to our mythology, does not complain. A good mother puts her children's needs, her children's health, her children's lives before her own. This message is reinforced from pregnancy onwards. Endlessly. And most of the time we dance, guiltily, unconsciously to its tune without actually questioning its validity.

There are as many different ways to be a good mother, as there are mothers. But instead a woman is shown endless checklists of qualities and achievements to which she must conform, by the non-descript parenting "authorities". This has been going on for centuries, yet, despite feminism, the dominance of "bad mother" guilt is just as strong.

No wonder many creative mothers experience guilt, confusion or isolation because of their often competing desires and roles: those of creative and mother. A large percentage of the population, perhaps including your immediate family, and even you yourself, might equate being a creative mother with being a bad mother, as it takes you away from your children and means you are not "properly" focused on them.

This quote from **Adrienne Rich**, in *Of Woman Born*, sums it up so perfectly:

> *Unexamined assumptions: first that a "natural" mother is a person without further identity, one who can find her chief gratification in being all day with small children, living at a pace tuned to theirs; that the isolation of mothers and children together in the home must be taken for granted; that maternal love is, and should be, quite literally, selfless.*

The total annihilation of self that is required of "good" mothers, is not expected of good fathers. When we have children we make a practical commitment to support and nurture them, but not to sacrifice ourselves on the altar of parenthood. As **Pam England** wisely says in *Labyrinth of Birth*:

> *You don't need to "get it right" to earn love or respect or to be a good-enough mother.*

For many mothers, myself included, who are instinctively drawn to the philosophy of attachment parenting (which usually includes natural birth, breastfeeding, sling-wearing, co-sleeping, gentle sleep and discipline techniques) the need to be our children's everything in the early months and years, can be deeply draining to creative spirits that are used to long periods of solitude, quiet and concentration. We aspire to be totally devoted mothers, and yet find that we cannot. **Leonie Dawson**, blogger, artist and entrepreneur, expresses this so well in her free *Biz and Blog Success* e-book:

> *I used to think I'd be a 24/7 attachment mama, but [...] I work best when I have time to integrate on my own each day. And I will move mountains to make sure that happens. A happy mama is as important as a happy baby. For me now, getting time out every day serves two purposes: I get my work done. And it's my happy time. My sane time. When I don't get it, my anxiety returns from its happy cave where I wish it would stay. I feel like getting time to myself every day is pretty much essential to my mental health.*

Jennifer Louden, bestselling author, shared with me her experience of trying to find support to be the mother she needed to be:

> *I found a mothers' support group when my daughter was a baby, it was an attachment parenting group, and I remember the first day I showed up and as I walked in the leader was saying "you must meet every need that your child has." And I turned around and walked right back out. I thought – I cannot meet every need my child has. I am a person too. And I found this every time I tried something monolithic with my daughter, it just didn't work, for her or me, and I always had this sense of not just: "What does she need?" but "What do I need?" too.*

We all want to be the good mother all the time. I have yet to meet a woman who claims to have managed this. To be a mother is to live in fear of being "the bad mother." In **Elizabeth**'s words:

One always dreams of a harmonious and smiling world – before and after children – I wanted to be that ideal mother.

But we have to make peace with the fact that we will not, cannot be the good mother all the time. For creative mothers, taking time away from our children is the best way to be a good mother more often, rather than trying to address their every need whilst further depleting ourselves.

The goal posts of the perfect mother are always changing – their one consistent is that they demand more than most mothers can possibly hope to give.

In 1953, the British pediatrician, Donald Winnicott, published his views of "the good enough mother", a far gentler, more human version than Freud's black and white views of the good and bad mother that had dominated cultural consciousness for decades. For Winnicott, the "perfect" mother, (that is one who does everything for their child, all the time) is actually not a good mother at all in terms of child development. When we seek to become our child's everything, there is no room for them to develop their own sense of identity or competency.

In 2010 authors Becky Beaupre Gillespie and Hollee Schwartz Temple presented an accessible, updated version of the "good enough mother", in their book *Good Enough is the New Perfect*, based on their research with hundreds of mothers. Some of my favorite recommendations, which are particularly appropriate for creative mothers include:

- Stop looking for external approval: define and remain true to your own definitions of success.
- You can do *anything* – that doesn't mean you have to do *everything*! Nor do you have to be the best at everything.
- Your sacrifices should reflect *your* priorities.
- Always keep in mind the bigger picture.
- Be willing to decide, know when to say "I Quit".

- Balance isn't about having perfect harmony each day.
- There are a lot of right ways of being a "good enough" mother – find yours!

Reconciling our feelings about ourselves as mothers is crucial if we are to free ourselves from limiting feelings of guilt and failure. It is an on-going process and one which our creativity can help us to explore.

Reflections

Complete these sentences:

- Mothers should…
- Mothers can…
- I feel like a bad mother when…
- I feel like a good mother when…

Now reflect:

- Whose terms are you judging yourself by?
- What are *your* terms for being a good mother?
- What do your children really love about *you* as their mother? What makes you special to them?

Grab your journal and list everything your children require in order to be strong and healthy, well-balanced individuals and, importantly, where do they, or can they, get it from?

Each time you find yourself thinking *I don't have time to be creative, I "have" to do this and this or I'm being a "bad mother"*. Stop. Take a step back and look at this list. How well are you delivering on their real needs?

If you're meeting them, then back off on yourself.

If you're not then figure out how you can adjust the time you are spending with your children to prioritize these needs.

How well are you meeting these needs in yourself?

And how you can enlist other significant people in their lives to help?

Creative exercise

Do you dare to create the bad mother? Perhaps in clay or paint. Take a little while to sit with the feeling of being the "bad mother" or "death mother". What does she look like? Allow her to be "ugly", "hideous", "grotesque", "angry", "mad", "crazy". Let yourself see yourself this way. What can she do? How can she destroy? Where does she get her power from?

Put her somewhere where you can see her and acknowledge her presence.

A woman in her own power

We need to explore what it is that makes a woman free to let creative forces sweep through her. How does it feel when we are in control? It is to be free to let go. Empowerment is not something one person can hand to another. What does it mean to be empowered?

Sheila Kitzinger, *Birth and Sex*

Most of us women are, if truth be told, afraid of power: of being seen as powerful or of truly engaging with our own creative power. That is completely understandable. For most of history the only creative power women have had is that of creating, and sustaining, the lives of others. Every other form of power was actively withheld from her: denied on moral, political or religious grounds.

History is scattered with women changing their names in order to work or be published, donning britches just to be allowed a voice: to be someone in the world, rather than just a woman.

When one reads of a witch being ducked, of a woman possessed by devils, of a wise woman selling herbs, or even a very remarkable man who had a mother, then I think we are on the track of a lost novelist, a suppressed poet...indeed, I would venture to guess that Anon, who wrote so many poems without signing them, was often a woman.

Virginia Woolf

There has been a long history of keeping women's power and creativity down through physical violence or threatening to remove her children, income or social status. A long, ignoble history of branding witches and flogging adulteresses, of enforced custody of children and bankruptcy: big and small acts which have taught women not to raise their voices.

Many times what threatens us today is more subtle than that which silenced of our fore-mothers. But the tools of control are the same: guilt, shame and fear.

Whether we have experienced this personally, or heard about it in history books, on some level we feel it in our bellies, in our bones. Consciously or unconsciously we know that to be a creative woman can entail huge risk. Take Dr. Christiane Northrup, who shares that after the publication of her first book, *Women's Bodies, Women's Wisdom*, she dreamt for weeks about being attacked. Novelist Amy Tan recounts similar dreams. I certainly experienced a feeling of intense vulnerability and nakedness as the writing of this book came to an end and I realized that my ideas, my creative soul was about to be laid bare on such a sensitive subject as creative mothers. It was in that moment I realized just how many taboos I was touching on, just how vulnerable I felt, and how easy it would be to shame me.

Indeed, for many women, the experience of motherhood has been the opposite of empowering, something which **Rachel Cusk**, a contemporary British journalist and author, articulates so well:

From the first moment of her pregnancy, a woman finds herself subject to forces over which she has no control, not least those of the body itself. This subjection applies equally to the unknown and the known: she is her body's subject, her doctor's subject, her baby's subject, and in this biological work she has undertaken she becomes society's and history's subject too. But where she feels the subjection most is in the territories, whatever they are, that in her pre-maternal life she made her own. The threat to what made her herself, to what made her an individual: this is what the mother finds hardest to live down. Having been told all her life to value her individuality and pursue its aims, she encounters an outright contradiction, a betrayal – even among the very gatekeepers of her identity, her husband or colleagues or friends – in the requirement that she surrender it.

And so I counsel you, dearest mother, to remain aware as you progress through the Rainbow Way, of how claiming time for yourself, valuing your creativity, sharing your voice, your images, your message with the world can feel threatening to others, and ourselves. Be mindful when these fears of your own power emerge to sabotage you. Be conscious of a woman's tendency to surrender. Be alert to shame as the greatest weapon to silence a woman who is just emerging into her power.

Reflections

What is your personal inheritance to do with women's power?

Have the women in your life been empowered or disempowered by the culture around them or their families?

How have they responded to it? How have you responded to their response? Do you accept it, try to comfort them, try to fight for them, argue?

How do you feel at your place in society as a woman and mother? Do you feel accepted, supported, lucky, angry, sad, disappointed, regretful? How do you express this?

Clearing exercises

Having read the women's stories in this chapter, and become aware of your own personal creative blocks through your reflections, I would now like to offer you a number of clearing exercises that you can do, to help shift and release long-held blocks.

If you are new to this sort of thing, perhaps you might do it with a women's group, friend or counselor so that you can have emotional and practical support. Don't let the idea of "doing it wrong" put you off. You don't have to believe that they will work. Just try them!

I hope you find healing, acceptance, and your own voice to write your own story of your life, on your terms. The exercises below should give you some ways in.

Body work

Often our creative blocks are expressed in our bodies – stiff joints, bad backs, coughs, sore throats, tight shoulders. Releasing physical tensions will go a long way to loosening you up creatively. You might:

- Get a massage.
- Go to a chiropractor, Alexander- or Bowen-technique practitioner or other body or energy worker.
- Start jogging, swimming or walking.
- Dance freely and expressively.
- Do some yoga, Pilates or other deep stretches.

If this idea is new to you and you want to increase your understanding of how your thoughts and emotions impact your physical health, I highly recommend Louise Hay's book *You Can Heal Your Life*.

Active imagination

Often the blocks to our creative flow are energetic: thoughts or feelings which have become stuck. These intangible things cannot be accessed with a scalpel or tablet. But they can be accessed using what Jung called active imagination. I offer a number of exercises here which use this.

1. One of the most powerful, yet simple ways to cleanse ourselves is through breath work, accompanied by visualization.

   Sit or lie down and allow your body to relax. Imagine the thought, feeling or experience that you want to release, really seeing it as a three-dimensional object. Recall a time when this feeling of disempowerment was strong for you. Really see that scene. Feel where in your body it is held and place your hands on that area. Then, breathing out, imagine it as dark smoke coming out of that area, rising up, up and floating away, really releasing that belief and dispersing it with your breath. Then, breathing in, imagine golden light flooding to that area and surrounding you. Feel yourself relaxed and safe.

2. Imagine you have in your hands a pair of golden scissors, strong but dainty, these scissors of love cut firm but true. As you cut each negative attachment, each thought and action that hurts you every time you remember it, you get a little energy back for yourself, to stoke your creative fire. Instead of losing your own energy into worry, anger, hate, resentment, frustration or psychic warfare with your loved ones, you call your energy back to yourself, for yourself.

   In the space that is left, from the part that was exorcised, energy is freed up to put into new life, a life that we consciously create, rather than subconsciously hold onto. The next step is to rededicate this reclaimed energy consciously to yourself as a creative mother. To make a conscious dedication of it to you and your work, to creating positive acts of love and beauty in your life, in your family, to yourself as a woman and as a creative spirit. I like to do this by lighting a candle for each area of my life.

3. Imagine yourself standing at the entrance of a labyrinth. Look closely at your labyrinth in your mind's eye. Perhaps the reason you feel blocked is that your threshold stone rather than marking the entrance to your creative path, is so big that it is blocking the whole way. Perhaps it is literally a lump in your throat, a pain in your head, a stone in your belly or your guts, a tight yoni, constipation, a contracted painful womb. All these are entrances to the creative labyrinths in our body. Imagine walking into the area that is tense and tight, allowing it to release and relax. Look around as you enter your body, what colors do you see? Are there any symbols?

Get a pebble from the beach or your garden, or if you don't have one, then draw one. What word of permission do you need, what would help you to unblock and enter into your body more fully? What could be your mantra? Perhaps it is "trust", or "flow" or "open". Paint it on the pebble. Hold the pebble in your hands. Feel its smoothness, its weight, its size. Hold it on your body, wherever you feel the blockage. And then remove it. Saying the word aloud. Imagining yourself stepping over the threshold.

Phoenix from the flames

Before we symbolically step into our creative power in the next chapter, take a final moment to release and let go of all that you can which is currently holding you back.

- Write all the things that you want to release down on a piece of paper.
- Read them aloud – you might want to put one hand on your heart to help you to really connect to your body and feel the emotion connected to the words that you are releasing.
- Either in your fireplace, garden or over a large metal bowl

or dustbin, set this paper alight and watch it burn. See the smoke rising, feel these old dreams rising up to the heavens, freeing your mind and heart from them.

Chapter 9

Initiation

Beauty is deep in the soul of a woman – the desire to make beauty, share beauty, to create, to nourish others.
Lucy Pearce

In every culture, people moving into a new stage of their lives undergo some sort of initiatory process. It is an important human way of preparing and celebrating a person for the next step on their life path. Marriage, baptism, first communion, bat mitzvah, mother blessing, all these are important rites of passage in our culture.

A rite of passage is like drawing a line in the sand, literally and metaphorically, and consciously calling up and envisioning a new identity that we can inhabit from there onwards. It usually includes elements of ritual, words of commitment, the passing on of wisdom, often a new name or soul allegiance, gifts (whether physical or spiritual), prayers and blessings, altered states of consciousness, and a tangible symbol of the initiation to act as a reminder, such as a piece of jewelry or skin marking. It is a sacred act that has deep soul meaning and significance.

During the first half of this book we have begun to let go of what might be holding us back from creating, and been shown new ways forward through the stories of other women and the archetype of the Creative Rainbow Woman. But none of this really means anything unless we embody the learning. In this chapter you will be initiated onto a new path: that of the Creative Mother – you can take or leave the Rainbow part as you see fit!

Just as in the initiation of the *Ultima Madre* recounted by Lynn Andrews, let this be the threshold of your initiation into walking the creative-mother path with a deeper understanding, openness, surrender and dedication. Let it open your heart to yourself, your eyes to your inner dreams and your ear to your own voice. This is the initiation of your virgin creative mother. The old meaning of a virgin was "a woman unto herself". This is what you are becoming. In every act of courage, sincere love and beauty. You are becoming more truly yourself.

This is a potentially life-changing shift, one which can transform you completely. And so, if you feel called, or to be honest, even if you feel a little uncomfortable, take this opportunity to create a formal initiation for yourself.

Preparation

Your initiation will take the form of setting your sacred space externally, entering into the sacred space within you, allowing yourself to travel "between the worlds", and then creating your own map and symbol of the creative and spiritual path: a labyrinth, as both initiation and guide to your future journeys.

All initiations have a threshold which marks the crossing point between the temporal world of ordinary life, and the world of ritual, a place where great truths may be bestowed. The space must be carefully prepared and entered with mindful awareness, openness and most of all, courage.

In order to enter into a deep state of concentrated creativity, it really helps to disconnect from the busyness of life and connect with the powers beyond our conscious control from which our creative energy, ideas, inspiration seem to flow. We are going to do this in a number of ways.

- Firstly by creating time for yourself. Either in the evening, or by organizing childcare. You will need a minimum of half an hour alone and uninterrupted.
- Gather up your materials – you will need: a piece of paper A3 or A4, some pastels if you have them, if not then chalks, pencils, crayons, even a biro. Or you can create the labyrinth

outside in the earth or sand, or in clay.

- Then by creating soul space – find somewhere that feels safe and comfortable to you, where you won't be watched or listened to – your bedroom, home office, a tent in the garden, a friend's spare room, a quiet spot in the woods.
- Make it feel sacred to you – you might spread out a beautiful cloth, light a lamp, a candle or some incense, pick some flowers, spray your favorite scent.
- Then find one or more images or objects which speak to you of creativity – perhaps a postcard of one of your favorite paintings, or a painter in her own studio, or some embroidery you love, a favorite poem or quotation, this book...and simply lay them out to create a miniature altar.

In these simple acts you have set yourself up for potentially deep, personal creative work. We will go into each of them in more detail in the following chapters. But for now I want you to see how easy it can be, if you just decide to do it. Don't do anything that makes you feel deeply uncomfortable, after all, this is your sacred process! But do be prepared to push yourself a little outside your normal comfort zone, for this is where the magic lies!

Initiation

Settle yourself in your space and into your body. Take a deep conscious breath. Breathe deep into your belly, into your womb. Imagine you are breathing a pure, golden light into your womb, like sunshine, or honey, filling your whole womb area with light. Close your eyes and breathe like this for a couple of minutes before you read or listen to this short, guided meditation.

I see you coming through the trees, peering over your shoulder to be sure the children are OK, that no one is following you. The dead leaves and twigs snap and rustle under foot. You stoop low to avoid the branches, catching your sleeve on the brambles, these snares pulling you back. Take a moment and name these snares and thorns. Then with your golden scissors you find in your pocket, snip at each limitation, each fear, each thing holding you back, watch them fall to the ground. Feel yourself completely free to move forward.

You come out into a grassy clearing, the rainbow beads of dew still burdening the blades of grass. Birds are singing, the sun is shining through the newly crimped lime-green beech leaves. The robin flies back and forth with scavenged crumbs to feed her brood in an unseen nest. A little cabin in the woods is before you, with dusty windows. The door is shut. You peer through the windows: no one is home.

It seems familiar to you, this door, covered in cobwebs. Perhaps from a dream. You remember being scared and slamming the door shut, locking it, promising never to return. Yet here you stand.

You and that door.

You reach out, hand shaking, a memory stirs, a disapproving voice. You take a deep breath, turning the handle and push. It opens wide, much more easily than you expected. Dare you step inside?

Your eyes take a moment to adjust to the dim light inside. There is a stillness, a peace within these wooden walls. There is a table and a chair. You sink into the wooden chair and slip your shoes off, wriggling your toes as they sink into the warm earth. You close your eyes for a moment, and hear your thoughts racing, all the busyness of your life spinning round and round. Gradually it begins to slow down, this whirlwind of ideas, and you begin to see the spaces between them. Little doorways into possibility.

You open your eyes and see a box beside you, which you had not noticed before. You reach your hand in, and out comes paper, thick white sheets of paper. On the table lies a pen. You reach for it.

The rest of the story is yours to write as you wish. You may reach into that box again and again, there is wool in rainbow colors, glue, pastels, glitter, clay, oil paints, scissors, needles and thread. The supplies are seemingly endless, they are waiting for you to shape them into your own creations.

And then you notice, behind you, in the shadows, a woman, her hair dark as the night, with a streak of moonlight through it. She slips a warming shawl around your shoulders, woven from rainbow-colored thread. It feels so safe and comfortable, like it has always been yours. You realize, somewhere, long ago it had slipped from your shoulders as you ran out of the wild woods. She opens her hands to you.

"Welcome to this space!"

She smiles.

"It is yours. It has been waiting for you. I have kept your rainbow shawl here, waiting, waiting for you to claim it once more. And now you are here. I am so glad. Come here often. I will be waiting. Whenever you need me I am here. Sitting in the shadows.

"Welcome, dear one. There are so many stories to write, pictures to paint, so much magic to craft. Let us begin!"

Creative exercise

Pick up a pastel and draw what you saw. Draw the space, your guide, yourself feeling energized and creative. Or if you really feel you can't draw, write down anything that you want to remember from this. Perhaps get yourself a shawl, or rainbow beads to remember this initiation by.

Now it is time to move on to creating your labyrinth.

The labyrinth

Labyrinths have been used around the world throughout history to calm the mind and bring the body into flow and are often used to mark important rites of passage. They are a symbol of our life's journey: twisting and turning, the path unknowable, often misleading, yet the destination is always certain.

A labyrinth has a single path which spirals in to the center and out again. The journey into the center is symbolic of death and release, and the journey back out represents birth and rebirth. This spiraling in and out connects us to ourselves, to the earth and to each other. The repetitive curling pattern alters our brain-waves and shifts us to another realm of conscious awareness: by occupying the rational, busy mind and body, thereby allowing the subconscious to emerge.

Passing on the seed

This seed has been passed from person to person, from midwife to mother, from mother to daughter, from one culture to another, for four thousand years. Now it is being passed to you.

Pam England, *Labyrinth of Birth*

All labyrinths, though they initially seem complex, are started with a simple seed, a diagrammatic guideline from which the form is built. Though the seed is simple, labyrinths require complete mindfulness in their creation and use. If you presume for a moment that you can do something else at the same time, or you get distracted, that's when you get in a muddle! So be sure to center yourself before starting out!

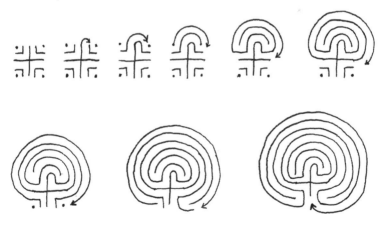

1. Lay your piece of paper out landscape way (so the long edge is facing your belly). Pick two colored pens or pastels that speak to you.

2. With the first color, just below the center of your space draw a large +.

3. Then a generous finger-width away (so that the paths are wide enough to run your finger round) draw four L shapes, mimicking the shape of the cross, followed by four large dots, again a finger-width away. This is your seed.

4. Now, with the other color, join the top of the + to the top of the right-hand L in an arc shape. This will be the center of your labyrinth.

5. Now, move left from the central cross, and join the top left-hand L arm over the top, looping over in an arc, a finger-width away, to the top right-hand dot. Can you see the pattern emerging?

6. Keep going in this manner, joining the top left-hand dot over the top to the remaining arm of the top L, keeping your paths evenly spaced. Don't miss out the dots! Continue like this until you have joined each part on the left to one on the right.

7. When you are finished you will see you have the entrance at the bottom left.

8. You can put a marker outside the entrance, at the threshold of the labyrinth, such as footprints or a threshold stone.

9. Now place your finger at the threshold. Breathe in and out. You can either hold a question in your mind or allow your mind to empty. Trace your finger in through the entrance, and follow the path, releasing, breathing the

whole way in. Pause in the middle. Would you like to make a symbol here, perhaps a finger print? Stay here and open to your source, become aware of your womb space, your source of creative power. Come out, tracing the path with your finger, returning with your calm and newfound wisdom into the world. Pause at the threshold once more. Breathe.

Welcome back dearest creative soul in all your rainbow colors – we are ready to dive so much deeper into the journey of the Creative Rainbow Mother together – let's get going!

Reflections

What feelings or thoughts came up as you drew the labyrinth?

What feelings or thoughts came up as you moved through the labyrinth?

What did you get from the initiation as a whole – is there anything you would like to treasure from it?

Are there parts of this ritual that you would like to use more frequently in your life?

PART II

Chapter 10

Creating Space

Women have not had a dog's chance of writing poetry. That is why I have laid so much stress on money and a room of one's own.
Virginia Woolf, *A Room of One's Own*

As you saw when we drew a labyrinth, the core of the Rainbow Way is laying down a structure, the guidelines for the path to emerge. Without this we would just have a maze of wiggly lines and dead ends. So it is with creative motherhood.

One day can very easily blend into the next, and before we know it weeks, months and years have flown by, with us still intending to "get around to doing something" someday.

The seed in terms of creative motherhood is threefold: dedicated work time, in your own space (the central cross), pockets of snatched time in your daily life (the corner bits), and co-creative time with your children, family and friends (the dots). Together, when they are joined up with your time, you have a complete Rainbow Way.

Clearing space

In order to allow space for creativity to emerge and take root, we need to clear space: physically, emotionally, mentally.

In the last chapters of Part I, we started the emotional clearing, set up a temporary physical creative space for our ritual. Now it's time to do this on a more permanent basis, so you can really get creating!

Many of the mothers I spoke to talked about needing to have a really clean, clear space before they can even think about getting creative. Most people find that working in a clear space allows them to have a clear head, rather than being disorganized and constantly tripping over junk. But, and this is a big but, the need for a clear space can be a block to creativity. If we cannot start until the house is perfect, chances are we won't start at all. We will spend so long cleaning, or making the perfect studio, that our time is over before we have even begun to create. Many women use the safety of the known: domestic cleaning, as a form of procrastination, so that they can further put off what scares them most: entering the unknown, getting creative.

A room of one's own

As parents we often prioritize our children's needs. For most families achieving a room each for each of our children is key – we want to give them space for themselves. And yet often this is what we do not have ourselves!

The idea of a room of one's own resonates strongly with most women today. When Virginia Woolf wrote about it almost one hundred years ago, having a room of one's own was a political statement, a domestic statement of empowerment. And it still is. For centuries a man has had his study, library, studio, shed or men's club, but a woman has not had a room of her own. Her space was the kitchen or the parlor – places where she served others. In honoring a need for space, we honor our need for privacy and interiority: having a room of one's own says, I do not just belong to the house but I have a space that belongs to me, I deserve to have space for my creativity, I deserve to be entirely me – separate from home, family and husband.

Having a physical space where your creations and materials are safe and untouched where children will not get their fingers in your wet paint or pull down your fabrics, scatter your sequins or press "delete" is vital. But this might not be a room. Most of us cannot afford to have a spare bedroom, let alone a dedicated studio. Your space might start as a shelf or drawer or cupboard that is totally yours, and the room of your own is the kitchen table after the children have gone up to bed at night. Do not let the lack of a dedicated, perfectly equipped studio space get in the way of your being creative. Again, this is a common form of procrastination. It's much easier to blame the lack of a room than our own fear of getting started.

One dear friend stated in our women's circle how much she needed her own space. She dreamed of a shed in which to paint, to re-connect with her creative side when her youngest started school. Through the power of the women's circle her wish was granted, another member had just moved into a new house with two sheds and was looking to dispose of one. The synchronicity was quite astonishing!

I too yearned for a room of my own, but with only three bedrooms for five family members and a husband working at home, this seemed a total fantasy. I wrote on my blog about my dream for my own creative space. I had a fantasy of a little cabin in the woods, like Henry Thoreau, or one of my favorite writers Louise Erdrich, who you met earlier. But alas we live on a housing estate and we owned no woods.

Then two weeks later a friend who reads my blog whose parents own the adjoining property said she had a little shed which she used to use for painting but no longer needed, would I like it? It was just over our boundary, in the woods. That was my first room of my own. A place where I could shut the door and not be mama any more, but me, free with my thoughts and my words. You know that special place I took you to in the meditation at the start of this section? That was my writing shed.

This has now evolved...when my husband went down to three days a week, and I was to get two full days creativity, I needed somewhere warmer and lighter to work. My father has a little Japanese style tea house at the bottom of his garden, a fifteen-minute walk from our house. Through the heavy-framed glazed sliding doors there is a panoramic view of a little lake, the bog, a silver sliver of sea, and the tall pine trees all around me. I walk under a bower of roses and down a meandering path between ten-foot-high bamboo to get to it. This was the same path I walked with my husband eight years ago, to our homemade wedding ceremony. The same path that we walked to bury all three of our children's placentas.

The herons swoop down from the trees and migrating geese call to each other as they cross the bog. It was here I wrote my first book, *Moon Time*. But whilst it was lighter and not damp, it was freezing in winter, and the internet access was intermittent. So I found another space, an unused office up in my father's business premises where I now work two days a week. Many of the women I spoke to shared this experience of an evolving work space.

Leonie started work up a tree, in her car and in local cafes, before doing up a caravan and working in there which became like a sauna in summer. When she moved house, a good studio space was part of the essential criteria. Both our stories show that firstly you need to prioritize finding or making space for yourself by thinking about it, talking about it, getting clear about what your requirements are, and being prepared to "do what you have, with what you have, where you are". You need to monitor what is working, and what isn't, in your space, before starting the process again by calling in another space as your needs change, your work and income grows, or you become clearer about your requirements.

Other mothers choose to adapt their work to their available space. **Laura P**, mum of three now grown-up children shares her experience of adapting her artistic process to her kids:

I began to do portraits with colored pencil. Setting up a palette of oil paints, only to hear one of kids wake from a nap before I could begin to paint, was too frustrating, and I didn't want to visit that frustration upon my kids. I had to realize what my priorities were. It was a real lesson for me. I could pick up a color pencil and draw for a few minutes at a time, leaving my artwork out on my drawing table, no set up, no clean up. I developed a style of working with

*colored pencil that my portrait clients couldn't believe wasn't oil
paint. I got more word-of-mouth work than I could handle.*

Creating a workspace

Laura's is an important lesson in not being too attached to
physical space. I have a number of workspaces set up in our
house for days when I am at home with the children and evening
times. So, depending on how long I have to work, what work I
am doing, whether the children are around, how much concentration I need, I always have somewhere to work.

I am currently writing this in my bedroom workspace. I have
a little laptop table, a gift from my mother-in-law, which goes
over my knees in bed. I have a snatched half an hour, because the
muse came to me last night as I was resettling the baby and she
would not let me move. So after having scribbled notes last night
on the paper I keep next to the bed, my dearest husband is now
in charge of children before he starts work.

I also have my spot in the armchair in the corner of the sitting
room with my laptop slotted down beside. It is this spot where
most of my daily work happens, and evenings too so that I don't
cut myself off from my husband. We also share a desk in our tiny
sliver of a home office space, where we have subdivided a
bedroom.

What is most important is that you have a space that you can
call your own, even just occasionally, to create, knowing that you
can make a mess, have fun, let go and not be watched, judged or
interrupted.

Factors to consider when choosing a workspace

- **Location** – proximity to home, is it easy to get to? Are you
  contactable by phone? Will you be constantly disturbed?
- **Light** – is there good day light? Artificial lighting? Ability
  to black it out if needed by your art?

- **Noise levels** – either from the noise that you are making or external noise disturbing you.
- **Space** – is there room for all your stuff and to move around?
- **Security** – are your work things and creations safe from others? Do you feel safe in your space alone?
- **Storage** – is there enough safe, practical storage for your materials and creations – or can you make some?
- **Damp issues** – many temporary spaces in sheds or warehouses can be damp – can you alleviate this or will it damage your work?
- **Working temperature** – if you are too hot or cold you will not be able to concentrate for long.
- **Ventilation** – is crucial if you are working with chemicals or materials that produce a lot of dust.
- **Flooring** – dancers and painters will have very different flooring requirements! Is it easy to clean?
- **Connection to utilities** – do you need electricity, internet connection, running water?
- **Cost** – if you are building, renting or buying a space, make sure you are not straining your budget – there is nothing more guaranteed to stop your creative flow than money worries!

I wish you well with finding or creating a space that honors your circumstances and needs.

Chapter 11

Creating Time

This caring for each other thing takes a lot of time. And there's other work to do, too.
Ariel Gore

Having focused on getting yourself some dedicated creative space in the previous chapter, I now want to help you to find time in your day.

It's OK, I am not about to get all bossy with you and tell you when you should do your creative work. Only you know the rhythm of your days, your children's needs, your childcare options and when you work best.

In meditation there is a technique where you look for the spaces between the thoughts, and that is where you find your way into true mindfulness. Creating when you have children is a bit like this. You have to scan your day for windows of opportunity and then grab them with both hands, be prepared to dive right in.

Often finding time requires deciding what to give up or to do less of. To do this look for what I call "energy sinks", activities which suck your energy and time with little reward. So you might choose to give up an hour's TV in the evening, or limit your social networking time. You might choose to only iron smart clothes rather than all your laundry, cook meals for the week in bulk, to stop reading the Sunday papers or trashy magazines, or wake up half an hour earlier in the mornings.

When do you have potential windows in your day which you could enlarge a little further to fit some creative practice in?

Are you a morning lark or a night owl? Are your children early risers or up late? If you are up all night with a baby, then you probably do not feel fresh in the morning, but maybe when the baby is having its mid-morning nap you are ready to go. Or if your children go to bed early, then you are ready to dive into your practice then.

I tend to work best first thing in the morning, before I have spoken to anyone, or late at night. Late nights are not a good idea for me as I have night-waking children, and so need as much rest as I can. But often I will stay awake after the last night-waking as dawn is breaking and start scribbling away. Or will settle the children with breakfast in front of the TV and get some writing done then.

Some people need a strict timetable to make them do something. If you are one of them, then write into your diary or calendar your daily practice time. Personally, I do not like things set in stone, there is no better way to make sure I won't do something! But once I feel like I have choice, the chances are I will do it most days at about the same time. I'm contrary like that!

When planning your creative work time, other important considerations are: how long does it take you to get settled and get into your creative work? How long can you create for before you need to take a break? How long does it take you to get out of it – both practically packing equipment away as well as entering back into family life mentally? And how much concentration do you need – how "alone" do you need to be? The answers to these questions will help you figure out how frequently you can do your creative thing, and where you can do it.

Creative activity

Draw a timetable, broken into half-hourly slots. Fill in the time you wake up and go to bed. Then fill in your children's waking and sleeping times, including nap times. Fill in work times, if you have them, meals, school pick-ups, time set aside for chores and after-school activities. Where is the space? Grab a highlighter and highlight the gaps. These are your spaces for possible daily practice.

If you have none, then highlight all the spaces where there is another adult in the house (if your children are small) or where your children will not be in urgent need of you (if they are older). These are your windows.

Next do the same for the weekend (or a day that you and your partner are not working). Block off any fixed activities such as soccer practice or church, and any commitments your partner has, and block off bedtime if your children are very small. Now, depending if you are a morning or evening worker, block off a two-hour window on one of the weekend days. This is for you: your creative time. Keep it there. Show it to your partner. Put it up on the wall. Get your partner to put it into his schedule – mental or actual. Encourage him to do the same. Once this is negotiated, it is just the same as you having a doctor's appointment. It can only be broken in an emergency. It cannot be eroded, forgotten or ignored.

Next you need to make sure in advance that you have all your stuff ready to go, if you are going out, or set up in your workspace. This is the beginning of getting your body and mind into the "zone". If you are staying home, get your partner to take the kids out – to the park, to visit family or friends, to do the grocery shopping...

This intention – both the marking out time and getting your materials prepared and the space ready and waiting is a strong way of visioning and setting intention for your creative spirit – it is like sending part of your spirit out ahead of you. This is your dreamer self – it can be planning, dreaming, visioning, scheming, whilst your daily self is going through the mundane life. Then, when you are in your creative space, you can reunify these parts of yourself, the doing part, which has been doing the daily practice, which I will discuss more later, and the visioning part which has been working on a different level. Now you are ready to create, to step fully into your creative space, raring to go.

A day in the life

Many women ask me what my day looks like. So I thought I'd share how I fit my creativity into my days.

Some days, if I've had a good night's sleep, and wake up with a buzzing brain, I get up before the children and either write in bed or creep downstairs to the computer. Otherwise I'm up when the children wake up. I take them downstairs, grab them some breakfast, which they like to eat watching cartoons or reading books, and I catch up with any emails I need to do, and write down my to-do list for the day. If I'm inspired and they're happy, I might publish a previously written blog post and update my social media. Some days if they're up super-early I run myself a bath, and listen to an inspiring teleconference whilst I'm in it, and they may well jump in with me. On other days I'm lucky to get three minutes for a shower.

Then it's lunches and uniforms and the school run. Some days this is quick and easy, other days it's hell on earth.

When I get home, we have self-directed time for an hour or so: the 3-year-old has her morning children's TV fix and I catch up on my world: so I might write a blog post, get book orders ready for mailing, read a couple of articles and do some admin, whilst stopping to dole out snacks and chat about what's on TV. If I do this now it sets me up for the day and then I can really give myself to them rather than feeling resentful. At some point the three-year-old drifts away from the TV and starts playing by herself and I feel a lot less guilty!

Then it's craft time: painting, drawing, junk modeling or playdough. Or we go for a walk, visit a friend, or the library. At least three times a week we will bake a cake or cookies and will cook something for lunch or dinner together. Cooking with my kids is really important. I love it, they love it and we love eating what we make.

Then home for lunch, a quick check of email, a story and then collect the older kids from school. I'll make them a snack and we decide what to do for the afternoon. I feel they miss out on creative stuff and outdoor activities by being in the school system so this is what we really focus on at home. Nature, craft, cooking and socializing are our usual activities.

Then it's "Scooby Doo O'Clock", so I can have twenty minutes headspace, to check emails briefly and do anything for my editorial role before the end of office hours, and then it's time to make dinner and get them to do the dreaded homework.

Bedtime is 7 pm for the younger children, but often it'll be 8.30 before they're all settled. When they're in bed tucked up it's my time! Evenings are often spent writing blog posts, articles, book reviews, Facebooking with friends, reading or art journaling.

I try and make sure I have a couple of nights a week totally off – to have a bath, or go to bed early, and very importantly to connect with my husband. I usually go to bed around 10.30pm.

Work days

I now have two full work days a week and since my creativity has become a proper job with allotted time, it has taken the pressure off my days at home with the children. I have a studio away from home that I go to after dropping the older kids to school, and am home at dinner time, whilst my husband stays home with our three-year-old. Just because I get to paint and write for my work, it's still work, it's what pays the bills, as does the admin, marketing and all that jazz that goes with being a professional creative. I turn up, I do my work. I am immensely grateful that I get to do it as a job – knowing how hard I found full-time motherhood. And sometimes (OK, often!) I have fun too!

Weekends

We have evolved our weekends to suit us all best. We used to have a constant competition for whose turn it was to have time off, whilst the other would stomp around being a resentful martyr. Now we have a system which works well for us all. I have 2-3 hours in the morning, my husband has 2-3 hours in the afternoon to do our own creative thing alone and uninterrupted. The other catches up with household duties, goes and has fun with the kids or meets up with friends.

We try, as much as we can, to honor a day of rest. Not for religious reasons, but for our own well-being, to have a Sabbath day to nourish our souls. We usually take it on a Sunday, but if one of us has a work commitment on a Sunday then we try to take it on another day. Our Sabbath is for togetherness, nature, rest, the garden, days out... We start with a lie in, followed by a cooked breakfast or brunch. And then we go swimming together, or a walk in the woods, share a family meal or visit the grandparents. This is one of the ways we build self-care and family care consistently into our lives.

Practicalities

Our days basically oscillate between "me time" (writing, reading, checking email, sketching out ideas, self-care etc.), "us time" (where we might cook or craft or go for a walk), "family time" (where my husband is involved too – watching TV together, playing on our local beach), and "practical time" (where I try to get as much housework as I can done in the minimum time).

I focus on providing as much food cooked with love for my family as I can. I hate washing up and most housework. As does my husband. Our house is pretty messy – though slowing improving as the children get older and I am no longer breast-feeding round the clock. We have a cleaner for two hours a week who is my sanity and a luxurious necessity. She earns as much as my husband does. But at least we know that under the mess the house is clean!

I spent years feeling guilty about my lack of interest in homemaking. I tried my utmost to fill that role. But I have come to the rather late realization that I'm never going to win any prizes at it. I choose to write and spend time with my kids over housework at all times. As a result there is usually a tower of dirty dishes, a cluttered dining-room table, works of art drying on every surface, and never a matching pair of socks to be found. But we are all happy, most of the time and I treasure my own books on my shelf and my paintings on our walls far more than a spotless house.

Fallow periods

You need to know, however, that the day in the life that I shared above is just an average day: a creative day, when I am in my creative zone, and one which explains "how I do it".

But what you wouldn't know, from the pages of this book and all the creative work I produce, are the spaces between days like these. The days where I wallow and do nothing. The days where I lie fallow, and we snuggle up with books and puzzles and a movie and we do not move from the couch, let alone the house. The days when I am in bed, exhausted. The many days that I, or the children are sick. The days when I am anxious or low. These days are just as real in the life of the creative mother. But rarely documented.

Show me a creative mother, and I will show you a woman who sometimes, or even often, takes to her bed and doesn't have the energy to make dinner. The woman who chooses to write, over going to a friend's party. We only have so much energy in a day, in our lives. If we live to create, if we are mothers too, there are days when there is no energy left for anything else. That doesn't make you a failure, just human. But this is the hidden bit of creativity. So please believe me that it is part of the process, it happens, and for every three big creative days I will have at least one down day. All of nature needs fallow time to revitalize. Modern culture with its "always on" expectations is the anomaly, not your need for days, or even weeks, of rest and quiet.

Multi-tasking and uni-tasking

I am a high energy multi-tasker. I love the buzz of projects, I work fast and I get swept up with enthusiasm for my latest thing: if there's no enthusiasm, it's unlikely a thing will get done. But as I have just shared, I have a lot of down days when I do nothing. My high energy creating comes at a cost, and I certainly wouldn't recommend it to anyone else.

Talking about my day in a linear manner doesn't really give you a sense of it – I am always multi-tasking: I will be planning an article whilst putting the children to sleep or reading on the toilet, or blogging and watching TV at the same time.

Rarely do I get a chance to do anything uninterrupted, so I use my time to the full. My life is woven of multiple strands, on multiple levels, and each is a crucial part of the whole tapestry. If I leave one part untouched for too long, a hole emerges in the fabric of my life.

I find it mostly manageable because it is inner-directed and home-based. When I was doing a lot of stuff outside of the house: trying to settle a baby in bed before running out to meetings or to teach classes, having to be at certain places at a certain time, that was really stressful, and more like trying to keep plates spinning on sticks. I prefer weaving!

The most important skill that I have cultivated as a creative mother is my ability to multi-task. But an equally important skill, and one that comes naturally in the early baby days when we are pumped full of hormones, is the need to uni-task: to fully give ourselves fully to our soul work.

So when you are playing with your child, when you are reading them a story, or crafting with them, be there. Completely. If you find your attention wandering, or have other competing needs, remind yourself that you have dedicated this time to them. When you are painting or writing, be sure to put all other distractions to one side and really be there. This is my surefire solution to burnout, overwhelm and regret: if you build multi-tasking time and uni-tasking time into your creativity and motherhood, there can be few regrets. Because you were there, really there. And that, at the end of the day, is all that matters. You don't have to be there every moment of every day, but your art and your children need to know that they can have your undivided attention when you are feeling rich and full: that they can have the best of you. **Amanda Oakes** expresses this really well in her e-book *Zen and the Art of Being a Work at Home Mama*:

> *If I am with my children, I am with them. If I am working, I am with my business. If I am with my mister, I am with him. If I am practicing self-care, I am with myself – but each of these things are subject to change in a hot second when you are a mama. Getting right with that was one of the greatest shifts I've had on this journey.*

Top tips for organizing your creative time:

- Have a regular time that is sacred and yours – like Saturday mornings that you do not have to re-negotiate every week.
- Put your creative time in your diary and the family planner.
- Adapt your creative work to short, sharp bursts.
- Ensure that your more concentrated or messier work is planned for a time and place that will not be interrupted.
- Develop memory techniques for holding on to inspiration that comes to you in the midst of daily life: use your phone, an i-Pad, journal, note pad, digital voice recorder, back of your hand to jot them down – or you will forget them.
- Learn how to get into "the zone" quickly.

- Do research in the corners of your days – reading, trawling the internet, don't let it take over your main creative time.
- Plan your projects on a big planner so you can see what's coming up.
- Have an acceptable minimum for housework – do a fifteen- to thirty-minute burst first thing in the morning and late afternoon. Then make creative time and family time a priority after that.
- Turn off your phone/social media etc. when creating so you don't get distracted.
- Have a clock nearby but not visible.
- Have your workstation and materials set up in a number of places.
- Learn to squirrel away pockets of time when your children need you less.
- Have deadlines – perhaps a piece for a magazine, Christmas presents, items that need to be ready for a craft fair or exhibition – a little self-imposed pressure, once you have gotten into your creative groove, is a great way to ensure you don't fritter away your time, and that you raise the standard and quantity of your creative output.
- Always have something with you in your handbag in case you get stuck somewhere unexpectedly and have a God-given extra pocket of creative time.
- Learn to say no: to social invitations, commissions, work projects that do not tempt you – your time is precious and valuable, spend it doing what you love, not what you feel you ought.
- Have on-going, absorbing creative projects that your older children can get out and work on when you are doing your own creative work.
- Get a cleaner!
- What other domestic work can you out-source or cut down on?

- Do you batch cook and freeze? Do you cook one meal that can be adapted for a number of days?
- Make friends with quality (preferably advert-free) children's TV – I know this is contentious for some!
- Limit the amount of times you check your email in a day (note to self!)
- Grab a quiet five minutes on the toilet at the beginning of the day!
- Keep a notebook and pen beside your bed for when late-night inspiration hits!
- Do a childcare exchange with other mothers.

Childcare

For many creative women, having to split time between the people that they love and creative work they want to do is a difficult and often wrenching choice.

This intensely personal struggle to try to develop their personal talents while they also try to meet the needs of those they love causes creative women the most conflict, guilt, and pain.

Sally Reis

Often it is the most practical parts which baffle us the most as creative mothers. How can I actually take time away from my child, especially if they are very small? This is why it's vital to find someone who you totally trust to care for your children. Be it a partner, a member of your family, friend or paid carer.

So much depends on your set up: the age of the child, whether you are breastfeeding, how dependent they are on you and how well attached they are to the caregiver you will be leaving them with.

Often the hardest part, for our children and us when we start to take creative time away, is the act of leaving. Though we may long for time off and time away in the abstract, the reality of escape can make us spiral into panic. Will they be alright? What if something happens? What if the baby won't stop crying? And even, how will I cope? I'm going to miss them!

For this reason it is important to start with small, local times away. Keep your phone on you, let the carer know where you will be, so you can be located if for any reason phone contact cannot be made. Make sure that the caregiver understands that you must be contacted if the baby needs breastfeeding or an emergency arises (you might want to explain what you consider an emergency.) Once mama's gone, the person in charge is in charge, you are not. And if you want to enjoy your creative time to yourself you have to learn to accept that and let go of being in control of everything.

Get yourself ready to go calmly, subtly, in plenty of time, perhaps even get your equipment together the night before. Let your child know, however young they are, in the preceding hours before you leave, that you will be going for a very short time and that you will be back soon. Then when you leave make sure you do a proper handover to the carer, letting them know where the child is in terms of hunger, sleep and other needs.

There are some days when my children are in good form, that I say: *Goodbye, I'm off to work and will be back soon.*

On others I find that seeing mama disappear tends to lead to tears and begging and sudden needs – so, having agreed my time away with my partner, I slip away unnoticed. If there is a real emergency I will be found, otherwise, mama is off duty.

The first time is the hardest. So make it short. And then do it again soon. The more regular your creative time away, the more comfortable, calm and familiar it will be for you, your child and your caregiver. And then you can build from there!

Chapter 12

Crossing Between the Worlds

Becoming centered is one of the most important aspects of your training on your path to power. If you do not live in your center, you live on the perimeter of power, never inside the world of power. [...] Center yourself in your power, and release your need for constant distraction from your center. Then you will have learned to choreograph the mighty energies of the universe.
Lynn Andrews, *The Power Deck: Cards of Wisdom*

You might have your space all set up, the materials ready to go, but then there might be this jangling uncertainty. You can feel your creative energy buzzing, a million ideas going round your head, but you don't know how to channel it into something, how to focus it. It is like a radio fizzing with white noise. What we need to do is to find some way to focus the energy, to tune it into a channel.

This is where finding your center is key. In its simplest form, it means coming back fully into your body, releasing your attachment to identifying with your racing mind, and settling into a calmer, more receptive state. You can always start this process through relaxed breathing (slow and deep, from your belly). When you do this your heart rate is lowered, stress hormones are not being released, your muscles are relaxed and your brainwaves are in their slower alpha rate rather than the faster, everyday beta-waves.

When we are centered in ourselves we become aware of our inner voice and inner eye, as clearly as the outer influences around us which are coming in through our senses: we can be guided by both.

For some women simply picking up their creative tools or

entering their creative workspace brings them to center. Others need a conscious centering practice to help them to transition from the busy world of mothering and endless distractions and help reconnect them with their own inner voice and creativity. Something to still the noise of the mind and allow their imagination to bubble up. For some it is meditation, for others it is breathing, or yoga. Others find it in affirmations or mantras, or in a devotional image. For many it is running or walking in nature which centers them. For me it is painting, writing, breath-work and dance that bring me back to my own inner poise, my still point of being.

One of the biggest challenges for creative mothers is needing to be able to "turn on" and "turn off" our creative flow very fast. We have small parcels of creative time, dictated by childcare restraints, nap times, or the length of the TV program our children are watching, so we need to learn how to get ourselves primed and in the zone, fast, and equally how to "come back down to earth" fast, otherwise we can find ourselves frustrated, an experience which **Karien** describes so well:

Since becoming a mum there have been a number of occasions when I've found myself blessed with a little bit of time to myself, only to sit staring at my supplies with absolutely no idea what to do. And I get so angry at myself for not being able to instantly turn on the creativity and just get to it, I hate wasting what precious time I get to work.

Having everything set up ready to go and keeping a daily practice going are two simple ways to ensure that diving into your creative practice is easier. But having a little ritual to help us transition us from mama to a creative frame of mind can help to minimize those days where we just can't get into the flow, and maximize the joy and productivity of our creative time alone.

Rituals for crossing the threshold

If you think again of the map of the Rainbow Way, the thing that we do before crossing into labyrinth, is to pause, to allow our mind and body to "yoke" together, to root into ourselves, to slow our thoughts, and allow ourselves to start to listen to the voice of intuition.

Here are some ways you can do this:

- Close the door, which is a symbolic way of shutting the world out.
- Stand in your space for a few moments, bringing your intention for the time ahead to your mind.
- Take a few deep breaths.
- Close your eyes.
- Take off your shoes, wriggle your toes and feel your feet sink into the ground.
- Put on a piece of clothing or jewelry which you associate with creativity, imagine it contains within it some way of accessing your creative self.
- Use scent – some creative mothers I spoke to spray the room, or themselves with some essential oil of rose, geranium, grapefruit or lavender to freshen their minds, or use a smudge stick or incense.
- Turn on some music which inspires you. Listen, or dance and shake out your body.
- Light a candle or turn on your work lamp.
- Have a cup of tea or glass of water.
- Write down your intention (maximum three!) for the session.
- Take out a previous piece of your creative work, or your work in progress and drink it in without judgment, through all your senses, just spend some time with it.
- Briefly tidy your work space.
- Lay out your tools in front of you, so that they are inviting you to work.

- Shake out and stretch your body. If you do yoga, do a couple of poses.
- Read or say out loud a prayer, blessing, poem, mantra or quotation which is meaningful to you.
- Sit in your chair and take a few deep breaths.
- Ring a mindfulness bell.
- Do a visualization or short meditation.
- Take a short walk in nature.
- Start by doodling, especially with your non-dominant hand.
- Pick a tarot or affirmation card from a deck.

All of these help to shift the energy and brainwaves from the faster, multi-tasking, beta waves which govern our daily lives to the slower, alpha waves which are more receptive. They also awaken all of your senses, relax the body and quiet the chatter of the mind. Whatever you can do to help your body and brain shift into that space is great.

Erin shares her techniques:

> *I'm learning what I need to entice and set the mood for the muse, in hope that when I do it with practice, she will know when I have time ready to work with her and fully bring it.*
>
> *I need: the right music, some Flower Essences on the tongue and spritzed on my body to breathe in, a hot cup of tea, a clean work space with all of my stuff set out and ready.*

My best creative work happens when I walk to my studio. The fifteen-minute stroll helps to clear my mind, and allows me to gently leave my home life behind and naturally transition into the creative work I am involved in. Being immersed in nature relaxes me, the walk gets my body and energy moving rather than static, and my brain starts working more creatively.

Many creatives have developed quite detailed rituals or

superstitions to get them in the zone and help them to woo their muse. For some it is an object, a kind of totem which they imbue with a sort of magical creative intention. I have a rainbow-colored scarf that I like to wear when writing – it is my "priestess shawl" which surrounds me, in my mind's eye, with the wisdom and love and protection of women throughout the ages, it embraces and comforts me with is soft warmth, its bright colors lift and inspire me. **Seonaid** has a ring...

I bought a ring that I wear to call me back. It is my work ring, and it has (I fear) replaced my wedding ring! I decided that I had to recommit to my own life, not the life that I had fallen into. So I wear a rather large ring on my left hand to remind me that I made a promise to myself, to the creative life, and to help me turn up, muse or no... Sometimes it works!

In his book *The War of Art*, **Steven Pressfield** shares his extremely detailed set of creative prerequisites:

I head back to my office, crank up the computer. My lucky hooded sweatshirt is draped over the chair, with the lucky charm I got from a gypsy in Saintes-Maries-de-la-Mer for only eight bucks in francs, and my lucky LARGO nametag that came from a dream I once had. I put it on. On my thesaurus is my lucky cannon that my friend Bob Versandi gave me from Morro Castle, Cuba. I point it toward my chair, so it can fire inspiration into me. I say my prayer, which is the Invocation of the Muse from Homer's Odyssey translation by Lawrence of Arabia, which my dear mate Paul Rink gave me and which sits near my shelf with the cuff links that belonged to my father and my lucky acorn from the battlefield at Thermopylae. It's about ten-thirty now. I sit down and plunge in.

Reflections

What centering practices do you currently use?

Do you practice them regularly? If not what is getting in the way?

What practices might you like to try?

Reintegrating

Because we get into a different brain state when we are creating, we need to take a few moments to allow our brain to switch back from alpha to beta, from zoned out and in the flow, to active, responsive and alert, otherwise the shift back into full-on motherhood can be a jolt which makes us feel stressed and resentful, and takes away any of the benefits we might have gained from our time away. So take a moment after you have done your creative work to transition back into your other life. Reintegrate fully back into your physical body, taking care of physical needs you may have been ignoring, and do it in your creative time, not once you get back into the whirl of family life. This way you enter the fray focused, embodied, and ready to go.

So before you go back home: go to the toilet, have a drink, a snack, a stretch and put your stuff away, take a few moments to breathe, to acknowledge what you have achieved.

Then turn your attention towards your family, opening your heart to them in gratitude for your creative time. Go home and greet them with love and presence, feeling connected and recharged. Share this feeling with them. Then they will come to associate your creative time not with your absence, but rather the full presence they gain from you when you return. For everyone, partners and children, this matters far more than all the distracted hours they could have had with you.

If you have reached the flow state during your work time, ideas might keep coming to you once you have arrived back home. Jot the notes down so they are not lost, and work them up when the children are in bed.

If you have been working in a more beta-wave state – editing, doing networking, looking after the business side of your creative work, researching, especially on the computer, or late at night – you need to allow enough time for your brain to ease into alpha, and then theta states necessary for sleep, so be sure to allow yourself some reintegration time before bed.

Chapter 13

Committing to the Creative Path

Until one is committed, there is hesitancy, the chance to draw back...The moment one definitely commits oneself, then Providence moves too. All sorts of things occur to help one that would never otherwise have occurred. A whole stream of events issues from the decision, raising in one's favor all manner of unforeseen incidents and meetings and material assistance, which no man could have dreamed would have come his way. Whatever you can do, or dream you can do, begin it. Boldness has genius, power, and magic in it. Begin it now.
W.H. Murray

So you have your space. You have your time. You have found your center.

Now what?

One of the biggest secrets about the creative life is that you're always starting again. There will always be another blank page. And it doesn't necessarily get much easier. You keep having to start again and facing the unknown. The difference between the novice and the seasoned creative, is the seasoned creative has gathered a bag of trusty "getting started" tools, whereas a novice feels the fear and takes it as a sign to stop.

I don't know how to start...

A truly creative endeavor is about stepping into the unknown where the mind has not previously been.
K Ferlic

Mary speaks for so many stalled creative mothers when she says:

I have no idea how to start, where to start. I don't feel creative, I don't know how to access that part of me that was shut down many, many years ago. I really don't know how to start.

This is one of the most basic, and most paralyzing fears shared by painters and writers, novice and experienced alike: the holy terror of the blank page. It feels confrontational, its unsullied purity calling for our perfect vision to bring to life our dreams. You may have a burning desire to paint but when you get there all you can think is – where do I start? What if there's nothing there? What if it doesn't work out? What if I make a mistake? For those just entering the pool of creativity at the shallow end this can present itself as an expansive fear of anything and every-thing creative...where, we wonder, do we dip our toe in?...where do we make the first mark?...and then what do we do after that?

Think back to creating the labyrinth for the initiation – how much resistance did you have to go through **before** you drew it? And then **before** you actually traced it with your finger? Thoughts like: *this is silly, I've done one before, this is boring, I don't have time, I don't know what to do.* But once you'd decided to start (because you have done it, haven't you?) and moved your finger over the threshold, the path almost sucked you in and guided your way. Starting was the hardest part. It required you to consciously give your intention and agreement, to move from automatic pilot into active participation.

The only place to start is the beginning – just start – and keep going! You can paint over it, rub it out, delete the words. You can start again, and again, and again, and no one dies. But you have to start somewhere. Moving from our heads into our bodies and out in to the world is the biggest creative step we can take. Truly. The biggest amount of courage and energy is that which takes us from self-doubt and inertia to initial action.

I know this all too well. When I started this book I had not painted in ten years, paralyzed by the fear of not knowing what to paint or how to start. I had gotten blocked up in my early twenties as painting after painting had stalled and I lost my faith in my ability to make art. It took a lot of psyching myself up and a powerful teacher, on an inspiring e-course to get me started again.

The artist Flora Bowley led us to work bravely and intuitively, asking that we not be attached to what we were making. She made us start out blindfolded, just making marks, any marks, on the blank canvas. When we start we want to be in control. We have such a strong sense of "wrong" and what it might be, that "right" has no chance to emerge because we are controlling and judging everything. The only way to start is to let the flow come through you, to let it start, to see what is there. Flora took away our fear of getting it right, by emphasizing that we were working in layers, that nothing, ever, was final or definite, that our job was to keep adding, keep loose and playful, safe in the knowledge that pretty much all that we would do at the beginning would be covered up.

Think of it like warming up before sport – you have to get all your muscles, creative and physical moving again. So smear the canvas with paint with your fingers, doodle and scribble with your pencil, pour out a stream of consciousness with words. Then put them aside, start again, or paint over them, but whatever you do, don't go thinking that this is "it". You're only just beginning!

I love this exercise from Christine Mason Miller's book *Desire to Inspire* for getting started. If you find that you procrastinate, and can never find time – then try this exercise:

- Write down a creative project that you have been wanting to pursue but haven't started yet.
- Pretend you have a month to prepare for it: list everything you need to do before you get started – the car tax, the shopping…
- Now imagine you only have a week. Cross off anything which is no longer a top priority.

- Now you only have 24 hours. Cross more off your list.
- From this list choose one item and commit to doing it in the next 24 hours!
- You're on your way! You have started!

Under pressure!

Waste no time questioning your own legitimacy.
Jennifer Louden

Knowing that your vulnerable first strokes of a brush or first words on a page are not going to be judged removes a massive weight of expectations and frees us to create. We need to feel confident that the first steps can go unjudged – most especially by ourselves.

Pressure and expectations can stop fledgling creativity in its tracks. Starting creative exploration is like the early stage of labor – your body can easily take fright and shut down. Just like the opening cervix during labor – you need to feel safe and unobserved for this to happen effectively. I have heard of so many births which stalled when the mother arrived in the hospital, just like I have heard of many mothers whose creative dreams stalled after they had invested a lot of "face" in their creative endeavors by sharing them widely in public, before really starting out. This is why I put such emphasis on having a private space of your own to create.

We need to be wary of others' expectations as we start out. So much of what we consider to be art is about the end result, the product. We are a product-focused consumer society. If you write, then people want to know when your first book is going to be out. If you take photographs, they want to know when you're going to have your first exhibition. Stop! Just create! Let the journey take you where it will. Let the products speak to you when they are ready to be born. Whether you are doodling a picture for yourself or a book illustration, you are still in the process of creation. Sure, one might bring you financial reward or critical acclaim, and then again it might not. Just keep focused on the creativity side of it without being wooed by dreams of glittering prizes or agents...the rest may well follow when you find your path.

Another of the ways we can put pressure on ourselves is by spending lots of money (that we don't have) on expensive classes or materials. If you lay out lots of money first you have immediately put yourself under pressure – pressure of your expectations and financial pressure – *I **have** to create something good now or I will have wasted it all*. This is never a good idea. It's a tricky one to judge, because sometimes a course or new tool is just the thing to rekindle our creative fires. Creating with good quality materials is usually more pleasurable and the results are usually superior. And what is more, investing in our creativity is such an important way of valuing ourselves as creative mothers. But my advice, when you are starting is **do**, not buy! Be proud of what you have made, not worrying about what you have bought.

So borrow a friend's paints, or sewing machine, write with a pen and paper, draw on standard printing paper or a cheap sketch pad, find some free classes online, or take an affordable local class so you can play with somebody else's full set of materials and learn some skills along the way. Starting out, the media you use should not be of much importance – what matters is learning to get into the creative zone, and finding your voice.

You have to start somewhere. And you have to be there, day after day, laying the building blocks. And that takes courage to follow a path for which you have no map, no idea where it is going.

Be it birthing a baby or writing a book, painting a picture or performing a song, you have to start somewhere. Somewhere deep, quiet, small. Just like you cannot push your baby out when you are only six weeks pregnant, nor can you birth the Mona Lisa from scratch. Your creative journey will take you there if you follow the path, step by step. Your body will change, your mind will change, your body of knowledge will grow, little by little, until one day you are there – your novel is born, your baby is here.

Mothering and creativity are enormous leaps of faith, day after day, taking another step, doing lots of work, not knowing how the end result will be. And the reality is there is no end result – a book, a child, an adult, a play is a constantly evolving, changing work of art, subject to revision, interpretation, the fluctuations of mood and moment... But it all starts somewhere. And you are that place!

Whatever your situation, I urge you to focus on what **is** possible, rather than what is not. We all have options which are currently "closed" to us. There is no point wasting your energy on wishing that things were different. I share with you my guiding motto which has helped me almost every day on my creative-mama path: *Do what you can, with what you have, where you are.*

This means **start.** Start today, start NOW, from right where you are. Don't wait till you live in the perfect house, until the kids are grown, until the house is spotless. You could be waiting away a whole lifetime.

You have permission

We have touched on permission a couple of times now. One of the ways we can touch what it is we really want to do, is to write ourselves a permission slip. It is a great way of learning to listen to and follow our inner, intuitive voice in a guided way.

I recommend that if this is new to you, that you start out by actually writing them out in your journal. Sure you might feel a bit awkward or self-conscious at first, but don't worry, nobody else is going to see them but you. Get into the habit, every day of writing yourself a permission slip. Think of it as a prescription, if you like, for your own mental health.

Before you write out your permission slip, center yourself,

take a couple of deep breaths, get settled in your body and ask yourself: what is it that I long for today, what do I need? You might give yourself permission to have a candlelit bath, read a romantic novel, go to the cinema, have an hour's writing time, go for a walk with your camera, confront your mother, listen to a favorite song, wear red…

Wait, quietly, listening. The answer might emerge loudly, instantly and it might take a while to float, quietly into your mind. Do not question or edit it. Write it down. This response is a key to your creative longings, to your mental well-being, to the lair of your muse. Chances are you'll try to resist it on some level, you'll want to rationalize it, sanitize it, ignore it.

But write it out. See your needs before you. Give yourself permission. Say it out loud if you need to. Then do it.

Creative Exercise

What will you give yourself permission to do, be, feel, know, have today? Do you give yourself permission to:

- Make a mess?
- Heal?
- Let the first sketch or draft be rubbish?
- Try something you've always dreamed of?
- Do something small, and let it be enough?
- Do something mad, crazy, wacky, far out?
- Do something loud?
- Do something just for you?
- Do something completely pointless but fun?
- Do something which feels scary?

This is an immensely liberating experience. It can be deeply challenging to begin with, as we often find it hard to even begin to admit what we truly want, let alone give ourselves permission to do, feel or receive it.

Exercises for getting started

The advice I like to give young artists, or really anybody who'll listen to me, is not to wait around for inspiration. Inspiration is for amateurs; the rest of us just show up and get to work. If you wait around for the clouds to part and a bolt of lightning to strike you in the brain, you are not going to make an awful lot of work. All the best ideas come out of the process; they come out of the work itself. Things occur to you. If you're sitting around trying to dream up a great art idea, you can sit there a long time before anything happens. But if you just get to work, something will occur to you and something else will occur to you and something else that you reject will push you in another direction. Inspiration is absolutely unnecessary and somehow deceptive. You feel like you need this great idea before you can get down to work, and I find that's almost never the case.
Chuck Close

In order to get started, you have to let go of the finished product, let go of how you want it to be, let go of your perfect vision and simply find a way into the process. Once you are on the path, it will carry you through.

It is a very Zen practice – you have to become non-attached to the product and learn to be one with the process in order for the product to emerge. Again a lot like birth! Once you get used to diving into process, you will find it is easier to get into it each time.

Some of my favorite getting started exercises include:

- Take a piece of paper, a pen and a timer. Set your timer for ten minutes. Start the timer and start writing. Do not stop writing for any reason (except if your house is on fire or a child is hurt.) If you can't think what to write then write that, over and over again…until you think of other words to write.

- Take some clay, start to mold it into a shape, keep working it, and working it…and then roll it back up into a ball. Repeat and repeat until something emerges.
- Paint a thick piece of paper with water. Using acrylics or watercolors or poster paints, put dots and lines of color on the paper. Keep building it up seeing how the colors dance together.
- Think of something you'd like to draw. Take a number of sheets of cheap paper or newspaper. Give yourself a minute to draw it on paper. Then screw it up into a ball. Take thirty seconds and draw it again. Screw it up. Take ten seconds and draw it again, screw it up… Now take all the time you want to do it.
- Write a word down the page, then write a quality for each of the words – you have made an instant poem. Like this:
Colorful
Reflective
Energetic
Artist
Tentative
Introspective
Vivid
Expressive
- Start with a dot in the middle of a page, then make a small circle round it, then a pattern around the circle, keep on building it up and up with pattern and color and shapes. There you have a mandala!
- Write a word and then start to doodle around it in color, adding patterns, representational imagery and branches onto to which you add more words that you associate with the initial word.
- Get some magazines and rip out all the pictures and words that call to you and make a collage of them in your journal – add your own words, doodles, drawings too.

- Take a class: online, with an artist in their studio, at a local college…

And lots of bite-sized ideas…

- Surround yourself with other creative people.
- Go to a gallery or museum.
- Go to a craft store and spend $50.
- Get cheap stuff so you're not scared to use it.
- Get expensive stuff that makes your heart race when you see it. Make yourself use it up in six months!
- Get paper, close your eyes and swirl with pastels or paints with your hands.
- Join Pinterest and get pinning!
- Take out all the birthday cards you have kept and do something with them.
- Give yourself an hour to create something that you've been wanting to do for age, start to finish.
- Write down every word your intuition says, no editing.
- Write a blog post.
- Paint your finger nails with more than one color.
- String some beads.
- Doodle a pattern.
- Take some close-up photographs.
- Go down to the beach and make something in the sand or with pebbles.
- Go to the woods or a park and make a pattern with the natural materials you find.
- Color a mandala.
- Put on your brightest outfit.
- Wear some sexy underwear.
- Get wet – have a bath, jump in puddles, swim in the sea…
- Loosen up everything – your jaw, your heart, your yoni, your breathing, your shoulders, your ideas…

- Stop pretending you can fail.
- Let yourself off your string, out of your box and fly!
- Do something completely different!

So put this book down, and go do: play, dabble, experiment, go wild, enjoy the process, make and keep, or if you must make and chuck, but just keep creating – don't worry about the products and do not invest lots of money in materials. This time is so important for finding your creative voice, your preferred media of expression. Try to put as few limits, or expectations on yourself. In every single way keep the pressure off yourself. Dive in headfirst, dearest mama. Have fun, be wild, be free...start now!

Chapter 14

Your Creative Toolkit

How many of us go through our days parched and empty, thirsting after happiness, when we're really standing knee-deep in the river of abundance?
Sarah Ban Breathnach

So here you are on your path. What do you have in your toolkit to support you on your journey?

When you're starting out, being creative can seem a bit of a mystery, and a rather hit-and-miss affair. But artists around the world have developed tools which help to support and nurture their creativity, building in a strong backbone or foundation in the areas where things can go awry: gathering inspiration, noting down ideas before they slip away, and organizing material.

Think of your creative toolkit as a place to come to refill your cup, refresh your spirit and refuel your fire, a bank of inspiration, your own personal menagerie of images and ideas. As a mama, whilst you may not have much time to create your final works, you have ample creative ideas and inspirations around you all day which you can harvest, and squirrel away for another day when you will.

Classic creative tools

Inspiration board

Most creative people have some sort of variation on the inspiration board, usually at the heart of their creative space, hanging over their desk or next to their easel.

The idea behind it is that when you start your work and need to find your creative center, or if you are feeling discouraged or stuck, your eye settles on the board in front of you and inspires you. Mine contains notes from people who have appreciated my work (affirmations of my abilities and their effect on other people to boost my spirits when I wonder what I am doing and why); some favorite images (a naked pregnant woman standing beside a beautiful lake, a couple of mandalas, a photograph of my grandmother Lucy, after whom I was named); my favorite quotations; a couple of precious greetings cards from my mother and soul-sister.

An inspiration board can become more three dimensional, taking the form of an altar-space which holds various objects that inspire you and help you to find your center.

Journal

Since I was ten I have kept a journal. It started out as a way of recording what I had for dinner, what I did at the weekend and the boys I fancied. It evolved into my Big Book of Ideas – where I noted down things I wanted to do, ponderings, quotes I loved. My journal is the place where I go to spill my thoughts – my anger, my fear, my inspiration, my feelings – they all get poured into my journal. I frequently feel guilty that I "should" write in it every day. But no, I am not a routine sort of gal. Instead my journal is an erratic way of collecting and collating my journey. I have recently started adding more doodles and drawings as part of my journaling. Art journaling has become popular over the past few years amongst creative women – it is a great combination of writing in a diary and making art. Using mixed media a dance develops between your words and images, it is a safe place to dream, play and experiment with new images and techniques, with the reassurance that they are completely safe and private.

Notebook

If you are a writer, then a portable notebook (or electronic notepad like an i-Pad) is indispensable. This is not intended to be deeply private, like a journal, but is rather an extension of your memory. Use it to jot down ideas as they come to you, the name of someone interesting you hear on the radio, a quote from a newspaper article you are reading, a statistic you don't want to forget, a book that someone recommends. Make it small and light so it can fit in your bag or purse. Always keep a pen with it. And when you're next feeling uninspired go back to it and let it light a spark in you.

Scrapbook

As children we are often given scrapbooks to fill with mementos from our holidays. As adults we tend not to do this. But scrapbooks are a great visual reference and record and mode of inspiration: fill them with everything you love! You can also use a folder system which writers call a cuttings file, to keep articles and images that you love in to peruse later at your pleasure. The benefit of scrapbooking is that it is more visually attractive and accessible. But they take more time and work – so a cuttings file is a great place to store your inspiration whilst you're waiting for a moment to put it in your scrapbook

A well-stocked library

Books of writing prompts, coloring books, books full of images and ideas you love, recipe books, pattern books, art books... Chances are if you're like most of the creative mothers I spoke to, you are a total bibliophile, and probably don't need to be encouraged. Fill your shelves with inspiration – a mixture of "how to" books for technique, and collections of the creative works of others to inspire the creative spirit and move it to action.

Your box of goodies

Build up a stash of materials you love. Get it out and be inspired by a piece of fabric or pot of glitter that you are longing to use.

Hi-tech tools

Digital technology has completely transformed the world in the past decade and a half, but for none more so than women. Our experience as creative mothers is so different from that of our own mothers.

Whilst many of us are guilty of too much screen time, for a large number of creative mothers the internet is our holy grail, and I recommend utilizing its incredible gifts in your creative life. It has been central to my own creative work, meaning that I:

- Can co-edit a magazine in another country from the comfort of home.
- Have created blogs which have helped me develop my writing, niche and readership.
- Have published books from first idea, to final proof from home, via digital print-on-demand technology. I can check my sales and order stock online.
- Have online shops to sell my books and art, which is infinitely cheaper than having a bricks and mortar shop and is accessible to a global market.
- Have interviewed heroines of mine face to face from home, via the magic of Skype.
- Have attended painting courses with top US teachers from my studio.
- Can listen to podcasts, lectures and teleclasses whilst cooking dinner or having a bath.
- Have joined and started interest groups to support my blogging, creativity and women's work and can communicate instantaneously with my growing global group of soul sisters via the wonders of Facebook, Twitter and Google+.
- Can access niche books, magazines, audio and movies instantly which are not available in our local area.

The internet is connecting us like never before – forums for like-minded people, exchanging ideas and inspiration, giving support and sharing our work. These are some of my favorite uses:

Online curating

I have fallen head over heels in love with Pinterest, an online pin-board utility. It is currently at the height of its popularity, and will, as with all technology, be superseded by something else in the near future. I use it in two ways: as a resource gatherer for recipes and craft ideas rather than spending a fortune on books and magazines, as well as an inspiration gatherer for my art and creativity. Facebook pages, Flikr and Tumblr are other great ways of compiling images and online links and sharing them with others.

Blogging

A blog is a "magazine of you", in the words of Susannah Conway. Many women find this to be the most powerful digital tool in terms of connecting with others, sharing their creative work, inspiring them to create and sell their work.

Originally the term comes from web-log. They started as online kind of journals – but they can be like an interactive website, a show case of work, a column, an online portfolio, a scrapbook, a magazine, your very own TV or radio station!

Blogging is a free way of getting your stuff out there without having to win the approval of publishers and editors. It's a great way of finding your voice, your style, your niche – and getting feedback from your customer base, finding your tribe and being part of a community. And most importantly just having a little corner of the world outside your door that sings your passion and style without your even having to leave home! It's also a wonderful way to document your creative adventures as a family and archive memories.

Camera

Cameras are the most indispensable tool for any creative. You do not have to be "good" at taking photographs – but they are a handy, instant way to "sketch" and record what you love, what inspires you, what is happening around you. They are also great for tracking your creative journey – taking images of your creations at various points in their process so that you can remember how you made them, and to give you faith when something is not working out so well that every work of creativity goes through an ugly teenager phase!

Voice recorder

These are great for recording ideas if you don't have a pen to hand, making pod casts, recording interviews or speakers at conferences, snippets of song ideas. I take mine everywhere with me.

Laptop/ i-Pad or some sort of portable computer

These are pretty much indispensable in this era. On it we can create, reproduce and record our art and daily lives. Word-processing tools mean you can create a book from home. Graphic-design packages mean you can create all your own marketing material, edit your own photographs. Now we can all create whatever we want, from the comfort of home. That is true liberation for all creative mothers.

I am so very grateful to live now. I would be a lot less creative without my laptop, it is my creative hub (though I'm sure my children would like me to be on it less!)

Reflections

What are your best-loved creative tools?

What impact has digital technology had on your creativity?

What have you yet to try? And what's stopping you?

How does screen time impact your family life?

Chapter 15

Step by Step – Making Creative Habits

A little step may be the beginning of a great journey
Anon

It doesn't matter exactly what the actions are, it matters that actions are performed regularly. Like warm-up stretches for dancers or scales played by musicians, art practice is done out of faith in the process of creativity. Practice is relational, it is about showing up to play with the Creative Source.
Pat Allen

You are really walking the Rainbow Way now! You have your space, your time and your toolkit. But how do you develop these fledgling scribbles, these free-flowing lines of text, or the homework exercises from your class into something more?

When we are children, learning to play an instrument, our teachers and parents often demanded daily practice from us, to ensure that we improved week on week. And research shows that in order to make a new behavior become a lasting habit, we need to do it for 21 days in a row.

Being creative as a mother is no different. If you are only creative sometimes, like running, it's much harder to start from a standing start, your creative muscles are stiff and you take a long time to warm up. Whereas if you practice your creativity every day, soon you begin to get into the "zone" more quickly and easily. It is no longer painful or slow. You find your rhythm and can build on your achievements.

I read this about writing, when I was first starting out seven years ago, and I got myself in the habit of writing for at least ten minutes, but preferably minimum of an hour a day. At first it was hard. I didn't know what to write about, it felt forced and a bit self-conscious. But the next day when I sat down, I would read over what I had done the day before, and there were bits I liked, little nuggets of gold in the midst of lots of mud.

Over time it has become completely natural and necessary part of my day. If I don't write I don't feel right. I love filmmaker, **Mary Trunk**'s experience of getting back into creative "fitness" which she shares on her blog:

I was lonely and my daughter needed most of my attention. I felt desperate for inspiration to get me back on track. It was as if my creative muscle needed a kick-start. With just the daily domestic activities of caring for a child, doing laundry, cleaning the house and making meals taking up all of my time, I came up with the idea of turning the camera on myself and recording ten minutes of my day, every day. I did this faithfully for an entire year, every single day. Somehow, by sticking to this routine, my creative muscle got recharged. I got back to my film and completed it within the next year.

In seeing us strengthen our own creative muscles, our children learn about what it takes to be creative too. My son who is seven was so excited to visit a friend's house yesterday. She was learning to sew her own creations and her enthusiasm was contagious. They slipped into the sewing room, and soon fabric, scissors and thread were flying, and they made two little scented cushions. The next day he wanted to make one himself, I helped him measure and cut the pieces, he sewed and stuffed it. But he looked glumly at the end result. "Are you pleased with it?" I asked "No!" he retorted, on the verge of tears. "The stiches are too big and there's a big gap here, and here. I'm no good at sewing!"

"But, love, it's only the second thing you've sewn in about a year. Whereas your friend is sewing every day. You just need to practice. "

"I've got no talent for sewing!" he sulked

"You just don't have much experience," I replied. "It's nothing to do with talent, just practice."

I highly recommend that you do your creative thing every day. Whatever your "major" is in the creative universe, be it sewing, writing, painting, dance or drawing, do a daily practice every day. Be it a little sketch in a journal, or working on a large piece. Keep your hand in, keep yourself limbered up. If you're a writer, something like the NaNoMo – writing a novel in a month is a great, and major, challenge – the marathon of the creative world, you might say. If you are a photographer, you might take part in an online photo a day challenge.

This active practice of your skills, the craftsmanship of your art, is vital so that you are refining your techniques and practicing new ones on a daily basis, and soon your art becomes an embodied part of your life. If you do your work every day in the same place, your body and mind will come to associate this activity with this place. So when you approach your desk, for instance, your brain will think – aha, it's time to get in the writing zone.

This is also true for the time of day that you choose. Just like with exercise or meditation, if you consistently do your daily practice at the same time, every day, after only a few weeks it will become second nature.

Reflections

What are your current creative habits?

Is there a time when you had daily creative habits established? What was the impact of that on your creativity?

What resistance do you have to making a daily creative habit now, either internal or external?

Are you good at keeping to a daily habit yourself, or would it help to do it with a friend, or join an online program that can keep you to your commitment?

Chapter 16

Perfectionism

Don't aim at success – the more you aim at it and make it a target, the more you are going to miss it. For success, like happiness, cannot be pursued; it must ensue...as the unintended side-effect of one's personal dedication to a course greater than oneself.
Viktor Frankl, *Man's Search for Meaning*

We are victims of our own internalized perfectionist, a nasty internal and eternal critic, the Censor, who resides in our (left) brain and keeps up a constant stream of subversive remarks that are often disguised as the truth.
Julia Cameron, *The Artist's Way*

After the exhilaration of starting out, there often comes a lull. The voice of the critic starts to creep back in once your initial voice of inspiration has quieted down a little: *You might be doing creative things*, it whispers, *but so what! It isn't like you're actually any good, is it? Look at those colors, the way you painted that. Anyone could do better!*

Does something have to be perfect, otherwise you won't even try? Do you need to be in control at all stages (have you ever wondered what would *really* happen if you weren't?) How good is perfect? What are you basing your standards on? Take **Leigh** for example:

I don't feel pressure at all to be creative, however, I do feel pressure to be really good and produce masterpieces.

Welcome to perfectionism. She is a close companion of most creatives. Women in particular really struggle with perfectionism.

We are urged as little girls to do our best, and so we interpret that as meaning, the best, in the whole world...ever! We seek to please, and so we push ourselves harder and harder in search of perfection, first in our actions, and then how we dress, and then we learn that our bodies must be perfect too, and our mothering and other relationships. We get wound tighter and tighter in the need for perfection, and long to scream, but we can't because it's wound so tightly round our throats that it is strangling the life out of us. **Sally Reis** has found in her research on creative women that:

> *One of the most common traits is perfectionism, which causes some girls and women to expend maximum energy at all times, attempting to do everything and do it well. [...] Creative women often wear themselves out trying to do everything well, often with minimal help from their spouses. Despite these accomplishments, they still feel plagued by guilt that they may not have given enough to their husbands, children, home, and career.*

Where does this obsessive need for perfection come from? From everywhere in our culture. I wrote a post on Tiny Buddha about this:

> *We are expected, according to conventional wisdom, to "give 110%" all the time. "Failure is not an option," we are chided. "You can always do better, be happier or richer..." Everywhere the message is the same, and it all boils down to one thing: you are not good enough the way you are. As women we are particularly susceptible to this message. And particularly targeted by those who spread it.*
>
> *And so we find ourselves trapped in the perfection spiral: creatively blocked, self-loathing, controlling, and alone. And it is not until we are chronically infected that we see that perfection is not an absolute, but always shifting, unreachable and undefinable – outside our grasp.*

When we absorb the law of perfection, we are infected with the virus of self-doubt which eats away at every area of our lives.

The more perfect we are, we are led to believe, the more valid we are as people. But with every advance in one area, we find ourselves wanting in another. We worry that we are not good enough, therefore on some level we do not deserve love, happiness, or even life itself.

Creativity, however, works in a different field to perfection. In the wise words of celebrated cartoonist **Scott Adams**:

Creativity is allowing yourself to make mistakes, art is knowing which ones to keep.

Our creations in fact have a sort of life all of their own. Often they surprise us, their "creators", by morphing in front of our very eyes, taking radical departures from what we had planned. We adapt them as we go along because of error or inspiration – both are powerful guides of the process!

If we are working to a pattern the desire for perfection is necessarily much stronger, as we have a finished product, a Platonic ideal form, to compare our own attempt to. I have just realized as I write this that this is why I never follow instructions to the letter but adapt as I go. It is my way of dealing with my perfectionist streak. If I do not follow the instructions precisely, then I don't need to face the part where I compare my creation to theirs and find it lacking. Instead it is always mine and unique!

Creativity is a potential way out of the strait-jacket of perfectionism, but only if we learn to allow perfection out by the back door. If we are ruled by perfection, our creativity too will simply cause us misery.

Amy found that motherhood gave her the permission she needed to try things and not need to be perfect:

Before babies I had never had the confidence to explore my creative potential, perhaps borne out of some ingrained self-critical belief that everything had to be perfect or why bother. Now, our house is now adorned with my creative pieces, from art on the walls and patchwork quilts, to DIY decorations and pieces of pottery.

Often our children force us to let go of our perfectionist natures just a little, by adding their own creative touches to our work, or by demanding that we speed up our process, spending less time on the polishing and editing of our work than we once would have. **Becky** says of crafting with her children:

I've had to let go of the idea of "perfect" art, and embrace the beauty in our collaborations.

The more we learn to dance to the tune of our own innate creativity, rather than following the missives of others. The more we can release our attachments to our creative products as reflections of our own egos, the more fun we will have and the easier our creating will become.

Reflections

Do you consider yourself to be a perfectionist?
When does it tend to emerge most strongly?
What impact does it have on you and others around you?
What fears do you suspect underlie it?

Chapter 17

Facing our Fears

Our deepest fear is not that we are inadequate.
Our deepest fear is that we are powerful beyond measure.
It is our light, not our darkness, that most frightens us.
We ask ourselves, who am I to be brilliant, gorgeous, talented and
fabulous? Actually, who are you not to be?
You are a child of God. Your playing small does not serve the
world. There's nothing enlightened about shrinking so that other
people won't feel insecure around you.
We were born to make manifest the glory of God that is within
us. It's not just in some of us; it's in everyone.
And as we let our own light shine, we unconsciously give other
people permission to do the same.
As we are liberated from our own fear, our presence automatically
liberates others.
Marianne Williamson, *A Return to Love*

Beneath perfectionism lie many fears. In this chapter we will take
some time to start to tease them apart and name them. Because, as
we saw earlier, to find words and images for the contents of our
subconscious is the first step in healing. When we bring everything that paralyses us in fear, out of the darkness and into the
light of the conscious mind, we begin to discover that it is not the
solid reality we thought, but simply an illusion, a ghost of truth.
And when we realize the non-truth of our fears, we can step
beyond them and into the fullness of ourselves and our creativity.

Our fears can include:

- Fear of failure.
- Fear of success.

- Fear of being exposed.
- Fear of being seen for who we really are.
- Fear of not being acknowledged.
- Fear of not measuring up.
- Fear of judgment.
- Fear of not being good enough.
- Fear of our own lack of skills or talent or experience.
- Fear of looking stupid.

I know a thing or two about fears. When I was twelve, I was cast in a leading role in our school musical. I had genuinely never considered whether I was good at singing or acting or not, I just enjoyed doing them unselfconsciously. But then in one of the final performances, one of my leading co-actors made a comment about me singing out of tune, and literally, my voice shut down. From that moment on I was never able to sing solo again. I was a powerful member of many choirs in my latter school years. But never a soloist. I then went on to a professional acting school for a year, however, when I discovered that at the beginning of my second year I would be required to sing a solo, I freaked out. I spent the summer crying and two weeks before we were due to start back, I quit. My terror was crippling. I have suffered nightmares for years where I try to open my mouth, to speak, to sing or scream in danger, and nothing comes out.

But, and this is the ridiculous thing, I can sing. I've got a great voice. I never once stopped to question this twelve-year-old girl's authority on the matter. Never once thought maybe her comment was rooted in jealousy, or unconsidered teen tactlessness. Or maybe even that on that note, at that moment she was right, but that it did not define me as a singer.

Others I have spoken to experienced this shutting down after critical comments from parents, teachers or siblings. It seems to usually happen in our late childhood or early teens, at a time when we are crossing from unconsciousness to self-consciousness.

Where previously we have not really thought about our creative output, suddenly we are made painfully aware, we are judged and shamed, and the magical freedom that we had is cut off at the roots. It is as though our natural state is that of the intuitive creative self, however, once the voice of the critic is switched on, we spend the rest of our lives seeking to mitigate it.

The voices

Let me introduce you to the voices...

- This is rubbish!
- I don't have time!
- I'm too old!
- Who am I to...?
- No one will buy your work!
- You're worthless!
- It's not as good as...so I won't bother!
- It's not important!
- I'm just fooling myself!
- It's just self-indulgence...

Do you recognize these voices? I know I do. They have kept me company through the writing of this book, through the publishing of two others, and through planning an exhibition. One of the most tiring jobs as a creative woman is doing battle with these voices almost every time I sit to create. Often it seem like it would be much easier not to go there.

In *Bird by Bird* **Anne Lammot** describes the critic thus:

Like a war-time government official he is planted in our heads with his black pen, striking through thoughts, dreams, ideas – "no" he says, brandishing his Censor's pen "too crude, too ambitious, too messy, way too stupid..."

We have a lot of internal characters: nags, critics, spiteful ones, know-alls, ones that delight when we mess up, the moaner, the martyr...

When you take a moment to breathe mindfully and center yourself at the beginning of your creative time you will hear them lining up to be heard, pushing and shoving and yelling to get your attention. What a band of misfits these voices are! Voices that we have internalized our whole lives from things that parents, teachers and other children said to us, things we heard them say to themselves and plenty of special ones we have created just for ourselves. What a cacophony! But instead of tuning them out, we turn up the volume and listen, and believe them, and they begin to take over the show. Rarely do we take a moment to stop, and listen, to question them, or just leave them to chatter away. No instead we believe them and react unquestioningly to them. The voice of unreason steers our ship: welcome to the ship of fools! But where is the captain?

Oh there you are! Ahoy there, Captain! Time to meet your crew. Their role has always been to protect you and keep you safe. But like a car alarm which goes off when there are fireworks, they are often false alarms, and in trying to keep you safe, they keep you small, limited and sad. Have you ever sat down and just listened to what the Censor has to say? Who does he (or she) sound like to you? Is it a parent, a teacher, someone you know in real life or a character in his own right? **Mary's** censor has convinced her over a lifetime, with a little help from teachers at school that she is most definitely not creative:

"Sure, what would you know about it?" the critic asks. "This is you trying to be somebody you are not. I won't be able to do it properly. I haven't a creative bone in my body. I can't draw, paint, bake. I am out of my league here. This is not your life, this is you trying to be somebody else..."

What about yours? How much power has the Censor had over your creative life to date?

Creative exercise

Sit for a moment and listen to the voices. Can you distinguish different voices? Can you name them? Perhaps you have: The Judge, or The Queen of Hearts, or Professor Peeved or Mr Jones your old Art teacher, or your mother... Can you draw a quick cartoon sketch of each of them?

What do they say? Write down word for word what the voice says. Does it have a long spiel, or does it just say the same thing again and again?

What does the character who says it look like/sound like? Speak it out loud, write it down. Does it belong to anyone you know? A parent, teacher, sibling?

How do you usually respond to this voice? Do you listen to the voices? Do you believe them? Do you have debates? Do you ignore them? Tell them to shut up?

Start a conversation! Usually these voices are monologues – but you have the right to reply. Now is your turn to answer back!

Doubt and self-confidence

Don't think about making art, get it done. Let everyone else decide if it's good or bad, whether they love or hate it. While they're deciding, make even more art!
Andy Warhol

When we doubt, we act as saboteurs to ourselves. Rather than being fully engaged we have one foot in and one foot out of our creative camp. We are at psychic war with ourselves, which is generally not very productive. Most of us are hounded by the mafia triplets: "Not Doing it Right", "Not Good Enough" and "Not Doing Enough". They make our life a living hell with their constant surveillance and threats.

Very often people assume that if you are creative you must therefore be very self-confident. The reality of many artists, especially women artists, couldn't be further from the truth. The fact the we are putting our work, our most precious soul creations out there can make us feel intensely vulnerable, to criticism and judgment. Most people feel that this is par for the course, being a creative. But the truth is it doesn't get much easier each time you put a new creation out into the world and await the verdict, your heart is in your mouth. To have it ridiculed or even slightly criticized is a hard blow to fragile creative sensibilities. It tends to reignite all our own inner critical voices. *Please like it*, we silently beg, *please be nice, be gentle*. But then if they are we don't believe the praise! We think they must just be being nice, so we push for more details, we inquire further until eventually a criticism appears, however mild – *ha! I knew it, I'm a failure*, the old voices crow! It is for this reason, I'm sure, why most artists learn not to read their reviews, good or bad, for when we learn to look at our art through the eyes of others, we lose sight of our own values and sense of self-worth, handing ourselves over to someone else on a plate – ready to be devoured.

Just like with our children, we want people to approve of them, to see how wonderful and clever and funny, and handsome they are, not point out their snotty nose and the dirt on their sweater or that they forgot to say thank you. Our children and our art are sensitive areas. We put our love and energy and very beings into them. If they are criticized, it is we who feel the sting.

The most important thing to do when doubt sets in is to realize it and either back off, step away, get a change of scene – take a walk, watch a movie, visit a friend, play with your kids – do something fun, engaging and nourishing which will shift your energy away from introspection. Or alternatively step right back in and start work. Not in order to prove anybody wrong. But the process of starting work again soon acts to silence the internal voices.

Deep vulnerability

The moment that you feel that, just possibly, you're walking down the street naked, exposing too much of your heart and your mind and what exists on the inside, showing too much of yourself. That's the moment you may be starting to get it right.
Neil Gaiman, 2012 Commencement Address to the University of the Arts

You will remember I told you earlier about how I didn't paint for ten years. And then when I restarted, it was almost a second sexual awakening. I created so many paintings, that I suddenly felt I must do an exhibition. But as the date approached, I found myself gripped with terror, a deep vulnerability. I wrote on my blog:

I feel like I'm going to be riding through our local area butt-naked. I cannot begin to tell you how exposed I feel.

If you feel deeply vulnerable in your body or sexual feelings the chances are the same factors will come up for you in your creative practice. There is undoubtedly a connection between our sexual and creative vulnerability as women, I have never read about it, but know deeply from my own experience. It is an opening of our most intimate selves. Although, unlike when we do this with a trusted lover, it is to the whole world, including those who can disparage, criticize and shame us. This is why when we are starting out, it is so important to only share our work in a way that feels safe, to a handpicked audience who will be respectful.

Whilst some brave souls relish the feeling of vulnerability – they who dive out of planes and do bungee jumps for fun, for most of us vulnerability is a discomfort we feel safer avoiding. And so we choose to stay in our comfort zones. But the truth is, in art, sex and life in general, our comfort zone is not where the magic happens. Vulnerability by its very nature requires an element of risk – be it physical or emotional. But intentional, mindful vulnerability is not the same as courting danger, or acting irresponsibly. It is heart-centered and intuitively-guided, not putting ourselves out there for others to savage. Instead it is taking a risk that your heart desires but your head is wary of. It is a risk, because the outcome is unclear, unplannable, and feels both terrifying and thrilling at the same time.

The lesson of the gingerbread man

Have you often noticed when you mention a creative activity to other people they tend to come out with "Oh, I can't..."?

"I can't" is like a stroppy two-year-old. It digs its heels in and whinges and whines, and won't even try. It begs to go somewhere else, do something else, anything but this – it chucks itself on the floor and flails about screaming: *AAHHHIIIIII CAAAAANNN'TT!*

We often struggle with the "I cants's" before we start out – *I can't do that, so I'm not even going to try.*

I have a wonderful example of getting over the "I can'ts" which I want to share with you, mainly because it involves cookies!

So, one day I'm with my children, icing gingerbread – not men, but robots – their creative desire that day! But I don't ice you see, I can't... I can bake sure, but I can't ice...my hands are too shaky, I'm an impatient person, I don't have the eye for it, icing bags are too messy, it never works... I nearly bought myself a super-dooper icing set the other day so that I could be the mama who ices...but I know that that's not what's really holding me back. I just can't. But the children aren't buying this, they have no interest in "can't"! In their eyes mamas have super powers. We can do anything. We know everything.

So I decided to play along and forget that I couldn't. They demand not one but four colors, so we mix them up, and I'm sitting down, and we're doing what we can with what we have, so using teaspoons and skewers to drip and smear icing. A dollop here, a smudge there, licking it off our fingers...when it suddenly occurs to me that I can kill two "I can't" birds with one stone! I have been wanting to draw or paint a mandala for years, but again the excuses come flooding up. So I decide I'll make a mandala cookie – never having seen one of those in my life I have nothing to compare it to! And then, I think smugly, if it's really good I can blog it on my baking blog. So I start with wobbly circles of red, some bits of the line are fat and blobby, others are missing. I fill these in and continue. Blue dots next. Then yellow zigzags. Some of the blue and yellow get mixed up a bit. I keep on going. It's alright. Certainly not blog standard – there are too many really fancily iced cookies out there in blog-land to let this humble critter out to compare unfavorably! But I look and smile. I enjoyed the act of making it. I enjoy the act of eating it twice as much! And in three bites it's gone. No evidence for my creative act, except perhaps around my waistline. But two invisible birds are dead – may they rest in peace!

The need to be original

What inspires you sets you free. The inspiration of others lights a fire which it is your sacred job to tend and grow.
Shiloh Sophia McCloud

What has stopped me so often in my writing is the feeling, the fear, that it's all been said before. When you start to go down this path you fixate on how many books there are out there on the subject you are writing about, how many articles, and how much better they are than my lame attempt. What moments ago seemed like a great idea, now feels hollow. The fear kicks in. It has all been done before. Lots of times. And better. And look. Lining the bookshelves in our homes, in shops, in libraries, lining the walls of galleries, on the big screen of the cinemas is the proof. We cannot do it better, so we shall not do it at all.

And in a way this has a seed of truth. There are only so many things in this world to feel and see and do. But our voice is unique, as is our way of seeing, our mode of expression – if we train it and act truthfully on it, finding our own way, rather than mimicking those of others then there is always space for it.

The message of love or beauty or hope needs to be said by a hundred thousand different voices, written by a hundred thousand different pens, at a hundred thousand different times in history, different places in the world, different sectors of society, in different genres and registers, simply to be heard by the billions of ears and hearts that lie waiting for a truth which fires their soul, answers their question, speaks to their heart. Think of the amount of love songs you have ever heard. And how many touch you, touch you so deeply you know their truth? There are only a few, maybe even only one that sets you alight. But for another person it might be another song, one you have never even heard of, or one that you hate. This is why we must honor our creativity. It is a sort of ministry to each other, and a ministry to ourselves.

Overcoming the voices

When I get anxious I make my world small and dark. When I open myself to beyond. When I articulate my dreams. When I put pen to paper and let fly – then the world opens to me in shimmering colors.
Lucy Pearce

Remember **Mary**, from earlier in the chapter? I asked her how she responded to the voices:

I usually let them win! There is so much else I can do that I tend to go – ah feck it, let's do this instead and don't 'feel the fear and do it anyway'. The times I do go ahead I usually feel great after.

Do you ever "feel the fear... and do it anyway?" Do you ever say *so what?!* or *what's the worst that can happen?* Why not try it today? The response I have taught myself is to step back and take a couple of minutes of deep, centering breaths and then, say gently, but firmly to myself: *It might be scary, but it isn't going to kill me.* With creativity we are talking inner risk, not physical, life threatening risks. And yet we respond, physically and mentally the same as though it were a physical threat. Many people feel so scared of being creative, of not knowing what to do, that they won't even sit and scribble with their own child, let alone start their own creative project.

I'll let you into a secret: the more power you give to your fear, or your negative voice, the bigger it will become, the more dominant and terrifying. Whereas each time you move beyond it, it becomes easier, and easier, the fear diminishes. The first time is always the hardest. The first step always the most momentous.

Really feel the fear – where is it in your body? Do you get a knot in your stomach? Are your hands shaking? Is your breath getting shallower and faster? Are you sweating a bit? Are the voices getting louder? Are you finding it hard to concentrate and focus?

This is just adrenaline. You feel under stress so your body is reacting in the way it knows how. You are preparing to run, to escape from this danger.

But it's OK dear one, this is not a danger. It is a paintbrush, not a snake. It cannot kill you. These are knitting needles, a blank page. Just breathe, allow your mind to quiet. Just for today do not believe the voices. Let them chatter away. Listen in the way you would a little child. Humor them, embrace them, reassure them, give them a drink and a biscuit and let them chatter amongst themselves.

Yes, really, give your scared inner child voice a cup of tea. Sit down with it like a dear friend. In your head or your journal, you could say something like this: "Hey, it's OK, I can see you're feeling really anxious, but I'm here for you, you're alright, what's really bothering you?"

Many creatives and therapists suggest treating the voices like a radio station. Anne Lamott calls hers WFKD, which I love! Once you can objectify it and see that you can have some control, you can reach over to an imaginary dial and tune into a different radio station, or simply turn the volume down.

The path of courage

When I dare to be powerful, to use my strength in the service of my vision, it becomes less and less important whether I am afraid.
Audrey Lorde

Creativity takes courage. Not just once, but consistently. Without courage we cannot be creative. Without feeling fear at some point we will not reach our creative potential. From first putting paint on paper through to selling our work on a worldwide stage there is plenty to be scared of. But this is where creativity lives – on the edge of our comfort zones.

These acts of courage go unseen. They are private battles that we fight within ourselves. But that does not make them any less important. When I asked one Creative Rainbow Mama what she was most proud of, her response brought tears to my eyes:

That I refused to quiet the inner creative soul urge. Because it runs that deep. It's not a whim, or a hobby. It's necessary. I could have said – no, mothering only. And, ironically, I would have been a worse mother for it.

Break the walls of your own fears and I will be here as doula to your dreams, holding your hand, listening to your fears and cheering you on the other side as one who knows the measure of your courage.

Chapter 18

Creative Doulas

We do not believe in ourselves until someone reveals that deep inside us something is valuable, worth listening to, worthy of our trust, sacred to our touch. Once we believe in ourselves we can risk curiosity, wonder, spontaneous delight or any experience that reveals the human spirit.
E.E. Cummings

We all need a creative doula in our lives at some point. A doula is a person who attends a woman as she prepares for birth, during labor and in the early days postpartum. Her job is not that of the midwife, but to be a practical assistant and soul-carer during the extended process of birth-giving. A doula stands beside us and helps us to face our fears, and offers techniques that will help us through the stage we are at. Many of us also require a midwife or consultant to act as an authority figure, and a supportive family member as an ally during the birth. Our creative births are no different.

It is up to you to know where in the process you need most assistance. Is it in getting started? In choosing what to do? In helping with the editing? Or is it in sustaining you physically and energetically, holding the space and external responsibilities for you as you dive deep and give your all to your creativity for a while? You may have a number of doulas for various roles.

Reflections

Who do you tend to turn to for support?

Do you have a variety of different doulas?

If you are still searching for one, what are the emotional and practical skills you need in a doula?

189

Know your allies

One of our chief needs as creative beings is support.
Julia Cameron, *The Artist's Way*

One of the most crucial, most valuable possessions for any creative person, and any mother, is a strong support system. Make building, and maintaining one a top priority in your life.

An ally is a supporter, one who at the very deepest level supports our highest intention for ourselves. We must find our allies, recognize them and acknowledge them for the reflected power they give us – they are good mirrors for ourselves, through them we see ourselves more clearly than we can by mere self-reflection.

Often we try to turn people into our allies because we feel they should be. But an ally cannot be converted, on a deep soul level an ally understands you, really gets you. Perhaps your partner is your ally, or one or both of your parents. Perhaps a sibling. Though often not. Often the ties of familiarity, human pettiness, competitiveness, jealously can poison these relationships, and so whilst these people are day-to-day allies, they may not be creative allies. So make it your mission to seek out your tribe of creative allies who will be with you on your journey, believing in you sometimes more than you believe in yourself.

Finding a teacher

For many of us our doulas take the traditional form of a teacher or mentor who can teach us precise skills, and whom we can apprentice ourselves to for a time as we soak up what we need to know from them.

But not just any teacher will do. Like in any spiritual discipline, you are looking for a "guru" type figure, someone who can inspire and challenge you in equal measure. Someone you respect, who embodies gifts and talents that you aspire to have and is dedicated to transmitting them to you. In order to choose the best teacher for you, you need some understanding of how you learn best, and which approaches are most successful in building your skills, motivation and confidence.

Having been both a creative teacher and creative student for nearly fifteen years, I know the magic that happens when a student finds a teacher at the right time, and is open to learning.

Finding a teacher as an artist is usually more than just finding someone who teaches you skills. You are finding a mentor, someone who sees a part of your soul, has walked this part of the journey before you, and can hold the space for you to develop as you need to. In order to really open up and learn from a creative teacher we need to feel some sort of connection to them, it is generally not just a matter of paying your money. There is a two-way transfer that happens between creative teacher and student, and both need to be open to that process.

This can make it feel daunting if we have no idea who the "right" teacher might be. My advice to you is to follow your heart, try different teachers and classes that pique your interest, and you will in time find your way to your real soul mentors as you learn more about yourself and your creative path.

Finding teachers is so much easier now that the internet has opened up e-learning, blogs, online forums and websites – suddenly you can learn with world-renowned artists, writers and teachers from the comfort of your own home, and with self-led courses you can learn at your own pace. For busy mothers who find leaving the house in the evenings nigh on impossible, this is truly a godsend. This year alone I have learned with four celebrated artists, and a writer. For someone who loves guidance, is an audio-visual learner, is quite shy, and lives in a rural area, e-learning has truly expanded my horizons. But for others nothing beats the chemistry that happens when they share the same physical space as a teacher or mentor.

Knowing what you need

Are you someone who needs to create alone? Or do you need others to bounce ideas off and collaborate with? Do you like teamwork for the early stages, then birth the work alone? Or do you need total solitude to dream up ideas and then don't mind having a bit of bustle around whilst you are creating?

Take **Heather,** she says that:

As much as I enjoy my circle of friends and am a chatterbox, I don't actually enjoy being creative with other people very often. I am often self-conscious and am the type of perfectionist who, if I can't do it well right away, will often talk myself out of doing it at all.

Are you someone who needs a lot of one-to-one attention? It is really important to know these things so that you can set up the optimal learning conditions to support yourself.

If you struggle with feeling judged, does this come more from worrying about what others are thinking? If you feel this way then a class is probably not a great idea as it will put you under pressure and actually stall rather than help creativity. If you prefer being anonymous and having company, then a large class or an online course would work well for you. **Mary** recalls her experiences of school art classes which have made her nervous of group-based creative experiences as an adult:

I remember feeling sick in secondary school when I had to go to Art class – I hated it. We were supposed to think of things to do – I could never think of anything. I am still like this when given a blank page or told to draw something to represent something else – there is a lot of that in community groups and the like – and so I steer clear of that sort of thing!

You may well identify with her. Maybe school-type learning situations totally put you off formal learning environments and so you need to find something more personal.

Important things to consider when finding a class are:

- What kind of atmosphere do you need in a classroom?
- Do you learn best by listening, watching or doing?
- Do you need someone watching you as you try something new or do you need to create alone and get feedback on the results?
- To what extent do noise, smells and other distractions bother you?
- Do you need lots of theory? Lots of practical work? An even mix?
- Do you have time to do the homework?
- How long is the course?
- How easy is it to get to?
- Is there a built-in support system so that you can build relationships with other students?
- Do you need personal support for learning difficulties or health issues?
- Is it a very specific skill you want to learn? Then be sure to find a specialist.
- Do you need to commit to specific times – will you be able to?
- How much will it cost?
- Does it need specialist materials or tools, or can you use the ones at the class?
- What do you need to know before you start?

Do bear in mind that our needs vary for different projects and media depending on our skill level, need for concentration, ability to handle stimulus, and our level of confidence. So, for example, you might find that you love crafting with other people, but can't stand cooking when someone is watching. Or you like taking a writing class but prefer learning to garden with a book as your guide.

Choosing your bridge over troubled waters

So let's take painting. A lot of people paint at school, then give it up. But at some point in their adult life they feel drawn to starting again, but don't know how. This might even be you! It feels like such a gulf between wanting to paint, and actually painting. I know, I've been there! So what you need is a bridge to get you across the chasm of impossibility.

There are hundreds of bridges, you will know the right one for you when you spot it. You can tell because it feels like it can take your weight. It can hold you. And when you are standing facing it, you no longer feel like you will fall in to oblivion. You can see the other side. And it looks so exciting it makes your heart race. Sure, it's still nerve-wracking, you're crossing a deep canyon, for goodness sake, but you have the trust in you that this bridge will support and guide your steps. So pick your bridge, and start walking!

- You might get a group of friends around to paint together once a month.
- You might chose to join a landscape watercolor class at the local college…
- Or a life-drawing class at a community center.
- Get one-to-one tuition in oils from a local artist.
- Join a local painters' group and exhibit your work together every year.
- Pick up an old box of acrylics from your college days and some scrap cardboard and get started this moment at the kitchen table.
- Get a book on the basics of portrait-painting from the library.
- You could copy a favorite work of art.
- Follow a YouTube tutorial.
- Look in your local shop or online for classes that inspire you.
- Volunteer to help paint the background scenery for a community play.

- You could paint a picture with your kids in the garden on an old sheet.
- Or with a large group as you create a big mural or some pavement art as part of a community event.
- You could make sketches of favorite photographs in private.
- Book a group sketching holiday in the South of France.
- You could paint on a stone, an old box, a primed canvas, a sheet, your hands, your child's face, a friend's pregnant belly, your kitchen wall...

To find your bridge, just keep your eyes, and heart open. It's out there.

Reflections

List five excuses you make when you think of trying something new – and give yourself answers.

List three classes you'd like to take – and investigate them.

List five projects you've started but not finished – where did you get stuck on them, and how might you revive them?

List the three most important qualities in a creative teacher, and three deal-breaker qualities.

Chapter 19

The Creative Process

Go, yield, surrender to the magical wilderness of your mind, the splendor of reverie, the lawlessness of imagination, where anything is possible.
Aimee Myers Dolich

I am aware that putting a chapter on the creative process so far into the book might seem a little unusual. But I believe that you need to have started the process in order to reflect on it, otherwise you will stay safely in your head, feeling that now you "understand it all anyway" rather than actually embarking on your own creative journey.

Whether you are writing a book, designing a dress, painting a picture or composing music, the process for creating any detailed piece of work is pretty much the same. If you are working at creative levels one and two, following a pattern or recipe (see Chapter Two for a reminder about the levels of creativity) the dreaming and planning stages are generally shorter, as once you have found the pattern to follow, the instructions are there to guide you.

However, if you are working with inner-directed, free-flowing creativity (levels three and above) then every time you start a new project, the process can seem like a new land: daunting, unfamiliar, overwhelming, disorientating and certainly directionless. Creativity is scary stuff! You are working alchemy with the unknown, making images, forms and words appear that have never existed in this way before!

This is why so many people get stuck before they have even started. They have a great idea, but then have no clue of the process to follow to actualize it.

There is a wonderful quote about writing from **E.L. Doctorow** that states:

Writing is like driving a car at night. You can only see as far as the headlight, but you make the whole journey that way.

Whilst this is true for each individual's journey, the journey itself has its own archetype, its own blueprint which is generally similar whatever medium you are working in, however experienced you are.

The creative journey is not a trek through the wilderness, but actually a clearly defined path, which though not visible to our outside eyes, can be felt with our inner senses. I have provided a map, so that you will be able to identify the landmarks on each section of the path, and know what is required for that part of the journey. This immediately makes things a lot easier and clearer for us.

As we follow the creative journey, we learn more and more to become reliant on our six senses (sight, sound, touch, taste, smell, and intuition), and less on the logical mind, or the responses of others. The more we can learn to follow our own senses, the more personal and original our work will be. There are parts of the process that require us to focus our full attention on our own judgment and senses for feedback, and parts which require us to open up to the voices and feedback from outside.

It was only towards the end of my own creative journey writing this book that I realized that the best map of the creative process is a labyrinth! The symbol of the Rainbow Way! It made me laugh out loud to finally realize, having walked the creative path most of my lifetime, having taught about labyrinths for five years, the rather blinking obvious – the process of birth, spirituality and creativity is one and the same: The Rainbow Way, the labyrinth. Though I felt a little less stupid, when I shared this realization with one of my mentors, an artist and author of a book on labyrinths, who proceeded to have her own a-ha moment! She had never considered that either!

Artist, Flora Bowley, talks about the spiraling in and spiraling out that is required as we create a painting and make decisions about how to proceed. In simplest terms this is what the creative process is, a spiraling in and out. But the labyrinth archetype makes this **seem** a less straightforward path than a simple spiral, because we cannot anticipate the path ahead with our logical minds. In reality, we are doing no more than spiraling in and out a number of times to reach the center, and then the same as we head back out. This is one reason why the creative process is often littered with false starts, parts where we lose our momentum, and parts where we race ahead, full of energy, having a clear view of where we intend to go.

Your roadmap to the creative journey

Feel yourself being quietly drawn by the deeper pull of what you truly love.
Rumi

Before we embark on our creative journey, we stand outside the labyrinth, in the wider community of creatives, in the fullness of the world and nature. We soak up ideas, images, inspiration through our senses, through our roots. This I call **creative bathing,** where we consciously, and unconsciously absorb the world around us, with no great intention for what we will get from it.

When we live in a rich environment this tends to happen quite naturally. When we choose to live more mindfully, our minds and hearts are moved by what we soak up as we go about our daily lives. If we take time to surround ourselves with inspiration, this happens even more frequently, rather like giving compost to plants helps to nourish them and make them grow stronger and faster.

We then take ideas and images from our daily lives into the **dreamtime,** consciously or unconsciously, we start to play with them in our imaginations. Quietly in the dark they begin to gestate. This can take days, weeks or even years. As they bubble into our conscious minds, we start to wonder: what if...?

Entering the labyrinth

And then, one day we receive the **call to action**. Inspiration calls to us, often in the most bizarre of times and places, and we think: I want to make something, I need to do something about this... We are called to the mouth of the labyrinth, to the beginning of this particular creative journey. At this point all we hold in our hands is some sort of a kernel of an idea – a mood, a medium, a color, a feeling, a word or a few lines. This starting idea has an energy that sucks us in with enthusiasm. We need to learn to hop on this initial wave of excitement (as I will discuss further in the next chapter) and then sustain the energy ourselves. Like a lit match on a windy night, hold the flame close and safe, protect, treasure it, lend it the shelter of your body so that it may grow strong and bright.

The call to action might also be given to us by a teacher, client, family member or event, rather than emerging spontaneously from our own inner world. It is a powerful moment. One which we can choose to honor or ignore.

And so you find yourself **standing on the threshold.** Flame in hand. Dare you step forward into it or is something blocking your way? Are you free to start your journey?

If you experience a blockage, be it physical or emotional, something that stops your throat, your thought processes, your emotions, then take a look back at the chapter on unblocking and fears. What boulders do you need to shift? And how do you need to do it? Do you need to be brave and just climb over them? Do you need someone to help you shift them to one side, such as a teacher, friend or healer?

We step in. It doesn't really matter when. We enter the process. We start to create. We take a pen, a paint brush and jot down some ideas, notes, a rough sketch – these are usually very rudimentary, broad strokes or tiny details. We begin by **doodling, sketching, planning.** It is as delicate as a seedling at this point. As miraculous as a six-week embryo. Share it only with your most trusted people, or not at all. It is so easy to miscarry at this stage: when even you are not sure of its real potential or final form. This is a stage of deep faith, surrender and playfulness, of openness to quantum leaps and seismic shifts. Magic is happening. Play your part and trust!

And so we allow our **dreamtime and intuition** to help us to add details to our basic outline. We look at what we have put down, we might go back to our original sources, we dream some more, wonder what else we are missing. And then we carry on going. Step by step. Doing the work. This is the weird liminal stage, just like pregnancy, you don't quite look pregnant, no-one wants to ask if you are, just in case they offend you! It's all blobby and a bit sketchy and messy, no tidy bump to proudly show off. No definite kicks of life. But we keep on showing up, doing the work. Sometimes it's so exciting, and sometimes we are just so tired and despondent. It's OK, it's all part of the process.

As more comes to us, we are able to translate it into the material realm. Some will be false starts, some will be major parts of the finished piece. What matters is that we get everything we can down, we lay down the building blocks. As we continue **getting down the bones,** (otherwise known as **pattern cutting, writing the first draft),** a more solid shape begins to emerge. We draw more detailed plans, looking at them from a number of angles. We get a reasonably firm working plan or pattern which will guide our initial steps. We are beginning to spiral in and out.

A-ha! moments of immense clarity occur throughout the creative process. Like hearing the heartbeat of your baby. It all makes perfect sense. We get a sense of the bigger picture, and how it all fits together. And for a moment or two we can hold it in our minds, rather than just touch it with a couple of senses.

A-ha moments usually emerge a little while after complete despair has set in, or after we have asked others for answers and direction. It is as though we need to fully surrender our own answers and possibilities, to really say "I don't know" before the co-creative power will step in to assist. These moments tend to be short and glorious. They can happen with our creativity and our parenting: we feel stuck, stagnant, frustrated, despite working hard nothing's happening, we aren't really getting any results, we wonder why we bother. And then suddenly a flash. Everything is clear. The whole vista is visible, shimmering in front of our eyes, as hypnotic as a mirage to a thirsty woman in the desert. Trust these moments completely. They are literal revelations. Now we know what we need to do, the action to take, and we shift our sails, adjust our course, our directions now clear and understood.

Now is the time to build the main body of the work, **fleshing it out, sewing it together.** Sail on the newfound energy and inspiration from your a-ha moment for as long as possible – it will take you far!

Sometimes we are following the plan we have drawn out, and sometimes improvising. The most important thing here is to fill in the gaps, even if we know what we are doing will not make it into the final creation. We need to make a coherent whole at this point.

This is when we think that we are finished! But in truth you are only halfway there! The baby might be perfectly formed at 24 weeks, but it is not yet ready to be born. Once out in the world it will struggle to survive. There is still so much more strengthening, growing, refining to go.

This is why people who consider themselves "not creative" are generally unhappy with their work: they will get this far and claim to be finished, and give up, either because they are not experienced or confident in the next act of refinement and polishing, or because they think that the quality of their work at this point is representative of what they are capable of. It is not. This is the center of the labyrinth. We see something solid and complete-seeming and we long to be done with it. Even though it is a little rough around the edges.

The turning point

The difference between a good artist and a great one is:
The novice will often lay down his tool or brush,
Then pick up an invisible club on the mind's table
And helplessly smash the easel and the paint.
Whereas the vintage man does not hurt himself or anyone.
And keeps on sculpting light.
Hafiz

You have reached **the turning point**. This is where you can turn your back on your creative baby, and leave it half-formed in the center of the labyrinth. You come back out of the labyrinth alone, and may carry feelings of grief or even shame with you. Or you commit to the tremendous work of the second stage, of editing, polishing and birthing your creative work out into the world: to emerging from the creative labyrinth **with** your work. Heed well the words of **Leonardi Da Vinci** well: *Art is never finished, only abandoned.*

This is the point where we choose to abandon our half-finished creation, or give it the courage and the energy needed to make it into the vision we first had…or something even more incredible!

In the words of **Florence Scovel Shinn**, artist and author:

Every great work, every great accomplishment, has been brought into manifestation through holding to the vision, and often just before the big achievement, comes apparent failure and discouragement.

So as we stand in the center we draw breath. We rest. We look back on the process so far and forward to the work yet to come. We regain our center. **Clarify our vision and intention.** We step back from the details, from the process.

When we have been close to our work, working intensely on it for a long time, it is really hard to "see" it. This is the time to put it away for at least a weekend, perhaps a few weeks, then come back to it with fresh eyes. What works and what doesn't will jump out in sharp relief once you have some emotional distance.

The path out

From now on we need to start to make judgments about our work, to begin to **edit, shape and adapt it**, **spiraling in and out**. We will be clearer in our vision for our creation at this stage. Or we will be guided by the creation itself, responding to bits that we like and don't like.

This part of the work can be taxing and time-consuming – it always takes far longer than you expect. It usually takes as long again as the process has so far.

The ability to do this comes with experience, support, and a deeper knowledge of the technique of our art form. It is guided almost solely by your instinct: an instinct that when experienced and well-trained can make gold out of the most unpromising of first drafts. Spiraling in and out requires that we look closely, focus our attention on the tiny details, be critical of our work, make decisions, then work some more, and then pull out our vision to see the bigger picture, to see if all the parts are harmonious and function well together, before working on it again. In and out our attention goes as we pull a finished piece of creative work out of fuzziness and chaos and find some sort of order.

Sometimes we only need small tweaks, sometimes we might need a total structural overhaul. This takes immense courage. Are you willing to hold your raw work up to scrutiny, to risk losing what you have worked so hard for, in the faith that something even better will emerge at the end? Are you willing to put in the time and energy for the second, pretty invisible, thankless and courageous part of the task? This is the step between first draft and final copy. Between sketch and finished painting.

Professional artists will often have professional advisers to direct their work at this stage – the client, agent or editor who will help to iron out any errors, wrinkles and inconsistencies. Non-professionals will have to do this themselves. Find yourself an ally, a mentor, a friend, a creative doula whose opinion you trust, who knows you well. Go through it together and alone. Talk out those parts that you are stuck on, let them shed their light. But be wary of asking for too many opinions. They are liable to contradict each other, and you will begin to get overwhelmed, to people-please, to lose track of your own inner voice.

You are now so close to the end that you can almost smell it. Like the 39th week of pregnancy, you are heavy with the weight of your creation. You long for it to be over, to be free of it. It keeps you up at night and haunts your dreams. And yet another part of you feels apprehension of what lies beyond. How will the birth be? Will the baby be as you expected? What will the response of the outside world be? What will we do, who will we be when we are not giving every living moment to gestating this creation? Will I love it? Will it be as I hoped?

Now is not a time for inductions. We need to carry our baby to term. To be sure that it is fully ready to meet the world, plumped out and beautiful. This is **the final polishing**: a proof read for any remaining spelling mistakes or punctuation errors; the varnishing of a painting; the polishing of a sculpture; the dress-rehearsal, tidying up the loose threads. The end is in sight, we have to step away from our need to change anything major now. We need to make peace with our creation, to begin to perceive it as something in its own right, no longer a work in progress. This is the beginning of detachment of artist from her creation, mother from her child.

The moment of **birth** is here. And so we step out of the labyrinth once more, down the birth canal of creativity and out into the world, emerging from our creative journey with our creation in our hands. That which we have been creating internally, in private for weeks or years, will now be unveiled. Birthing can be exhilarating, exhausting, daunting, depending on the creative process, the support at the birth and what sort of labor you have.

Though you emerge on the same path, you are not the same person who entered the labyrinth at the beginning of this journey. The seed of the vision that you carried in your heart, hands or womb has transformed into a material creation, into a reality that you can finally share with others. Notice how the process has transformed you as well.

Every creation needs to be **witnessed** and appreciated. Sharing our work with the world is a vital part of the creative process. As creatives we often struggle to really "see" our work as we are too close to it – we are usually simultaneously too generous and too harsh with our creations, rather like our children! Feedback is vital to most creatives. Though we might feel vulnerable, we also feel affirmed, and our hard work acknowledged. Take time to celebrate your achievement with yourself and others. Acknowledge the hard work, the commitment, the courage it has taken. Appreciate yourself and your work. Take special care of yourself. Rest.

And in a beautiful act of completion, the act of witnessing leads you, and whoever else witnesses, back to the first stage of the cycle – that of creative bathing. Your work will seed other works – in your life and those of others.

Reflections

For a strong finished piece of work, none of these steps can be missed, however much we might prefer to give them a miss.

Which parts of the process do you enjoy the most?

Which do you struggle with the most?

Are these the same parts of pregnancy, the spiritual journey or mothering that you find difficult?

How might you make them easier or more enjoyable?

How might you leave yourself reminders of these stages, for next time?

- Bookmark the chapter in this book if you found it helpful.
- Keep your labyrinth to hand – write on it the various stages of the creative process.
- Get your creative doula, ally or partner to remind you that you have been here before, that this is where you struggle, and that you will be OK.
- Have a quote which helps you pinned to your wall – use it as a mantra or affirmation.

Chapter 20

Nurturing and Supporting
your Creative Self

No one – not us, not our children – benefits if we become burned out, miserable, or exhausted. In order to avoid travelling down that stressful road, we need to bring some balance to our lives and keep the batteries of our souls charged. Taking time to create art can help.
Shona Cole, *The Artistic Mother: A Practical Guide to Fitting Creativity into Your Life*

A woman has to make a real effort not to dissolve into everything that needs her.
Lynn Andrews, MetaArts magazine.

To be all-giving is to be mindless of one's own needs. To give mindfully means recognizing fatigue depletion, my own limits. I am not good at this. I give to my family, my students, my clients, but I am less able to receive.
Pat Allen, *Art is a Way of Knowing*

How are you doing? Have you gotten so excited to be creating again that you're starting to stack up late nights? Are you spreading yourself too thin? How well are you taking care of yourself right now?

Burnout

Most of us are not very good at it. We're very good at taking care of everyone, and everything else. We know we should do it, of course, it's on our to-do list in fact. But that list is long. We are busy. And no one encourages us to nurture ourselves, if we're honest it seems a bit self-indulgent. So it's not a priority. And we keep on putting it off. Ignoring the warning signs and burning the candle at both ends. Until suddenly it's too late: we burnout, or get sick, or melt down. Breakdown or depression take us in hand. Then the only way to recovering ourselves is through even more intense self-care. The thing we saw as negotiable suddenly becomes essential!

When we become women, the first thing we should be taught is about self-care. As mothers, we need to be taught even more about how to care for ourselves. As creative mothers this is doubly important as your precious life force, your energy, is the source of both of your soul callings. Do not underestimate how much energy creativity and mothering take. Sure they fill you up on one level, but they require lots from you too.

Find a way to monitor your energy levels. Ask a trusted friend or partner also just to keep an eye on you to ensure that you are not burning the candle at both ends. Ensure that you are creating from your overflowing abundance, from fullness, rather than draining an already depleted mind and body dry. When we run on empty, we are actually running on adrenal energy which gives you a rush and then a slump, depleting our immune systems, and often causing weight issues as well. Adrenaline is our friend to get us through extreme times when life suddenly demands our all. But it is vital that we do not live or create from this place on a habitual basis.

What are the signs that burnout is on its way?

- You're finding it hard to concentrate.
- You feel tired all the time.
- You're thirsty or hungry and you ignore it!
- You feel the beginning of a bug.
- You feel overwhelmed by deadlines or a lack of time.
- You feel despondent, hopeless and like you don't have another drop of energy.

- Your libido is flatlining.
- You're using caffeine, alcohol or sugar to keep you going.
- You haven't had a break for weeks or even months.
- You're feeling particularly angry or emotionally turbulent.
- You find yourself bursting into tears at the drop of a hat.
- Your muscles feel tense and tight – especially those in your back, hands, feet and jaw.
- You are sleeping poorly and find it hard to relax.
- You keep getting sick.
- You feel you are on an endless treadmill…

You can trust me on these. I feel every single one of them at this moment. So I'm heading straight off for a break to follow my own advice:

- Stop. Right now. Yes, you can!
- Drop everything. Now!
- Step away from all digital appliances. Put down the book. Turn off the radio.
- Get outside if you can.
- Move your body briskly for a few minutes: yoga, dance, a walk…
- Take a few deep breaths.
- Go to the toilet, have a big drink of water and a healthy snack.
- Take a few herbal supplements and a multi-vitamin.
- Go to bed early tonight.

If your burnout has been grinding on for a while, then you're going to have to do these things consistently for a few weeks, until they are an automatic part of your daily regime. Burnout happens because we have been ignoring the body's signals that it is tired and needs to rest and replenish for an extended period. Its basic message is that we need to get back into our bodies, into being, not doing.

We live in a world where we have to decide our own enough. Children will always want more, need more, that is human. And society will always require more of us too. So it up to us to decide and clearly communicate our limits, it is our sacred duty to ourselves and our children if we are to share a loving and healthy relationship. **Laura P** reflects on her own experience of this:

> *Holding my life up to the light and deciding what was important to me, and what was **not important**. That was a challenge, because what I learned was true for me did not fit my preconceived idea of what I **thought** was true and important in my life.*

Learning what really matters (the hard way)

I'm fiery, creative, passionate, and independent and the demand of the earlier years was difficult for me. I resisted. I thought that there was something more important "out there" that I needed to accomplish or express. I felt this urge from deep within, to do something that had nothing to do with my role as mama.

For a short, but important time in my daughter's life I did just that, but I also missed the moment. I was experiencing the most outer success that I ever had in my life. I was getting a lot of recognition and expressing my creativity for a global audience of women, but I wasn't happy. I was a sleep-deprived mama, and there was no way for me to accomplish what I did without ignoring my body. But even worse was that I ignored my daughter.

I can never get those six months back when I was diligently working on my "big" project and ignoring my body and my daughter's needs. But the pain of what I discovered fuels me every day now to pour all of my energy into making my kiddo and my whole family healthy and happy.

I still run an online global business for women, but I offer my services when there is a surplus of time and energy available that my family and homestead doesn't need from me. Mostly, I am using my creative forces to make great meals, keep my home and body beautiful, be present with my daughter and husband, plant and maintain gardens, raise animals, and home-school my amazing daughter!

I know the creative work I am doing now will not last. In another short six years, I will have plenty of time on my hands to create something "out there". But this time is precious and temporary, and I will not miss the beauty of these moments.

Indigo Bacal

Is your creative work draining you?

I feel it is important to note that whilst some creative work can be soothing, healing, relaxing, other creativity can require vast amounts of energy and be exhausting. Be aware how much energy you have when starting out and your purpose for creating at this time, and then when you are in the creative process, check in with yourself and see whether what you are doing is draining or recharging you.

Creative work which we can find draining includes: commissions, deadlines, high-pressured or highly detailed work, high levels of physical strain, concentration and decision making, lots of noise or chemical fumes, highly emotional work, dealing with trauma, lots of teaching or giving to others, long sessions, late nights, struggling to find creative solutions, screen-based and sedentary work, generally anything which requires high levels of concentrated cognitive work, detail or emotion.

Creativity that is recharging is that which is: free-flowing, deeply enjoyable, personal, healing, repetitive and reasonably simple, soothing physical activity, short bursts, using color and gentle movement, including centering or meditative elements, working outside in good weather.

We are deep but not bottomless wells. There are high clouds and deep ground waters of creativity. When we are cut off from them, it says nothing about our abilities or potential – just that we are dry, and in need of creative rains or to sink a deeper well. Take the pressure off yourself to produce – because really creativity should not be about producing things. The products of creativity – the books, the paintings, the sculptures – are whispers from your soul or the communal soul: they are by-products of the journey. When we run dry it is because we have fallen for the mistaken belief that they are *it*, and that we are the source of our creations. We only have two jobs – to turn up with our skills, and to get out of the way and let the process guide us.

We need to stop, and listen, not just with our ears but our whole beings. To sense, to drink in through our senses the world, her beauty and color, to taste our tears, to see our love, to touch our pain, and then express them through the tools given to us in the material world – to play with our media of choice, like children to revel in the feel of the clay, the squelch of paint between our fingers the smell of the soldering iron, the joy of seeing stitch after stich create cloth.

When we lose this childlike joy, we have lost our way and drought and despair are only around the corner – even when we create professionally and it becomes our work. We need to reconnect with this joy of sensation and delight in our tools. We need to have that flutter of excitement as we try a new technique, as we attempt the impossible. When we lose this, we lose our taproot into creativity. We must always be forging new paths into the wilderness of the impossible, if we stick to the tried and trusted places, we become lost. It is in the wild places that we find our creative selves.

Creativity flourishes on both order and chaos, in equal balance. If you are stuck, then figure out what are you needing? Is it more structure and clarity? Then tidy your workspace, start an exercise regime, make plan, take a class... Or do you need more chaos? Are you being too staid, structured, safe or downright boring? Then do some wild dancing to music, sing a song that makes you let loose, do a free write in your journal, paint blindfolded ...

Recharging

In this world of electrical appliances, recharging is part of our daily lives. We know that if we want to use our cell phones or laptop computers all day, we have to charge them up the night before. Otherwise we'll find them running on low battery and then blanking on us just as we really need them. Same goes for our bodies. Recharging is non-negotiable for creative mothers. The more energy you expend in your creativity and mothering, the more time you will need to commit to recharging. I used to feel weak, guilty and a bit pathetic about my need to recharge. But we don't expect our appliances to run indefinitely without recharging, so nor should we expect that of ourselves.

In your dreams

By allowing open sexual expression in dreams, it seems to me, we may actually be freeing creative thinking on all levels of consciousness.
Patricia Garfield

Dreams have been acknowledged throughout history as having great importance – as aids to spiritual guidance, artistic endeavor and healing. They are one of the best ways to recharge the physical and creative self.

Dreams are where our sensory experiences of the world and our inner psyche are fused into magical apparitions which can give us insight, ideas, and messages. Without them, we are creatively firing on fewer cylinders – relying purely on our logical brain and our ability to shift between the brain hemispheres, between the worlds, in our waking state.

There is a sense of open-ended possibility within our dream life. Here the laws of reality no longer apply: time, gravity, age, physical strength have no bearing on what can occur. In dreams we can speak without language and know things without the need to recourse to logic. We can see the most fantastical landscapes, costumes and events which do not need to rely on engineering or economics to justify their existence. In short our dream lives are our creative playground, and our creativity is our faculty for making our dreams real.

As mothers, the early years of sleep deprivation can be particularly hard, as it is not just a lack of sleep, or even the wakings which are the issue, but rather the lack of deep sleep and the episodes of dreaming sleep which are sandwiched between them that we are missing out on. Recent research at Duke University, North Carolina, found that women need more sleep than men to keep our hormones in balance, stating that for women: "poor sleep is associated with high levels of psychological distress, hostility, depression and anger."

Other research has proven what indigenous cultures have known intuitively forever: that when a woman is menstruating, her need for dreaming sleep is much, much higher in the few days before her period and during her bleeding. Lack of enough rich dreaming sleep leads to much stronger PMS symptoms. So do whatever you can, for every aspect of your health and wellbeing, to optimize your chances to dream.

Reflections

What do you need to do to ensure a good night's sleep? Do you (and your babies) sleep better with them in bed beside you, or in another room? Do you need to sound proof or light proof your room better? Do you "power down" early enough before bed? When is your optimal bed time? Have you tried a gentle herbal sedative like chamomile tea or lavender oil on your pillow to help you to drop off?

How good are you at recalling your dreams?

Do you have any recurring themes or images? What are they? What meaning do the hold for you?

- Which are the most powerful dreams that have stayed with you over the years? Why?
- Try keeping a notepad beside your bed and scribbling down the images, words and narratives that you recall, directly on waking in the morning.
- Encourage your family to share their dreams with each other, and learn to reflect on the various meanings that the dreams might hold.

Retreat

It is not where you go or for how long you go. You don't have to go anywhere. It is all in your intention and commitment.
Jennifer Louden, *A Women's Book of Retreats*

Another vital recharging tool is retreat. We all need time out, and as we get older our need for this increases. A retreat space is a sacred container for spiritual growth or artistic creation, protected from the interruptions of the outside world.

Both women and artists have a special need of retreat. Many artists throughout history have lived almost exclusively in a form of retreat, whereas for women it has been a luxury rarely denied them.

Retreat is really the conscious creation of a space for yourself to receive what you need, rather than to be giving to others. Whether you create this for yourself at home, or book an artistic or spiritual retreat away, retreat is the best antidote I know to burnout! It allows space for profound self-care, rest, and deep reflection where important insights, healing and creative spurts can emerge.

Reflections

Have you been on retreat?
What did you get from the experience?

How do you feel when you think of retreats? Scared? Envious? Excited?

How might you create a retreat for yourself in the next month? Set aside at least two hours where you will be completely uninterrupted.

High sensitivity

The truly creative mind in any field is no more than this: A human creature born abnormally, inhumanly sensitive. To him...a touch is a blow, a sound is a noise, a misfortune is a tragedy, a joy is an ecstasy, a friend is a lover, a lover is a god, and failure is death.

Add to this cruelly delicate organism the overpowering necessity to create, create, create – so that without the creating of music or poetry or books or buildings or something of meaning, his very breath is cut off from him. He must create, must pour out creation. By some strange, unknown, inward urgency he is not really alive unless he is creating.

Pearl S. Buck

Chances are high if you're a creative mama you are probably a highly sensitive person as well. If you're highly sensitive then you tend to get more overwhelmed more quickly than your average person. The same things that make you creative: your sensitivity, your heightened awareness of color and feelings, can also lead to regular overwhelm.

Elaine Aron, the authority on high sensitivity and author of a number of books on the topic, describes a highly sensitive person as someone who:

- Is easily overwhelmed by such things as bright lights, strong smells, coarse fabrics, or loud noises.
- Gets rattled when they have a lot to do in a short amount of time.

- Needs to withdraw during busy days, into bed or a darkened room or some other place where they can have privacy and relief from a situation.
- Makes it a high priority to arrange their life to avoid upsetting or overwhelming situations.
- Notices and enjoys delicate or fine scents, tastes, sounds, or works of art.
- Has a rich and complex inner life.
- As a child was seen by parents or teachers as sensitive or shy.

Her extensive research suggests that between 15-20% of the population are highly sensitive. In the past, people with these traits have been called "shy," "timid," "inhibited," or "introverted," but these labels are often inaccurate, as around a third of highly sensitive people are actually extroverts.

If you or your child are "highly sensitive", as my whole family are, be sure to build this awareness into your life, factor it in rather than denying it. And do get your hands on Elaine Aron's wonderful books – I have found them invaluable.

Sugar, sugar

Being highly sensitive means you pick up more from your environment – you feel things more strongly (both your own feelings and those of others) and reflect more upon what you pick up before acting. Because of this high level of processing and thinking, you're more easily overwhelmed, overstimulated and overaroused than someone who isn't sensitive.

Where food comes into play is this – we often use food to soothe ourselves when we feel overwhelmed.

Karly Randolph Pitman, *author Overcoming Sugar Addiction*

Rainbow Women and Highly Sensitive people need to be careful to balance their sugar, caffeine and alcohol intake, and other things which add to the adrenaline swing cycle. Often when you find yourself with a sugar craving or downing coffee or margaritas "just to get through the day", you have one of two issues. Either you have feelings that you are wanting to medicate, to push down so you don't have to deal with them. Or you are wanting to rest or zone out and you are not listening to your body's needs, so are fuelling it with sugar or caffeine, to keep it buzzing and going, which leads to adrenal burnout. I have recently recognized that throughout my life I have chosen to self-medicate with sugar, rather than go near anti-depressants. I felt more comfortable with that choice, but in truth, both have serious side effects.

When we choose to eat sugar, often it is a way to bring us into the now. Stop, listen to your body. What does you really need? Give yourself **that** instead. If this is an issue for you, there are a number of very helpful books on the market to do with sugar addiction and balancing hormones, see the "Resources" section at the back for my recommendations.

Sweets for your sweet

Creative women also need to be aware of relationship dynamics – throwing so much time and energy into a project often can overtake you, leaving little time for partners who can feel left out and overlooked, hurt and confused. Often a creative mama finds more solace and understanding in her creative projects than the people around her. Until she crashes. And then she needs their support deeply. Be sure to give time and energy to your partner.

Laura, a mother of three, shares her experience of how her creativity impacts on her relationship with her partner:

I would like to be creating all the time, I am so bursting with ideas that I can only create a fraction of what I want to. I simply don't have the time. When I try stepping it up a little I find that my health and my relationship with my partner suffers. I have to be very strict with how much time I spend on creating.

Laura's experience was echoed by many of the other mothers I spoke to. For many women, this was top of their struggles: how to balance their needs and their partner's needs bearing in mind the limited time that parents of young children have. It is not easy. But what makes the whole thing navigable is to learn to express your own needs clearly, without excess emotion. And for your partner to really hear. And for them to be able to do the same. And then together to carve out a plan.

Top tips for having a healthy partnership as a Rainbow Mama:

- Explain your creative process to them, how you hunger for it, how it fills you up, gives your life meaning and keeps you sane.
- Explain just how important your creative time is and what time of day you work best at.
- Negotiate time away so that you can have it and keep them to their side of the deal. We, and other friends, find that dividing Saturday between us works wonders.
- Be sure to be grateful and loving when you return, tell them how much it means to you. But no need to grovel or feel guilty.
- And reciprocate – just like making love physically, making a loving, creative life requires give and take – be sure to let him have his creative, sporting or down time too.

I hope this chapter has given you lots of insight into managing your energy and caring for your precious self. It takes a total change of mindset to move from mother-martyr to self-care queen. But if you are fully committed to your creative and mothering selves, it is the only way which ensures health and sanity. Do be sure to check out the "Resources" section at the back of the book for great books and articles to support you in learning self care.

Reflections

How are you nurturing your creative self right now?

What areas do you need to focus on more?

When was the last time you dried up? Do you know what preceded it? And how did you get out of the dry patch?

Chapter 21

The Spiritual Gifts of Creativity

To live life creatively, you have to let creativity lead you. End of story, beginning of story.
Sheila J. Ramsey

I begin with a few scribbles... I keep thinking somehow the art process is all going to order itself in my life one day and become neat. I will wake up one morning and know I am a painter who paints mothers and children. I wish for an orderliness that doesn't occur. This river meanders and goes where it wants, taking me with it.
Pat Allen, *Art is a Way of Knowing*

So now that you're really engaging with your creativity, let's dig a bit deeper into it. What does it feel like? Can we find words to begin to touch the mystery of what creativity is?

This is where we start to get to the edge of language. To the end of the visible and the beginning of the spiritual. It is the spiritual aspect of creativity which feeds us as creators: the sense of freedom, energy, timelessness, flow.

The spiritual. It is a loaded word. A challenging word. It has been muddled up with religion and politics and charismatic moneymakers for centuries. But that makes it no less precious or real. When I use it, it is to refer to everything that is **not** part of the visible, material world, everything that can be known only by experience. And often as a term that refers to something greater, vaster and more transcendent than daily life. Already words are escaping me...

It is a world that we are taught little about in our Western culture, it passes by unnamed and unvalued, unproven by science. But this is what our creativity calls forth from us, if we are willing to take the challenge. It invites us to be intrepid explorers of unknown inner worlds, mapping our experiences. We have to find words to signify that which has never been seen, nor touched nor smelled, nor heard before.

Where to start? Where else but with all that I can know for sure, but cannot prove objectively: putting language to my own experience. You might find that my experiences validate your own. But if they do not, I hope that the next few pages offer you a greater vocabulary and confidence in your own experiences to be able to articulate your own.

A personal experience of the spiritual

In creativity I find complete focus, harnessing of mind and body towards an unknown yet passionately yearned for goal. I get a sense of making something new, meaningful, beautiful, of seeing thoughts and feelings which I have not even previously guessed at writ large before me in my own hand. I find a deep intellectual stimulation, a harnessing of heart and mind, like the fluttering of first love, the adrenaline rush of a sky dive, but all from the safety of my own chair. And I feel connection, a deep soul connection to those whom I am creating for as I imbue the best of me into my creations.

At times there is the most precious moment of getting lost in the process. When my hands and the needles are one and the knitting is doing me, the piano is playing me. It has the strength and depth and clarity of an orgasm. But just as I realize what is happening, it is just me again, sitting by myself painting or writing.

Every time I sit to write, or hold a paintbrush, the possibility is there, just a heartbeat away, if only I can fully bring myself to it with all my being and surrender myself to it. If I can let go of my ideas and flow with it, then, for a moment it is holy. I am holy. I and it and everything is God: pure undivided energy and color. We are one great beauty, pulsating in joy. Through my creativity, be it painting or birthing my babies or making love, I have felt for a moment here or there, that I am connected to something greater than myself. That there is a heart in all things and for a moment I have touched it, held it, written it.

Creativity is a path to transcendence. And my paintings, books and babies are living proof for ever more to me of that fleeting experience which touched me.

Spiritual electricity

Spirituality is the sacred center out of which all life comes including Mondays and Tuesdays and rainy Saturday afternoons in all their mundane and glorious detail. The spiritual journey is the soul's co-mingling with ordinary life.
Christina Baldwin, *Life's Companion*

Energy is something I refer to a lot in this book. What is energy, what do I mean by it? It is certainly key to my understanding of myself, of creativity, of the world, of parenting, of what works and what doesn't. For me energy is at the core of all things.

I remember being on a bus driving down a mountain road through the Malaysian rainforest, out of the tea-growing hills, through the cloud line where the cooler mountain air hit the humid jungle heat and the fusion of steam and the word "energy" just hit me between my eyes. It is the core of all things, the connector, the most basic form scientifically speaking, of all things, living and inanimate. It is the most basic principle, the building block of existence. Energy: it underlies everything visible, everything we can pick up with our senses, and every-thing we can sense with our sixth sense, our intuition. It lies beneath the solid structure of things, it is undeniable. Quantum physics has shown it to be so – that everything which exists is bouncing between particles and wave energy. Radio waves cannot be seen. But we do not deny that they exist. Some people call this energy "God" and they often add a personality to it. I do not. But I understand it to be the foundation principle of the way things work. Others call it instinct, or intuition, the creative soul or even consciousness, this ability of ours to contact and commune with the intangible, but real, force field around us.

Energy is a felt level of life force or tiredness. It is a buzzing or fizzing or vibration. It is what the Chinese in their medicine and martial arts and philosophy refer to as *chi*. The Indians in Sanskrit philosophy as *prana*. It is life force.

In *The Artist's Way* Julia Cameron speaks of spiritual electricity. And certainly my experience of creativity is, once you get going, something takes over. Suddenly you are just the person typing, not creating ideas, it is like putting your finger into a light socket: the power that comes through is not your own. Like a river it flows. We can feel when it is in flow, and when it is sluggish, congested, and when it is so weak it is almost not there at all.

If this idea resonates with you then I do suggest you work with it, in your parenting and creativity – because in the end that is the underlying root of most of what this book is about – becoming more consciously aware of your own energy, and allowing it to flow and to recharge, so that you are left feeling good rather than depleted, so that you are feeling fulfilled in your life and your work, rather than drained. When you create and mother in flow, you have the full power of the Universe as your source, the work you do is power-full and will change lives, including your own!

Finding flow

Flow helps to integrate the self, because in that state of deep concentration consciousness is unusually well ordered. Thoughts, intentions, feelings and all the senses are focused on the same goal. Experience is in harmony. And when the flow episode is over, one feels more "together" than before, not only internally but also with respect to other people and the world in general.
Mihaly Csikszentmihalyi, *Flow*

Flow is a positive state studied by former Chair of Psychology at the University of Chicago, Professor Mihaly Csikszentmihalyi. He studied the optimal experiences of painters, rock climbers and athletes from around the world for over 25 years to discover the universal elements of flow, which he described as:

> *The state in which people are so involved with an activity that nothing else seems to matter; the experience itself is so enjoyable that people will do it even at great cost, for the sheer sake of doing it.*

Flow is the point where you stop thinking about what you are doing and just are it, do it. Like riding a bike, it's when you stop thinking about changing gears and pushing the pedals and keeping your balance, and are just aware of the beautiful scenery whizzing by and feel drunk on the awesomeness of life and the feeling of power in your own body.

Flow is where the spiritual side of creativity comes to the fore and it becomes a peak experience, like the most incredible meditation session when it seems we are suspended outside time and space and reality. For a moment we "get it", we are at peace with ourselves and the world. This is what creatives and spirituals throughout history have quested after. This is the same experience our creative endeavors, when they succeed, bring to others. This is why we apply ourselves diligently, working, straining, turning up and fine tuning our creations. A few moments of flow make hours of work worthwhile. According to Csikszentmihalyi:

> *The best moments usually occur when a person's body or mind is stretched to its limits in a voluntary effort to accomplish something difficult and worthwhile. Optimal experience is something that we make happen.*

And yet the irony is that whilst it is our conscious decision to do the activity which makes the flow state possible, we are not in control of the flow state itself. Whilst there are a number of things we can do to help to encourage it, after that it is a fickle beast and often comes when we were least expecting it, and at other times deserts us despite all the candles and incense that we might have invested in it!

According to Csikszentmihalyi, the elements of the flow state include:

- A challenging activity that requires skill.
- The merging of action and awareness.
- Clear goals and feedback.
- Concentration on the task at hand.
- A sense of control.
- The loss of self-consciousness.
- The transformation of time.

If we analyze these, we find that many tend to be lacking in day-to-day parenting, and they are the factors which mothers list most as being the frustrating aspects of their mothering role. And these are the very things that most creative women report getting, even in small doses, from their creativity. No wonder we yearn so much for creative release!

Reflections

In what activities have you experienced flow? Can you identify how many of the above factors were active when you experienced it?

Have you ever written about your experience of flow? Take ten minutes and do that now – be sure to mention the situation, circumstances and your felt experience.

Kairos

Time is kairos in feminine consciousness, rather than the chronos of masculine time.
Ann Ulanov

Creativity means entering another dimension, guided by our inner senses, we enter a timeless zone, of the eternal now known as *kairos*. It makes us feel boundless, unconfined, simply flowing with the experience of life. This timeless space can be reached in meditations, peak experiences such as birth and orgasm, in dreams, and often out in nature. *Kairos* cannot be reached against the clock – that is why orgasms and inspiration cannot be forced or hurried, and time awareness shuts down our access to *kairos*.

I am a very time-bound person, always aware of how much I need to be doing and how little time I have. But the experience of getting in flow with creativity often takes me completely out of clock time and into a timeless space of creation where I am one with the experience of creating. Once I start painting or writing I am so focused that often when I look up a number of hours have passed in what only feels like minutes.

Freedom

To be creative, is to be truly free. It's a constant struggle; creativity is freedom, and it requires freedom. […] Creativity if it holds you in its thrall, is worth every sacrifice, every risk.
Rice Freeman-Zachery, *Living the Creative Life*

Freedom is a feeling which we as mothers, especially of young children, yearn for, like oxygen. The constant physical needs of infants can be an energy drain, leaving even the most patient of women begging and pleading for: "Just half an hour by myself, please!" As **Paula** says:

I want to be free, to connect, to be part of something bigger, the big wide world and all its beautiful creative craziness, and all the fantastic people out there.

Our creativity gives us the possibility for almost infinite freedom if we allow it. Freedom from rules, from external pressures and demands, freedom to be the people we envisage ourselves to be, freedom to make mess, freedom to reflect, to express ourselves, to have fun: freedom to be.

The muse

Many artists speak of the muse. Originally conceived of by the ancient Greeks, it refers to a personification of that which inspires an artist. For many male artists their muse has also often been a female model and lover. For others it is the embodiment of the divine feminine, a personal goddess of creativity: a spiritual permission-giver and font of inspiration. Interestingly for most women the experience of the muse is also female, (whereas the critic tends to be male). She is perceived as an internalized voice or sensation which seems to touch or even inhabit the woman's body, bringing (divine) inspiration and ideas seemingly from nowhere, unconnected to the creator's previous rational thought process.

The muse appears at that point of my writing where I sense a subtle shift, a nudge to move over and everything cracks open, the writing is freed, the language is full, resources are plentiful, ideas pour forth, and, to be frank, some of these ideas surprise me. It seems as though the universe is my friend and is helping me to write, its hand over mine.

For me, that spiritual-mental high would be sufficient reason for writing. And while I have experienced it with each book I've written, I have never been able to decipher its pattern so that I might repeat it as often as I would like. Whatever it is, I am grateful when it happens, fearful that it may not happen again.
Amy Tan, *The Opposite of Fate*

Shiloh Sophia McCloud, a celebrated artist and teacher talks about creativity as the "seventh sense" (the sixth being intuition). She speaks of creativity as making a bridge between the two sides of the brain. The left brain, the logical linguistic brain is the home of the critic, the right side, that of pattern and flow, is where the muse resides. If we think again of the labyrinth symbol – which is a similar pattern to the brain – at the entrance stand two gatekeepers: the critic, the left side, and the muse on the right. Both are powerful spiritual guardians, but perhaps one has grown stronger and over-powered the other. Perhaps the one that says "Beware!" is louder than the one which tempts us in.

It is up to us to strengthen the right side. Because our dominant culture focuses almost exclusively on the left, we disregard the value of the right, until at some point in our development, we begin to associate the voice of the critic with our own inner voice and begin to identify with it. We become the critic, until we restart the creative process which we all naturally flowed with as children, and learn to reawaken the voice of the muse, and to speak her language once more: that of pleasure, symbol and intuition.

Intuition

As women we are rarely encouraged to heed our intuitive voice. As a creative and as a mother, it is, without the shadow of a doubt, the most powerful tool you have, and one which both mothering and creativity will help to strengthen no end. If you listen to it! It is both a font of ideas and inner guidance system, a spiritual sat-nav.

I have always listened to the voice of my intuition keenly. It is my compass. But I know that a lot of people don't follow theirs, or have much contact with it and so it was interesting in writing this to try to focus on its qualities.

The voice of my intuition is crystal clear. Where my own thought process is either linear, or inchoate and contradictory, the voice of my intuition cuts clear like a knife. It also often says unexpected things, certainly unrelated to the thought process that I am going through in my rational, planning brain. Often it is a single word or phrase that seems to appear from nowhere, its sound ringing in my head like a bell, unlike the monkey chatter of my mind. Or often it presents as a three-dimensional form, dangling in front of my eyes – a book plan, an event – almost fully formed, that I can see all angles of. It is invigorating, energizing, exciting – this sudden emergence of something I may have been mulling and struggling over for years. It is a literal eureka moment.

The voice of intuition also comes through the ear in hearing with a supernatural clarity. It does this by adding an echoing resonance to the word or phrase or idea that I or another have said, so that it seems to resonate round and round my mind – echoing, recording, making the phrase stand out from normal communication.

The voice of intuition likes:

- Late nights and early mornings.
- A contemplative cup of tea or wine.
- Being out in nature.
- Illness.
- Dreams and the moments before sleep and in the darkness of night.
- Relationship discord.
- The first flush of love.
- Sacred spaces.
- Quiet.
- Toilet time.
- Baths, and water in most places – the sea, a river…
- Reading.
- Galleries and performances.
- Bike rides and walks.
- The changing seasons.
- Pregnancy and birth.
- Candlelight and firelight.

- Menstruation.
- Death.

We all have this insight. But many choose not to listen to it. This is your gold, this is your answer book, your guidance system.

Catching creativity

Creative inspiration often comes to us at the most un-spiritual of times. Not in the midst of meditation or when we have a whole day devoted to ourselves, but rather when you are driving the kids to school or changing a nappy, making dinner or falling asleep.

Creative mothers recalled with a laugh their experiences of writing ideas down on the nearest thing to hand, old envelopes, shopping lists and even toilet paper, so that they did not disappear forever. This is what I call catching creativity.

Like falling in love or giving birth, the experience of creative inspiration has been described by thousands of voices over the years. But it doesn't make it any easier to access!

I get the bubbling of ideas coming up, one, then another, then another, like swamp gas, emerging from the depths, from an invisible, untouchable, infinite energy source below. I need to grab a pen fast as the ideas keep bubbling and if I fall behind it is hard to capture them all. I feel buzzy, slightly vibrating, my head is both racing and ultra-still. There is a tangible energy which is exhilarating. I am different to how I normally feel, I am hyper-alive and it feels wonderful. It is like I have a surge of energy which needs to be poured out, I stream it onto paper – notes, mind maps, lists, doodles, sketches, it is as though I am downloading information: I am not in control of what it is or where it is coming from. My only job is to be note-taker, not try to steer it or interfere. This only blocks it. My role at that moment is to step into the pure bubble of energy and inspiration, before it pops, and to sketch out as many of the details as I can.

And once it's stopped, it's like the tap is turned off by some unseen hand, a tap that I cannot reach. I am left to work with the information that I have, to fashion it into something – an article, a picture, a project, an event, a book. I know when I am "on the money" because the tap turns on again. What was previously invisible becomes visible, what was unclear, unknown becomes obvious, piece by piece of the puzzle fall into place as if by magic. My fingers are the ones typing, yet there is something just ahead of me: divine dictation, and I am struggling to keep up.

Catching creativity is like catching butterflies – fast-flying, bright-colored sparks darting here and there, it requires quick wits, good eyes and desire to net them. And once you have them, you need to act fast. An idea, like a butterfly doesn't last long: it is ephemeral. It is here, and now it is gone – so quick, grab your laptop, your pen and paper, your Dictaphone, your sketch pad, whatever your mode of expression or recording, swoop and catch.

Another metaphor which comes to mind when I try to explain the creative urge is it is like spotting wild horses in the desert. All is quiet and calm on the horizon of the desert mind, a dust storm here, a vulture here, then suddenly over the horizon there thunders a herd of wild horses. Where they came from is not known, nor where they are going. If you spot them you can follow them on foot, running fast to keep up, you might get a sense of their size, their energy, their number and color, and then they are gone, as quickly as they arrived. You are left with the bones, the bare bones in the desert. Your expression will never **be** the horses, it can never match them, it will be your impression of the horses. You will always be matching it up to that illusive, •
fleeting perfection of their vision when you saw and felt them. No one else saw them, so no one else can really know. Only your expression can, in some way, communicate these wild horses to the world. And if you choose not to chase them, because you're too busy, you didn't know how or you weren't ready, the image of these escaped horses may haunt you, lurking in your creative

mind forever more – you will see other horses, other landscapes, but those horses, that desert, that day, are gone for good.

Divine dictation

There is an intangible energy which guides me. I can sense it. If it is there in the work I am doing, it flies, if it is not I can feel myself forcing myself, it is like wading through treacle, it is slow, frustrating, and dispassionate. When I write without the energy there, I fish around for each word, making self-conscious and dull sentences. When the energy is there I fill page after page until it is done. A light edit and I have some of my strongest work: heartfelt, honest, and usually the most popular with my readers. And when I read it, it touches me too, because it is better than what I can write myself. It is inspired. And I can take little credit for it.

Once I had such an extreme version of this whilst I was at university. I had about six hours solid "divine dictation", followed the next day by another couple of hours. I wrote and wrote – in a cafe, in the toilets in lectures, the information was coming at me. I had no idea where from, I wasn't carefully planning or formulating ideas, I had no idea I was going to write anything that day. The same happened with this book and my first. It just came to me, unfolding, by itself. And just as I feel despairing and stuck, disillusioned with myself and the project, I keep plodding away and suddenly whoosh, another tidal wave of content appears at my fingertips and I simply have to keep writing before the energy is gone. Afterwards I feel deep joy and contentment. I feel spent, and drained in another way, like wild horses have cantered through me, but I feel happy, so happy. I am a vessel and I have done what I am here to do. It feels right.

Paula describes her inner experience of like this:

My creative style is probably best described as impulsive, erratic, organic, and cyclical. I need to feel quite passionate about an idea to be spurred into action and then I become frenzied and unstoppable! My favorite creative moments are when I have a writing idea I just have to run with, and all the ideas slowly snowball - they're like a chain reaction of light-bulb moments or phrases or quotes that just shout at me! And it is so satisfying when it's done, like I have grown or transformed in some way through some new understanding. It becomes a kind of therapy, an almost spiritual experience, if you like.

I have heard many writers and artists refer to it as a form of channeling. It is more challenging to believe this if one does not have strong ideas about a spiritual realm (as I do not). It can also seem a little as though creatives are not taking responsibility for the content of their own work, or trying to get attention. But my experience of it is as I have shared, and I have heard so many others speak of it in these terms that I know I am not alone in it.

I may understand the sensations and know how to respond to them. But this does not mean that I am in charge of the process. I can set up my inner and outer environments to best attract this state. I can stick out my thumb and try to catch a lift to the land of creativity. But just as often as playing catch with creative butterflies, in fact more often, what I am doing is doing the work: turning up, sitting down and putting pen to paper. Struggling, wading through treacle, grinding out uninspired prose. For the act of working, the act of applying oneself and showing willing attracts the butterfly muse to our sides. We must work in good faith. Writing awkward sentences, doodling unpleasing scribbles, practicing our scales, tidying up the hems. And then, one day soon, whoosh, the magic happens once more, taking us to the transcendent.

Creativity
It's where I live, in all senses of the word. It isn't a process that's separate from everything I do in my life. But when I do get the chance

to make focused work, then it's listening to the undertow, following the things half seen. It's writing into the heat and heart and ache of things. It's moving into shadow and out into light, and back again. It's urging half-felt things into presence. It's surfing, and delving. It's listening to rain falling, and wondering about the strange light behind the mist. It's rage and laughter. It's the sprinkling of red freckles under the leaves of the scarlet pimpernel. It's all kinds of longings. It's cackling so hard I almost wet my knickers. It's the light on the water. It's the feel of the ocean holding me. It's brown bodies in my arms, and the yearn of them. It's gooseberry and elderflower crumble. It's Peter hugging me on the way to the car and saying 'you did us proud.' It's slow baths, wide Sundays, chaotic mornings. It's the grip and tension of not being able to cope. It's a cacophony of blossoms in the spiral garden. It's being raw and wide open enough to let the world happen to you, to listen to its stories, and the stories locked and creaking in our own bodies. It's in the voices that were bred here, and the ones that weren't. It's in the drip of elderberry juice, deep impossible black-purple. It's in the kisses of my children, the twinkle in my husband's eye. It's the long conversation, the hunger for connection. It's here. It's right here.

Jools Gilson

Reflections

Can you describe catching creativity from your personal experience?

What does the muse look like or feel like for you?

Where do you tend to get moments of inspiration?

What do you attribute them too?

How well do you listen to your intuition? Have you ever been led astray by it?

Chapter 22

The Womb – Crucible of Creativity

The womb is where you birth and create from, the center of your unique power as a woman. It contains within it a concentrated nucleus of living, fertile, vibrant aliveness and sensual power that once released floods the whole system with its life flow.
Padma and Anaiya Aon Prakasha, Womb Wisdom

Our inner grail

Thinking of creativity as being embodied within our wombs is actually pretty revolutionary. Creativity has traditionally been considered a "gift" or "blessing" from the divine, and the divine is usually seen as external, and tends to be described in masculine terminology. So for women to connect their creative drive as being rooted not only within the human body, but within the sexual organs of every individual female, is powerful indeed.

Let that sink in for a moment! The idea of the womb as an embodied sacred space is at first a new idea for many women. But many esoteric and mystical traditions have considered the womb to be the "Grail" which myth and legend refer to, the magical, life-giving cup of rejuvenation and knowledge.

Many women instinctively experience a direct connection between their womb, the biological crucible of creation, and their artistic creativity. It is not something they were necessarily taught, but that they sensed. They speak of feeling physically pregnant when they are gestating an idea, and they instinctively hold their bellies when they speak of it, or place their hands and their attention onto this deeply feminine part of themselves as they try to tune in to their deep inner voice of intuition.

Very little attention has been given to the experience of creating in a female body, and so few links are made between the female creative urge and our wombs, or between our sensuality in creativity and in sexual experience. And whilst one might think it is because of our culture's discomfort with the erotic, actually, the connection between creativity and sexual libido has been a well-documented fact in the life and works of male artists. It has often been observed that celebrated males' creativity flourished when their sexual lives were full of passion.

But women were considered different. Women were not (or not supposed to be) artistic. And women were not (or not supposed to be) sexual. And mothers were not supposed to be either. So the impact of women's physical bodies, their sexual experiences, the impact of the menstrual cycle and birth process on their creativity has remained relatively unstudied by the establishment.

Instead, the ground has been broken by brave pioneer women, guided by their own instincts. The first visual artist to start exploring feminine imagery in the modern era, explicitly connecting her art and her sexuality was Georgia O'Keeffe. She was a woman far ahead of her time, whose erotic close-ups of flowers are so feminine and sensual they still seem avant-garde to us a century later! Frida Kahlo explored this territory of the feminine soul in her painting too with arresting results.

Meinrad Craighead, an ex-Catholic nun turned artist of the divine feminine, speaks in *Birthing from Within* of arriving, through her painting, in a land where:

What my eyes saw meshed with images I carried inside my body. Pictures painted on the walls of my womb began emerging...each painting I make begins from some deep source where my mother and grandmother, and all my fore-mothers still live; it is as if the line moving from pen or brush coils back to that original place.

I don't know about you, but my womb was never once mentioned in my art classes at school, and it was certainly never suggested that it contained images which I might want to paint!

But I discovered it intuitively, as I followed my instincts – allowing images, even then at school, to come up intuitively – women jumping from cliffs and turning into birds, an erotic snake-woman wrapped around the apple-world and consuming it. And a painting called "The Tragedy of Woman" which showed a woman's face, serene and emotionless as she stood on the stage of life, her distress revealed by a lens held up to her face. One tear rolls down her cheek, it takes the form of an egg. Even then, at just seventeen, I instinctively knew: the tragedy of woman, my personal tragedy, was my ability to have children, and therefore abandon my creative dreams. These were the images that were "painted on the walls of my womb", though I did not have that language for it then. According to authors, Padma and Anaiya Aon Prakasha in their book *Womb Wisdom*:

> *The voice of the womb is a voice long forgotten, but once contacted it becomes a staunch ally and your inner guru. This is more than the voice of your intuition; this is the voice of your feminine essence, where you birth and create from, the center of your unique power as a woman.*

Many women connect the voice of their intuition or muse as being rooted in either their heart, or their "lower heart": their womb. In ancient Indian philosophy, the creative power lies coiled in the womb and when awakened this *kundalini* energy uncoils like a snake, shooting up the spine, bringing immense power through all the chakras (energy centers) on the way up before emerging through the top of the head. This is known to be accompanied by spiritual awakening, intense visions and pleasure. **Lisa Dieken** shared her experience of this on her blog, *Wild Creative Heart*:

> *As I focused on my uterus one night in a meditative state, I felt an immense power rising up from within me. A power I had never felt*

before and I don't think I have felt since. I was nearly frightened the energy was so powerful. And along with the power, came a message:

"The power of the feminine force...the power of creation is here within you. Strong within you. You merely have to listen. The driving force can move mountains. Create from your womb. Use the energy that is there for you – shifting things, moving things, changing things, destroying things.

"It is a wise choice to use this power. Never take it lightly. Harness it, tap into it and create from it. All things flow from here... Let it rise up from within you."

But it is important here to note that whilst creativity is energetically associated with the womb in women, losing your womb, or suffering from biological infertility, does not mean losing your creativity. As writer **Julie Daley**, explains from her own personal experience:

I had a hysterectomy at 29, so I've had a lot of pain, and a lot of healing to do in that area. I've done a lot of work, connecting the heart and the womb. That's so important, it really helps with your creativity. But more than that, it's like embodied self-love, you can really connect the heart and womb and belly, the places that we can hold so much pain and grief, so many of the ways that women have been abused. So waking up the heart, and sending love to those areas for me has just been so important.

Reflections

Have you ever thought how your creativity is connected to your womb?

How much does your creativity express your experience of living in a female body?

What is painted on the walls of your womb?

Does your womb have a voice? What does it say?

Have you ever experienced your *kundalini* rising?

Creativity and our cycles

Women are guided by cyclical processes, the feminine is characteristically dual: waxing and waning. If they are not in tune with their own rhythm then it shows itself in sharp and inappropriate breaks or alternations, rather than as a steady cyclical unfolding.
Ann Ulanov

In my blood there is poetry,
In my blood are ancient stories,
The red line all the way back to the beginning.
{...}
The holiest of chalices,
The spiraling path of birth and death,
The womb is a cradle of both,
We are a gate between worlds.
Bethany Webster

Our menstrual cycle has a number of connections to our creativity. It is our inner weather, situated in the crucible of our creativity, our womb. And just as there are some times when we are biologically fertile and ready to create life, and others when our body is shedding the old cells and regenerating, so these phases are echoed in our energy levels and our creative lives.

Understanding our menstrual cycle can inform both our mothering and our creativity hugely. When we can anticipate where we will be in our cycles, we can plan our lives to support our needs and work with the energy we are experiencing.

In our male-oriented world we are expected to live at the same pace day after day. There is little understanding, respect or allowance given for our monthly fluctuations in energy, our non-mothering impulses and our less nurturing characteristics. Penelope Shuttle and Peter Redgrove discuss this in their eye-opening book on the menstrual cycle, *The Wise Wound:*

To masculinist science and religion, women are essentially breeders of children. They have only an ovulatory function. Their other half, the menstrual half, is neglected. In this side of their being they are the conveyors of imaginative and creative energies, and initiators into creative modes of sexuality.

Our cycles start at the center of the labyrinth, in the domain of the Crazy Woman. We sit in the darkness, in our dreamtime, our moon time, resting, releasing, intuiting, shedding the old. Our blood flows, and with it, if we give ourselves the time to rest and dream, our wisdom.

And then as red becomes white, and we twist along the outward path, we find ourselves becoming more expansive and outward looking. Our energy rises, our fertility and arousal levels come to a crescendo. We are turned on to life, born again to ourselves. This is the territory of the virgin – a woman unto herself.

As we approach the entrance, this is the time of ovulation, and the domain of the mother. We release an egg, our feminine biological creation, into the womb. If it is fertilized by a sperm, our creative energies are directed towards it and our mothering energy is aroused in the gestation of a new human life. If not, our mothering energy remains full, expansive and nurturing, and the intuitive insight we brought forth during our bleeding can be brought to life. Our energy can be turned towards creative projects, and now is the time for late nights and collaboration. At this point in our cycle we are able to be fully in community, in the world, full of energy to care for others. But as our hormones shift again (around day 16 in a 28 day cycle), we are called slowly back into the labyrinth, back towards our centers, towards the womb. This is the pre-menstrual phase, the inner turning away from the world. Our mood can darken, our energy levels get lower, our patience shortens. Until we find ourselves once more, in the center of our own labyrinth, it is our moon time, our dream time, once again.

We focus so much on the negative aspects of our cycle, the

angry, tearful pre-menstrual energy, that we overlook the other parts of the cycle – the parts of deep introspection, eroticism and raised intuition during menstruation and the high levels of energy, creativity and arousal during ovulation. Nor do we plan our creative times around our shifting energies, instead just expect ourselves to be "always on" and then feel angry with ourselves and the world when our bodies are calling us to be more reflective and intuitive. In feeling frustration, disgust or disconnection from this part of our bodies, in resisting our own internal rhythm, we lose a lot of our potential creative power.

It is an exciting adventure, discovering more about our inner tides of creativity. We have lived with them throughout our adult lives, and yet still know so little about them. Many women who I spoke to were thrilled, evangelical even, about how under-standing their cycles helped them to tap into much deeper creative work, and helped them, often for the first time, to find a way of working creatively which worked for, not against themselves, on a physical, emotional and spiritual level.

If this is new to you, and you would like to learn more about it, I recommend my book *Moon Time: a guide to celebrating your menstrual cycle* as a creative guide to further understanding and celebrating your body's cycles. If you are not sure where you are in your cycles, I recommend starting to chart your cycle, jotting down a couple of words each day about your emotional state, energy levels and any physical symptoms. In this way you can be a conscious ally to yourself rather than a helpless passenger pulled this way and that by the unseen tides of your cycles. I sell moon dials, which are a great way to start charting your cycle on my website. I also offer an e-course to support you in learning more about your cycles. www.thehappywomb.com

My womb journey

The first moment I recall noticing a connection of womb and creativity was while I was deep in my (in)fertility journey. The moon was full, and

I bled. Any other moon of bleeding felt defeating, met with tears and disgust, shame, in how my body failed me again – but this time, it felt different… this time, I felt like a goddess. The blood dripped from my thighs and left a spot on the wood floor, which I left. It felt like a baptism, something sacred. I didn't know of any blood rituals at the time, so this was just enough… I sat in bed, and felt like a goddess – truly… I felt glowing, my body felt like a lioness, and that I had a thousand hands holding me, stroking me. I purred.

I cradled my stomach, and wonderful tears rolled down my cheeks with overwhelming gratitude. I felt full up and in love, I felt the rush of energy through me. Perhaps it came with accepting more and more of myself – my body – as a woman, as I had been journeying through self-healing with fertility – to accepting my womanly body. The blood that moon felt like a gift, and I welcomed it – made love with it, and let go with it. It was after that moon, that I started looking forward to the creative energy that would whoosh in as my blood approached, instead of dreading it. Creative energy to create a baby – and to release the energy I needed from my fertility wounds. Painting soft images of mothers and babes. Waiting for the moment that that image I painted would be the image I painted while unknowingly pregnant.

My first moon cycle after my daughter was born was on the first quarter moon, completing her birth on the last quarter moon. This was my first true calling and feeling like I needed to do something creative with my blood. I wanted to honor it, but was unsure of just what I should do. So I sat in the shower, watching the vibrant red swirl from between my legs into the water letting it slip through my fingers and honoring that my womb was held silent, while my body created milk to feed my little goddess. Honoring that this blood was birthed from the same womb my babe grew within… celebrating that my body bleeds, that my blood is a life force. And what could be greater creativity than life?

Erin Darcy

Reflections

Have you noticed how your creativity and energy shifts according to your cycle?

How do you nurture and care for yourself and balance your family responsibilities leading up to menstruation?

Sexual energy and creativity

The creative process has an inherent sexuality to it.
K Ferlic

As we dive more deeply into our creativity, and begin to understand on a physical level how our creative drive is intimately tied up with our female cycles, pregnancy and birth, we can begin to accept, often for the first time, this uncomfortable truth: our libido and our creative drive are one and the same.

This is one reason why women were kept away from the arts throughout history, because society knows that when a woman is inflamed from the inside by her creative spirit, her libido rises, her inner voice is strengthened, and her willingness to submit herself to others is diminished: she becomes vocal, erotically charged, expressive, irrepressible. She then knows that she is powerful, with a power drawn from an inner source which cannot be mediated or controlled from outside.

Both creativity and our sexuality have the ability to make us feel fully alive to ourselves, and more deeply connected to the soul of another. Both are sensual, embodied experiences which are capable of unleashing uncontrollable, ecstatic forces from within, rooted in pre-linguistic, instinctive parts of our being.

In her literary studies, leading feminist, **Naomi Wolf**, wondered why so many of the well-known women writers and artists that she studied had bursts of creativity (leading to their most highly-regarded work) shortly after a sexual awakening of some sort, either the loss of virginity, the taking of a new lover or the awakening of newfound orgasmic potential. Her research became the book, *Vagina: a New Biography*, which explored cutting-edge neuroscience and women's experiences to piece together the connections between the brain and vagina and their impact on women's lives and creativity. In it she states:

> *The vagina's experiences can – on the level of biology – boost women's self-confidence, help to unleash female creativity or present blocks to female creativity. They can contribute to a woman's sense of the joyful interconnectedness of the material and spiritual world – or else to her grieving awareness of the loss of that sense of interconnectedness.*

She elucidates her findings further in an online interview by Adam Leipzig:

> *There isn't a substance called "creativity" that gets unleashed by orgasm or arousal, but this is what does happen: when a woman is supported by herself, by her culture, by her lover, in anticipating pleasurable sex, it boosts dopamine in her brain. Dopamine is a neurotransmitter that boosts drive, focus, motivation, energy, and assertiveness. When a woman has an orgasm, it boosts opioids, which elevate a feeling of transcendence. The part of the brain in women that relates to self-consciousness and self-regulation goes quiet during orgasm.*
>
> *These are things we know take place in the female brain. It's my interpretation, that these are powerful potential mind states, and powerful sources for creativity.*

Since the birth of my second child I have begun to recognize the connections between my experiences of birth, creativity and sexual arousal. Each time I have a new sexual awakening or break-through, it is mirrored in a flurry of new, expressive creative work which feels like it has gone up a level in terms of soul-depth.

Putting to one side for the moment this upwelling of inner creative power, there is also the sensuality of the act of creativity itself. For me the experience of painting, especially the free, early stages which I do with my hands, is an intensely sensual experience. As is the feel of wet clay slipping through my fingers on the potter's wheel. And the race of energy when I am totally immersed in my body through dance.

I have noticed that this is something that women often feel uncomfortable discussing in public, or even amongst close friends. There is still such a taboo about women speaking openly about their pleasure and arousal, (and about mothers experiencing them at all – all that's supposed to just quietly die once you're a mother), that even admitting to the sensual pleasure that we gain from creative acts, let alone sexual ones, is seen as discomforting to others. So, if we don't admit to it, then it doesn't exist. And therefore we can leave the act which is sex safely locked behind the bedroom door "where it belongs".

But these bodies that make love, that experience orgasm, are the same bodies that paint pictures, breastfeed babies, make beautiful food, and put out the bins. We do not, in the words of Saida Desilets, leave our genitals on the bedside cabinet in the morning. This womb, this vagina, these breasts, these hands and cheeks and hair, are with us all day, sensing, responding, absorbing, enjoying. The sooner we stop parceling out the different portions of our lives and bodies, and learn to weave them together, to see our experiences as interconnected, the • richer every aspect will be, as it effortlessly feeds the other. And the less conflict we will feel as we try to find the time and space to express and enjoy each different aspect of our creative, emotional, sensual and mothering selves.

Discovering eros

As women (and perhaps more so, as mothers) we are neither encouraged in our sexuality or to express our sensuality through our creativity. The more each of us can do this, the more we empower ourselves and give permission to other women to heal and express this hidden but vitally feminine, powerful part of themselves.

I first began to explore my body/sexuality in performance when I directed 'The Vagina Monologues'. It was as part of [Eve Ensler's] V-Day celebrations and I worked with a group of seven other women, none of whom were professional performers, all of whom were passionate about speaking 'the body'. I did this for two years and it has opened up a huge space in my performance work for exploring this type of territory. My next project will be exploring the experience of birth, from a bodily and consciousness point of view.

In my solo work I am drawn to movement-based practice as it allows me to connect with my body/skin on a level that I only ever feel when I am making love. It allows me to bring an intensity, of what I would call eros, that I am unable to perform in everyday situations.

Therefore my performance body and my sexual body become the same thing. There is something about having the freedom to reveal myself, to be witnessed, and be held (as opposed to the voyeuristic gaze) that is deeply erotic and necessary for me.

Freud said eros was the drive for life, love, creativity and sexuality. So I see sexuality and creativity as the same thing – or driven by the same energy.

As a parent, one's libido is often affected in a major way…exhausted bodies and minds don't always feel sexy. I find that I need to have sensual/sexual contact with my husband often.

The energy of the orgasm, what Wilhelm Reich called orgone, is so powerful and beautiful. It is expansive, healing and generative. I feel great after having an orgasm. My body is more relaxed and open. So sometimes when the balance between home/work, mother/artist is in a high state of tension – an orgasm whether with a partner, or by yourself is the perfect release.

Tracy Evans

Maternal libido

Often as mothers our libidos are low, even worse if we are struggling with depression or are on antidepressants or the Pill, and the last thing we feel like is "having" to have sex. But being awake to our sensuality, not just product-focused sex (i.e. worrying about having an orgasm efficiently) but our total embodied physical sensuality is something we can focus on every day. It doesn't require a partner, or any genital contact, but rather is awakening a sense of aliveness, feeling, pleasure through all of our senses. **Saida Desilets**, a woman devoted to women's sensual, and sexual education, puts it like this:

> *Our sensuality, our sexuality is a daily choice. We must tune ourselves to recognize it. Am I completely numb to myself? Am I perhaps even over-stimulating myself? Or do I have a deep, honest, delicious relationship with myself? And that's a daily question.*

The same is totally true for our creativity. It is a daily choice. Not one that requires guilt, or lots of end-products, but is a process that we inhabit and embody every day. It is a fundamental way of responding to life and expressing our aliveness.

But often we refuse this daily choice. And when we ignore sexual or creative expression consistently, our body finds other ways to make its needs heard and release its tension. Headaches, stomach problems, throat problems and depression are very common examples of creative and sexual stagnation.

When we begin to trust ourselves and our voices, our inner yearnings, once we allow ourselves full expression – of the voice, the images within us, the energy, the words – then we enter physical and emotional flow. We experience greater physical and emotional well-being. Our bodies become looser, more relaxed, and the flow can come through us even more powerfully, be it through orgasms, powerful pieces of writing, expressive dances, paintings or relationships which really communicate our essence deeply to the soul of another.

Reflections

Have you experienced your life force/creative energy/ sexual energy physically? What did it feel like? Can you express it in words or images?

Are you resistant to it? Where do these blockages come from? Are they a result of what people have said of you, lack of self-knowledge or experience, inherited family or cultural beliefs?

Pregnancy and birth

Women are the primary resource of the planet. They give birth, we come from them. They are mothers, they are visionaries, they are the future. If we can figure out how to make women feel safe and honor women, it would be parallel or equal to honoring life itself.
Eve Ensler

Pregnancy and birth are another of the embodied teachings of the womb, initiating us as women into the miraculous possibilities of our creative potential and personal power. I discussed the analogies between the creative and birth journeys in the earlier chapter on the creative process. I love what Christiane Northrup says about it in her book, *Mother Daughter Wisdom*:

I have come to see that every significant creation in our lives, whether it be a child, a work of art, a home, a relationship, or our life itself, requires an investment of life energy similar to that of a human pregnancy And each of our own creations like each of our children, is also shaped and influenced by our own consciousness.

Birth was regularly used as a metaphor by the women I spoke with to describe the process of publishing a book, launching an event, putting on a performance or creating a painting from their deep inner world, even by those who had never physically given birth themselves. Those who had often remarked on how the skills that they used to navigate the birth process, and the insights they had during pregnancy, informed their creativity as mothers. It seems that women instinctively know that the process of gestating new life, be it human or artistic, is one and the same.

I found birth to be the most surrendered, and yet powerful experiences of my life. I truly felt my own power in a way I never had before (or since) as I roared my babies out at home. Much of this I attribute to the transformational creative approach to birth which I followed, Pam England's *Birthing From Within*. So I am particularly honored that she agreed to contribute to this chapter.

What making birth art can do for you

When it came time to write my master's thesis, because I enjoy making art, I created a study to look at the drawings of pregnant women in their first and third trimesters. That's how I accidently discovered that making birth art as a process of prenatal preparation is a surprisingly powerful "teacher."

Through the process of making art and her reflections afterward, a woman often finds her Heart's Question and gains insights about herself, what she knows, believes, and needs to do next. What birth art teaches is rarely what the artist expects; what she discovers she might never have learned through ordinary means of prenatal preparation such as books or classes.

In the same way that a woman might be inclined to plan her labor experience so that it turns out the way she imagined it would or should, when it comes to making birth art she may also try to produce the image or idea she has in mind on paper. And yet, life, birth, and art are spontaneous and unpredictable; there are always surprises. When what is drawn or sculpted looks different from what was intended, the artist-mother may think she failed, or that it didn't turn out right. She may worry what other people will think of her and begin to censor a creative impulse.

We censor creative impulses in many ways: by not speaking up or by not including a symbol in our drawing because we don't like what it represents, or we don't know how to draw it. And yet, there is something we want to ask or say, or there is a symbol wants to be included in our drawing. The birth art process cultivates our capacity to be daring, to do what needs to be done next even if we don't know how to do it.

Birth art should be an authentic expression of what the artist is feeling or believing – in the moment. It does not have to be pretty; it is not to be confused with crafting, ribbons, and glitter.

Fortunately, it is not the "finished product" that matters most. We can take our cue from the Tibetan monks who make elaborate sand paintings, then quickly sweep up the sand. They know that the point of making the sand mandala is the meditation, not preservation of the mandala itself.

Especially for women who do not typically make art on their own, exploring the birth art process as part of birth preparation can bring unexpected insights. When she doesn't know "how" to draw, paint, or sculpt – or how to give birth – she discovers she learns as she goes.

In both the process of making a painting and laboring, a woman will find herself at a threshold where she doesn't quite know what to do next. The birth artist may want to quit before she goes too far and ruins the drawing, or because she doesn't know what to do next. In a similar way, women in labor often "quit" and defer to others when they come to an unexpected moment and don't know what to do next. Fear and curiosity feed the imagination; where imagining an unwished-for outcome can stop us in our tracks, making art leads us across inner thresholds, thereby teaching us to "keep going."

The birth art process allows us to experience coming up against the unknown and discovering what we tend to do next when we don't know what to do. Making art allows us to experiment with what we can do and to see what happens next. This kind of experimentation can only happen if we are not attached to the art "product." Instead, we become fully engaged in the process.

Birthing women, their attendants, and the dominant birthing place do not routinely utilize the power of art-making in the complex rituals surrounding childbirth.

Hanging pretty commercial art on the walls is not a substitute. It is the process of making the art and the power of primordial images that come from the soul of the artist that speak to the heart of the mother on her inner journey.

Pam England, author of *Birthing from Within*

I am all too aware that many women have not experienced birth as powerful. Instead it has been terrifying, agonizing, and they have felt victims of their bodies or the medical professionals charged with their care. So many women have, through choice, social conformity or necessity, been drugged or operated upon. Have you considered how this might either reflect similar patterns in your habitual creative process, or how the experience of birth may have impacted your feelings about your competence and sense of power in your own body?

Whatever your birth stories, positive or traumatic, your stories of infertility, pregnancy, miscarriage or abortion, they matter, deeply to your creative process. They have impacted your creative self and your mother self indelibly. They live on still in your body, most especially in your womb. And so I invite you to be courageous and explore them – by yourself, in communion with other women, with a healing practitioner – to find your truths, to release the moments in them that hold you still, to find the places where you felt your power, and where it was taken from you. To relive these moments, create them, recreate them, transform them.

This work, though it seems so self-centered at the beginning, ripples out far from us to transform other lives. But first we have to start in our own stories, our own bodies, and experiences.

Reflections

Have you written down your birth story(ies)? What insight did you get from them – about you as a person, your power, your creativity, your need for support, your relationships, your feelings about your body, your feelings about motherhood?

If you have suffered a pregnancy loss or traumatic birth – have you written and drawn your experience?

If you are pregnant, how can you relate creatively to your pregnancy? Make a belly cast, paint your bump with henna, paint a picture of yourself, journal your feelings, write a poem, make clothes for your child to be, or a patchwork, take beautiful photographs of yourself.

Dark days

Women's depressions and out-of-control emotions used to be connected to the womb in medical terminology. Many of the female patients seen by doctors in the nineteenth and early twentieth centuries were treated for *hysteria*, believed to be an imbalance in the womb. Modern science has shown that much of woman's depression is hormonal, and where are the main female hormones of estrogen and progesterone produced? The womb!

Depression in many guises is common for the Creative Rainbow Woman – from minor episodes connected to her cycle, to the shifting seasons (SAD), to more ingrained episodes related to deeper soul issues, traumas and life experiences.

One of the less-spoken-about forms of depression which many creative mothers experience is post-natal depression – it seems to go with the territory. I have experienced it to varying degrees after all three of my children's births, and during the whole of my middle pregnancy. I know first-hand just how challenging finding yourself again after the maelstrom of the early days of mothering can be when you feel on the edge of sanity. (To read more about my experiences of it, as well as the other "weather of motherhood", may I point you to my second book, *Moods of Motherhood*.) It is hard when we don't feel like a new mother "should": we don't glow, or feel full of love, or feel our instinct hitting in, we are exhausted and drained, or perhaps we do not feel the bond with our child that we were promised. We feel angry, sad, frustrated, alone, despairing, and scared. **Leonie Dawson** is one Creative Rainbow Mother who shared openly about her experience of this little-talked-about experience in her book:

> *My daughter is now 15 months old. I've slowly made my way out of the labyrinth of deep new mamahood and caring-for-a-baby. I only need one my-energy-is-running-low-so-I'm-going-to-choose-to-sit-on-the-couch-for-a-few-hours Day a week now, instead of five (or seven) I'm-so-exhausted-I-can-do-nothing-else-but Days. I've healed from birth and from post-natal depression. I'm starting to feel like myself again.*

Just because having a baby is "natural" for a woman's body, doesn't make it any easier. Some births are hard, they shake us to our roots, making us question everything we previously knew about ourselves. This is even more likely if the birth process has been traumatic as **Tracy** shares:

> *After having a child, my confidence was very low for about a year. This was not just about being confident to take new things on. My body still was physically hurting and felt vulnerable and fragile, as I'd had a Caesarean. This fragility echoed through all aspects of my life. During this time I wrote a lot: I was reading, drawing, dreaming and planning performances. It was a very solitary process as I looked after G... I'm proud of allowing myself to keep moving through the dark places and the joyous miracles of being a mother to an incredible little boy, and accepting that there needs to be both darkness and light and neither one is more important – it is all necessary!*

As Tracy, Leonie and I have experienced, whilst the days of depression seem interminable and unnavigable, they are the equivalent of a caterpillar going into a chrysalis. Though it may take months or even years, it seems that it is only through the total breakdown of our old selves, in the form of depression, that a new self can break through, the bright-colored Creative Rainbow Mother self, bigger, more vibrant, more compassionate and wiser than the woman we were before. This is a dark initiation of the rainbow soul. It is a hard, hard process. It breaks us open. So many times we think we will not even make it. But if we can use all our creative tools to help us through the dark times, surround ourselves with support, health care, nurturance and help with childcare we will find our way through to join our rainbow sisters on the other side.

Chapter 23

Individuation

And the day came when the risk to remain tight in a bud was more painful than the risk it took to blossom.
Anaïs Nin

I celebrate myself, I sing myself!
Walt Whitman

The main aim for healthy individuals, according to the father of psychoanalysis, Carl Jung, is individuation. The same is true for creativity. When we are guided by own intuition, rather than by external authorities, we begin to find ourselves, our true voice, our own style and a new life force emerges within us.

Individuating is one of the most time consuming and courageous acts we will ever undertake. It is an organic process which cannot be forced. It simply flows from within us, and as we gain mastery over our tools, we begin to find a mode of expression which feels natural to us, which allows us more often than not to enter the flow with authority and distinctiveness.

When we think of Degas we think of ballet dancers and pastels, when we think of Picasso we think of his cubist distorted faces in oils, when we think of our favorite writer we can hear their voice in our ear: it is unmistakable. At the beginning when we are still finding our own authentic voices it can feel frustrating: *Who am I? What is it that marks me out as unique? What do I have to say?* we wonder.

Finding your voice

The urge, starting out, is to copy. And that's not a bad thing. Most of us only find our own voices after we've sounded like a lot of other people. But the one thing that you have that nobody else has is you. *Your voice, your mind, your story, your vision. So write and draw and build and play and dance and live as only you can.*
Neil Gaiman, 2012 Commencement Address to the University of the Arts.

We each have our own unique voice. But when we start to create we first have to work through the layers that we have accumulated:

- How we have been taught to create.
- What is correct.
- What is acceptable.
- How everyone else creates.
- How our favorite artists create.

We have to slough off these layers to find our own unique voice, hiding beneath. This takes time and practice. The more you allow yourself to create freely, the more opportunity your own voice has to peep through the chinks of the armor of convention and acceptability.

I started out writing wanting to be the next big cookery writer – I had visions of myself as Nigella Lawson or Delia Smith! I wrote to them and asked their advice on how to be a food writer when I was in my late teens. Then in my late twenties I wrote articles which I submitted to food magazines, got a food column in a parenting magazine, and started a baking blog. I loved cooking, loved reading, food writing, loved writing, so being a food writer seemed a natural step. Except that's not where my creative passion ended up being. I soon discovered that food writing bored me silly, it required a precision that did not come naturally or pleasurably to me. And in the end, when I wrote my first book, both the content and the style made me dizzy with delight, but were completely unexpected. My first book, despite seven earlier attempts at everything from poetry to a spice cookery book, was on the menstrual cycle. I did not see that coming! But by letting myself write freely what was in my heart and mind, in refusing to box myself in anymore and try to define what my interests or the focus of my creativity should be, my authentic creative voice suddenly emerged.

This is why it is so important not to censor ourselves, because our creative soul is often different to what we have seen before and what we have been taught. Like a hunter we must be stealthy, we must keep our ears and eyes open. If we catch sight of our voice we must be calm. Like spotting a rare bird on the fence, we must not frighten her. She startles easily and will fly off as quickly as she emerged. In fact it is often only in hindsight that we recognize her traces in our earlier work, her footprints in the snow. We know her because she makes us cry or laugh at our own work, she sends shivers down our spines and hits us round the face with a powerful truth. And she startles others too – people will respond to our work when it contains our deep voice. So when we identify her, we must track back and try to recall, what was it that brought her out, who is she talking to, what does she like to talk about?

Another of my intentions was to be an academic, and write intellectual books about living philosophy. But again I found my voice was dry and dull. And I had no desire to live in an ivory tower, writing endless papers for academic journals, trapped in a narrow academic discipline. It was only when I stated to write books about woman-craft, about the inner life of creativity and womanhood, about sexuality and sensuousness that my voice began to emerge. And oh, how I wished I could be writing books that you could talk to men at dinner parties about. But no, my voice is my voice, and this is what she needs to speak of. The following poem is taken from one of my journals, I wrote it when I was mama to just one, and it was one of the first times my woman voice emerged.

Womb voice, Womyn's voice
Deep from my uterus pushing out, out...
I call on my power
I summon my depths
This urging, pushing, moaning, writhing, guttural, visceral power
Is being urged to life,
Sung out, danced out, birthed out.
It is of me, but is it mine?
It has its own form, its own face.
Its own very being.
It is here within,
Yet I must search to find it,
Hunt like a tigress: ears pricked, body primed.
This is my voice,
Buried under the oozing depths
The layers of accumulated detritus.
Not fossilized, not quite, but living in a cave far from light.
Buried under niceness, cleverness, tidiness.
Sitting quietly under a pile of carefully folded judgment.
Sitting at the center of my onion,
Green shoot right through the heart.
New life, waiting, patiently to be discovered,
Not by agents or readers – but by me.
I see her – I think,
I feel her – I know.
This is my voice.
But to me she is silent...
I read her in the words of others,
Hear her emerging from mouths
Which are not mine.

Sometimes I catch her by surprise,
Revealed in something I have penned.
I stop and blink.
Unaware that she had been there during the writing.
Unaware that she had silently taken the pen,
And shown herself in silver snail traces on tree pulp.
This page was her sacred space, her hallowed ground.
For a while she and I were one.
But once again she returns to her cave,
White string haired crone
Wrapped round with a shawl of stars,
Hunched over the embers of my heart
Gently keening and crooning to herself
Strange tongues and mysteries.

Feminine archaeology

Art is important for it commemorates the seasons of the soul. Art is not just for oneself, not just a marker of one's own understanding. It is also a map for those who follow after us.
Clarissa Pinkola Estes

This process of finding our creative voices as women is one of soul archaeology. For centuries we have been denied our words, • our images, our stories, our fields of expertise. We have been told how to write, how to dress, how to speak, in order to please others, not to honor ourselves.

So be gentle with yourself and understand that in unearthing your own creativity you are entering an archaeological apprenticeship, digging down, down into self-expression which generations of women have been denied. It is not just your voice you are finding, but those of your forebears that have been lost or silenced. With each creation, with each act of expression you are reclaiming your voice, your soul, your birthright.

Voice

We hold our stories in our bodies. Stories and memories that have been hushed live in our flesh and bones, pull cords on our heart and spasm our backs out. They contract our wombs, trigger our hips sway and remind us when to cum and when to walk away. Untold, they expire like anything else waiting for movement, dissipation, alchemization. Untold, we are left with stagnancy and crafted illusions about our experiences that we tend to believe and pass on.

The Vagus nerve, which literally means, "wandering" does just that, it sends and receives information from our centers, wandering our chakra system, collecting wants, needs, emotions at Cosmic Milliseconds. The nerve is born from the rootlets of our medulla, zipping news along like an inner Internet, our high-speed Information Highway. It wants to deliver to us, so we can process and communicate, even if we just show up as facial expression, as it did to our tribes before there was even language. It's the information we share to keep ourselves heard and safe, this is how it's worked for millions of years.

*Voice wants to connect with this information nerve, but it works slow, slower than the nerve, it's like dial-up or rotary dial, that's why we often **feel** before we can attempt to express. Language for emotional experience takes its good old hot and sticky island-time to develop, this is why it's sexy and alluring when it gets heard, when it sounds itself like a temple bell. If fully marinated in adventure and expressed with intention, it's a hot market for healing and self-love.*

Sometimes the slowness of my voice's reception can make it feel lost in the depth of the dark forest; Shadow seems to have swallowed it whole. My contact with the vagal nerve can get interrupted and the messages wander my body waiting for me to grab on, but accessing seems impossible. My voice isn't ready to hear or the story isn't ready to unfold.

I am learning to breathe through these times. It's sometimes called writer's block, or being "stuck" but for me it's just the inhale. Fully inhaled all the way up from my root to my crown. The eventual exhale is more sensual, filled with wild truth {and the good stuff our mothers never really want us to talk about}.

I remember to breathe and take notes by pen or heart, even finger-writing in the air or imprinting the sea with my gaze and asking the vast water to help hold all this for me until I'm ready. Eventually, and sometimes it takes a god-awful long time, I get that moment of spasm, Voice is shaking my flesh, river rushing me, hand in hand with muse naked at my door.

I am on the edge of the release, and it's time to take the layers off, light the flame and blow the smoke. It's alchemy time: time to work it, making Imperfect art, allowing Voice to take over. I become its submissive possession. Voice is ripe and ready to pour forth some nectar and flame.

I see the voice as its own part of the body, a central system long ignored that not only speaks, but has the challenging job to listen. Voice is alive, a living entity of Soul's walk.

When my voice is given exercise and permission to be the sorceress for the stories of my body, it takes on the role of Expresstrix of Experience, Motherline from Material to Spiritual, it becomes a crystal-lined time machine for generations of past and future to release.

When intention is made, our voices can heal our bodies. The place in my throat that's a numb knot stuckness, because if I talk about what I need or crave, I'm at risk of rejection and abandonment, so instead I just stick with the silent shame. Well, I say fuck off to shame. I send that message with the nerve right to the center of my throat. That's where my story starts.

There is no way but your way, no rights or wrongs. There is no teaching, it's what we know and have always known. We were Sound before we were flesh. We were perfect before we decided to listen when they said we weren't.

Our bodies are worth letting Voice take its chance. If even just for that, forgetting about who hears or reads it, but for the sake of our body freedom.

Marybeth Bonfiglio

Discovering your own personal symbology

Often as mothers our lives are so full with remembering our children's and partner's and parents' and even friends' preferences, that we forget about our own. What is it that lights you up on the inside? What is it that makes you shine, that fills you with joy? What makes your spine tingle? These are the clues which will lead you towards your voice, your language, your own unique imagery: in short they will take you to your soul's work, if you follow them.

I discovered my own personal symbology as I started painting again. Images that had previously meant a lot to me, that I was drawn to in my life: peacocks, pregnant bellies, hummingbirds, spirals, rainbows, labyrinths would keep emerging on the canvases. It was only later that their deeper, subconscious meaning unfolded for me. At the time I was simply painting what emerged from the patterns of colors on the canvas, like making shapes from the clouds in the sky. The sense of the emergent, of trusting intuition, of literally going with the flow, of tapping into the inner world, are feminine skills. And if we are to get to the richest seams of our creativity we must allow ourselves to cut ties with what we "should" be doing, the forms we should be using and find our own inner vocabulary and syntax, our own personal feminine language and style.

Creative activity

What images/colors/symbols/music/paintings/poems really speak to you? Surround yourself with them, dive deep into them again and again – journal about them, sketch them, perform them, make an altar of them, hang them on your wall. Explore them inside and out, inhabit them, embody the medicine they offer you.

In your journal make a list of everything that lights your fire, inspires you, fills your heart, draws you in, that you collect, feel attracted to, that is a recurring theme in your life...what flowers, animals, symbols, myths, characters, artists, places in the world, natural forms, elements do you resonate with?

What stories or associations do you have with each? Follow the vein of a couple of these through free association. Write the word down and then just keep writing, all the words and ideas that you associate with it, don't worry about making sentences, punctuation, or even sense, just let the ideas flow out onto the paper.

Take yourself back on a sensory memory journey – think back to your happiest, most indelible experiences as a young child, and then moving forward through the years – what hobbies engrossed you, what colors sucked you in, what images have called to you through the years, which stories really resonated?

Make a collage filled with images of all these things.

Chapter 24

Women Creating Together

We are meant to midwife dreams for one another. We cannot labor in place of one another, but we can support the labor that each must undertake to birth her art and foster it to maturity. It is for this reason that the Sacred Circle must exist in any place of creation. It is this protective ring, this soul boundary, that enlivens us at our highest level.

Julia Cameron, *The Artist's Way*

A safe circle holds the dream of what a woman could be in confidence and nourishes the possibility.

Jean Shinoda Bolen, *The Millionth Circle*

Have you felt the power of creating together? Though many creative women are lone wolves, most benefit from some sort of shared creativity with other women on an occasional basis to add new energy and ideas to their practice and gain inspiration and support from others. For most of the women I spoke to, creating together with other women is an integral part of their practice and one which they would not be without.

The possibilities for women creating together are limitless:

- Book clubs, writers' circles, sewing circles, choirs, music groups, drumming circles, painting groups...
- Sacred women's circles, red tents, moon lodges, prayer groups.
- Creative collaborations.
- Creative classes.
- Taking part in or organizing creative events.
- Craft workshops in friend's houses.
- Full-blown creative retreats.

Some of my most favorite creative work has been collaborative – directing and acting in plays, creating an arts festival, singing in choirs. There is a power in the energy of many people creating together towards one aim, which makes it so much more powerful than anything we could do alone.

This is not exclusive to women – but what we gain from a single-gender group is quite different to that from a mixed-gender group. Some events can be intentionally women-only, and others tend only to attract women.

I have been a member of a women's group for five years now. It supports me in so many ways, I would not be without it. Nor would any of the women in it. I have also belonged to many different women's circles online – some very specialized for painters or bloggers, and others more general, but all have hugely supported my creativity and personal growth. For me, over the past few years, being in women-only creative environments has meant I have felt safer to get down into the depths of my own process and creative work.

A women's creativity group is like a container and mirror for your creative self, a womb where you might nurture your seedling ideas and bring newborn creative children to share. It's where you can feel safe, let your hair down, have fun and learn new skills from peers. **Wendy Cook** runs Mighty Girl workshops in person and online for mothers and daughters, and it's a process which she understands so well:

> I believe that it is vital for girls and women of all ages to have opportunities to gather and explore and nurture their creative gifts, to see and be seen. Women's circles are ancient in origin and are powerful and transformative because of the intention and commitment to wholeness. We all have unique and beautiful gifts, stories and wisdom to share that inspire and heal. We need these connections in order to discover who we are and who we can become.

Many women remark that it feels really good and natural to work in this way alongside each other and find it very satisfying and nurturing. Perhaps the tradition harks back to historical times of women sharing domestic tasks together such as sewing a trousseau, weaving cloth, preparing a feast, gathering food and preserving the harvest.

One such project which brings together women through creativity is the Pebbles Project which I first heard about on BBC Radio 4's *Woman's Hour* radio program. Run by the Firstsite gallery, and facilitated by Ange Leinster, the project centered on making clay creations with army wives in Colchester, UK. They spoke movingly of how therapeutic the process was. Not only in bringing them together and getting them out of the isolation of their homes and enforced single parenting, but also allowing them to open up about their shared situation and express feelings of isolation, fear and loneliness which they otherwise had to bottle up. Says one participant:

Preparing the clay is a physical way of debunking everything, and leaving everything at the door, you can almost feel it as "Phew, I can leave it all behind, this is OK, this is what I do here."

This permission to feel, to be, rather than constant doing and caring for others is powerful. Often women feel guilty doing creative things alone, or get stuck, or don't know where to start. The distraction and company of others is what many women need to open the door of creativity. Taking part in communal creativity often also gets you out of your own domestic space and into another place devoted to creativity – be it another woman's home, the village hall or wherever. So suddenly the worries about making a mess or keeping the children out of your stuff also disappear. For **Joanna** it is these practical aspects of creating in a group which appeal to her:

I find creating with a group of women I know less intimidating. So when I want to try a new skill or technique, money is tight and I am nervous about investing my time and money in a class, it is a great way to dip my toe in the water.

Now that my children are out of babyhood, creating with other women is something I hope to get back to. I used to do a lot of it. Two of the reasons I chose to were that whether other women were visiting me or I was at someone else's house the expectation would be that the group would stay for as long as the painting/crafting lasted. And secondly, that there was no expectation of serving food that involved a lot of preparation. These were important things to me because I really like my time on my own too and it made the experience just that, an experience – and a wonderful one at that – but not an imposition.

Being with a community of women seems to give women the permission and support they need to be creative. It can also fill the silence which many can find disconcerting when they start creating. There is someone to chat to, so rather than listen to the voices in your head, you have the voices of others, as well as their input and feedback when you get stuck. As another mother in the Pebbles Project says: "It gives you a release, a switch off, a sense of calm". There is something deeply soul-nourishing about creating in community. But it isn't just "worthy", it can also just be great fun and a welcome social activity, as **Amber** shares:

Crafternoons have been a way to connect with my crafty womenfolk once a month that is both nurturing for the spirit as well as for the creative mama inside all of us. This has been a lovely way for all of us to engage with minimal pressure on the host (each host provides food and craft once, and then attend the other five events within six month period to enjoy freely). The host is tasked with coming up with a simple cute idea that can be completed within a two and a half hour period so that there are no UFOs (unfinished objects) flying around to add stress!

I've loved this creative gathering as it is so different from creating and hosting a paid creative event that I do so much of in my business (which I also LOVE dearly of course but comes with other responsibilities). Creating with other women is inspiring, and life affirming. We all succeed with the power that is generated in the room.

For many women learning to create in a group gives them support beyond just their creativity, they make lifelong friends with shared interests who are there for them through good times and bad. Creating with women gives us a ticket out of our limited and often desperately lonely domestic sphere, and into a world of others who care. Along with exchanging stitches, we exchange our life stories, our worries, our needs – and find listening ears and words of advice. **Grainne**, an organizer of the Big Lunch project, which brings communities together through eating together, shares her experience of this:

I held a felt-making workshop and didn't know what to expect! But I found being in a room full of women of all ages trying something new together was a great way to unwind and make local connections.

This sense of connection, a shared sense of being, was one which came up again and again in the words of the women I spoke to. **Tracy** speaks about her experience on discovering the joy of working with other women on in a project to explore the relationship between mother and home in rural Wales:

Witnessing their strength and beauty, their fears and wisdom, is a huge gift for me. I learn so much about myself from our encounters. Although we are all very different, in different situations, I'm amazed at how many similar threads there are that connect us.

What we can accomplish increases exponentially when we find the right community to support our creativity and collaborate with, as **Lorian**, a mother of five shares:

I've spent the last 24 years collaborating with groups of creative women while we home-school our children together. My sisters in this venture have been the most supportive, loving group I have ever known and I think that when mamas are working together creatively there is almost nothing they can't accomplish!

Finding a group that fits

- The best way is by word of mouth. Ask friends who know you well for their recommendations.
- If you are joining a group or class after seeing a poster or advertisement, make contact with the leader to get a sense of it and whether they, and the group, will make a good fit for you.
- If it's a specialized group then be aware of that. There's no point in turning up and then trying to turn it into what you initially wanted. So if it's a group on Egyptian bellydance and you want to learn tribal – you are not going to change it into that by wishful thinking or complaining – I know from bitter experience!
- Listen to your intuition as you research the group and when you attend gatherings. But also allow for the fact that intuition can often be overladen by the voices of fear.
- If you can't find a group that works for you – then start one yourself!
- It is crucial that you feel safe and supported in your group, that each participant gets a fair amount of attention, no one is overly dominant or competitive and that feedback is given in a constructive and caring manner.

Joining a group of women requires an additional level of vulnerability to that of the normal creative journey. Entering a group situation can feel scary, even threatening for many women. It can reawaken all of our fear voices: am I good enough, will they like me, can I do it, will they laugh at me? Do not underestimate this. If you have had negative experiences of art or dance classes in school, or of being on the outside of a clique it can feel especially stressful.

Sometimes we can be so stuck that we need the help of others to help us to find a creative community. Whether it is a friend dragging you out the door to come to choir with her, or, in the case of **Francesca**, your family giving you the gift of a creative retreat to nourish yourself, take the chance of creating with other women:

As someone who creates at home alone most of the time and doesn't show my work to many people, attending a women's art retreat was really interesting. Within the safety of the group I was able to connect and express from my heart, and leave my thinking behind. I came away feeling a deep connection with some of these 60 women, knowing that even if we never saw each other again we had created a very special bond.

Reflections

What are you yearning for? What is it that communal creativity can offer you?

What kind of creative groups are they in your local area that you know of? How can you find out about more? Which friends could you ask? Which local publications run ads? Where are there good bulletin boards?

Which would you like to join?

Do you prefer to have a facilitator or have a group of equals?

Do you prefer mixed groups or women only?

What are your concerns? How might you address them?

What has been your experience of group creativity before?

How do you feel about starting your own group?

Chapter 25

Nurturing a Family Culture of Creativity

At the heart of every mindful and loving family lie the seeds of endless creativity. With patience, support, and just a bit of guidance, that creativity can flourish and grow in beautiful ways.
Amanda Blake Soule, *The Creative Family*

Creating together

Fingerprints on your photographs; stitches unraveled and wool knotted; words deleted; pages scattered, scribbled on, cut up; guitar strings untuned; equipment stolen away – these are the dangers of living and creating around children.

Previously in this book children have taken the role of obstructions to creativity, but it would be tragic if this is the only way we perceived them. In order not to resent our children for keeping us away from our creative work, we need to bring our creativity into our lives together, to allow it to inform our family's life and fill our homes with beauty and togetherness.

One of the best bits of having children around is having the "excuse" and the materials on hand to be creative almost all the time! And what is more, you have companions who do not know the rules, who have imagination and energy by the bucket load. You have the chance for a second bite of the cherry of childhood. Being parents gives us so many wonderful opportunities every day to connect with our own creativity again and explore a huge variety of art forms which in the adult world we are cut off from because we are not "good enough" to indulge in, but which make the human spirit soar: *singing, dancing, storytelling, improvisation, clowning, painting, sculpting, collage, playing percussion, dressing up, puppet shows, model making…*the list is endless!

There is so much joy to be had, as **Elizabeth** expresses so beautifully:

Allowing our children to discover their own creative selves, their own process, to teach them skills, provide them with materials, inspiration, a space for their own creativity is one of the greatest gifts we can give them. Because the bottom line is, when we honor their creativity we are saying: "You are an interesting human being with valid ideas and expressions which the world wants to share and enjoy, I truly appreciate this expression of who you are."

And then they learn to appreciate this in themselves to. They learn to connect with and trust that small inner voice, the pictures in their head, their intuition. They learn to be able to express their inner world through the movement of their bodies, their hands, their words. And in learning to express this they seek to hone their skills, learn more about their world, to connect, to dive deeper into life.

Our role as parents cultivating creativity, as I see it, is four-fold: firstly to provide a rich environment – not necessarily of expensive paints and costumes, but basic materials. Secondly, to step back and see how they intuitively choose to use them and join them in this. Thirdly, to share ways that we know to use these materials, and share our skills with them. And fourthly to model our own creative process to them – both by letting them see "behind the scenes" in our creative lives, to share how our creative process works, and allow them to see us fully absorbed in it.

What do children gain from creativity?

- Fun, fun and more fun.
- Strengthening their imagination.
- Development of hand-eye co-ordination.
- Honoring of their ideas, voice and self-expression.

- Important practical life-skills: sewing, cooking, writing, drawing...
- Creative thinking which builds brain plasticity.
- Aesthetic appreciation.
- Developing their ability to reflect on their work.
- Collaborative skills.
- Special time with you.
- Lifetime memories.
- Learning to listen to their intuitive voice.
- The chance to make a mess.
- An appreciation of creative work and time that goes into making things.
- A sense of generosity as they learn to gift their work.
- A sense of entrepreneurship as they learn that they can sell it or their skills.
- A sense of mastery.
- Joy.

Creating together is not just about today's painting or model, but about setting the tone and feeling for your child's creative ability in their own soul, perhaps for the rest of their lives. When we can see it as a privilege to engage creatively with our children, our time together becomes richer and more rewarding for us and them.

Nurturing a culture of creativity allows your child to regularly experience autotelic experiences (those which enable a flow state). Csikszentmihaly's research into flow states found that:

> Early childhood influences are also very likely factors in determining whether a person will or will not easily experience flow.

So in creating a culture of creativity, not only are you passing on valuable skills, confidence in their own creative ideas and abilities, but you are helping to wire their brains to more easily experience optimal experiences for the rest of their lives.

A culture of creativity honors and requires:

- Space for silence to bloom: for concentrated work, and contemplation.
- Space for sharing our voices, visions, experiences and dreams.
- Appreciation and enjoyment of the process, not judgment of works in progress.
- Courage and respect for trying new things. Being allowed to like them...or not.
- A need for responsibility.
- A time for mess!
- A respect of basic safety guidelines and rules.
- Prioritizing fun.
- Support for developing abilities.
- The understanding that creativity has an intrinsic value, beyond its extrinsic practical worth.
- Self-reliance.
- Dreams, possibility and the fully-fledged imagination.
- Celebration – of big festivals and small mysteries, and knowing how to mourn the losses and failures too.

When we choose to nurture a culture of creativity, we commit to giving our children the support and appreciation necessary for the breathtaking unfolding of their unbounded intellectual, aesthetic, collaborative and imaginative capacities. We show them that we are responsible for creating our own lives and that we can have a direct impact on every area of them. Our creativity can be used to create our living spaces, the food we eat, the clothes we wear, the gifts we give to each other. But most of all, that life is good, and that joy, celebration and beauty are to be nurtured and treasured – that life is not all work, hardship, suffering, nor should it be dominated by practicality and money-making. In nurturing creativity we give our children the practical and emotional skills to be productive, engaged authors of their own destinies.

Messages

We spoke earlier about the voice of the critic, and how it is often an internalized voice of someone close to us at a critical time of our development. So I want to take a moment, before we embark on how to practically create together as a family, to clear the space, emotionally, and bring us to awareness of the environment in which our children are creating.

What messages do you communicate to your children, consciously and unconsciously when you create together? I have put together a few of the messages that I and the other creative mothers have found ourselves saying:

- Hurry up!
- Don't make too much mess!
- That doesn't look like a...
- That's a really good...
- Stay inside the lines!
- Strawberries aren't blue...
- Don't be stupid!
- Sit still...shut up!
- Be careful!
- Not like that!
- Do it this way...
- Oh, for goodness sake!
- Do it like John/ Mary.
- Why don't I just do it for you?
- Oh well, we can't all be artists!
- I was always useless at singing too!

It's not that we intend to damage our children's self-esteem, nothing could be further from the truth. But in the stress of managing the mess of children creating in the midst of an already busy day, perhaps fending off fights, dealing with disappointments and frustrations and sibling rivalry and destruction, these messages often slip out. And often we hear ourselves saying them and recognize the voice of another who communicated these things to us many years ago. Or it is what we say to ourselves in our own heads. This is why the work we did earlier on the critic, and creative unblocking is so important. Because once these voices are not lodged in our subconscious, they are unlikely to be vocalized towards our children.

Even though we might do our best to be kind and understanding to our children, we tend to chastise ourselves: *Oh what an idiot I am!* forgetting that little ears are listening, eyes are watching. Treating our children with compassion and acceptance starts with ourselves.

What a mess!

What are the most off-putting elements of creating with children for most of the mothers I spoke to? **Heather** speaks for so many:

Time, space and energy and a compulsive desire for tidiness!! When doing something with the kids it's definitely the tidiness issue, when I put that aside there is no negativity.

The biggest misery for us mamas in getting creative with our kids is the blasted mess afterwards. We spend our days constantly trying to keep our houses up to scratch, and the thought of inviting more mess in can be soul-destroying. Being the adult requires a level of boring responsibility for cleaning up glitter showers and playdough stepped into the rug, wiping paint off every surface and making sure we don't damage the carpet. **Mary** is another mama who struggles with this:

I will be honest the mess sometimes holds me back. For example if

Sadbh wants to paint – taking all the stuff out, getting the paint all over the place having to clean up after, sometimes that really puts me off. Or baking – the same – she loves playing with the flour and all of a sudden the place is in bits. It is hard enough to keep the place going without doing extra bits that will add to the mess.

I find myself tending towards activities like weaving, sewing and drawing, or painting outside in summer which have a limited mess factor. I only get the poster paints or full-on craft activities out when I've had a full night's sleep, they're in good form or the cleaner is on her way!

Paula has a great solution to this. As a home-schooling mama of four lively boys, she has plenty of experience:

I personally think that art attacks out in nature, not in the home are the way to go with young children. Playing in the woods or on the beach, making something beautiful out of natural things that you leave in situ.

I find it really stressful initiating activities with glue and paint and bits of paper everywhere because I am attached to the outcome and get annoyed when they make other stuff than I have in mind. With art in nature it doesn't matter if you walk away and you've lost nothing!

Top tips for less-stressful family creating:

Setting up space and time, and learning to hold the space in a calm way are the most important three factors for successfully creating with kids.

- Keep your expectations simple.
- Do not embark on ambitious creative projects when pre-menstrual, severely sleep-deprived, you are expecting visitors or are working against the clock.
- Make sure everyone is fed and rested before you start.

- Have a selection of long-sleeved, waterproof painting smocks and cooking aprons – one for each family member. Be insistent that nothing starts till everyone is kitted out.
- Insist on old clothes for messy work.
- Have stools or chairs for everyone before you start.
- Clear off your work surface – move things that can get knocked over or messed up.
- Make sure your work surface is covered with a plastic table cloth, and/or newspaper.
- Get all the materials together, away from the workspace, before you start. Only give them access to the materials when they are calm and centered and you are all clear on what you are doing.
- Once you have started stay in the workspace. Have a cloth or paper towels to hand.
- Give appropriate tasks to keep little hands busy doing something you want rather than making mess!
- Have clear ground rules: tell them what's hot, what's sharp, what comes out fast, what is a grown-up job.
- Be clear that each person is only allowed to work on their own thing, unless they have been given permission by its creator.
- Model and discuss appropriate ways to give feedback on other people's work.
- Celebrate what's going well.
- Share the clean-up responsibilities with your children so that they know that this is part of the creative adventure. Children love water play, so factor this into your process. You might get them to wash up the paint brushes in the sink, a washing-up bowl outside or in the bath! Get them to wash up the safe items after cooking together whilst you stack the dishwasher and wipe the surfaces.
- If it's not fun, stop! You can try again another day!

What are we going to do?

There is often the onus on you as mama to come up with an idea or project to engage little minds and hands and fill a few hours of a rainy day, when they're feeling bored or can't come to an agreement on what they'd like to do.

We have a veritable library of craft and cookery books that we use for inspiration in this situation, and also to teach us specific skills and techniques. My kids know if they're bored they can ask to take down a couple of books, flick and dream until they find something they want to do, and then we discuss the practicalities: timing, energy levels, equipment and ingredients and negotiate if and when it is going to be feasible in the next few days. Maybe we can do it there and then, maybe tomorrow after we have been shopping, or maybe not at all! This way we have made ghost meringues, coconut mice, a red velvet cake, our own advent calendar, flying angels, paper windmills, egg-carton spring wreaths and felted animals.

Let creativity be a time when you share the lead, and as much as you can, ask them what they want to do and allow yourself to follow their cues. Children are astounding in their unfettered creativity, which may well feed yours. If you are wanting some inspiration I offer plenty of simple ideas later on in the chapter!

Setting creativity free

One of the main reasons I decided to home-school my kids is because for me, public school was torture to my creative mind. I had to "imprison" it to survive there. Creativity was looked upon as a second-class citizen, so to speak. I felt constantly repressed and lived only for art class. It took a while to heal after graduation until I could feel like my creativity could flow again.
Lorian Rea

There is a danger in the product-based way that children's arts and crafts are presented in books, blogs and TV programs. The children are shown a wonderful finished product, one which was made with care and lots of time by professional adult artists for presentation purposes. They are then given the exact steps, and some, like the seemingly innocuous "draw a face", with major oversights to children's levels of ability and the time it takes to actually do the process edited out. So when the time comes to make the object, the child quickly becomes bored because its taking too long, frustrated that their skills aren't appropriate, dispirited because the presenter made it look easy, and disappointed that theirs doesn't look as good as it "should". This is product-based creativity.

I much prefer skill-based or free creativity. Skill-based creativity is the learning of one skill set, like weaving or cross stitch, where first just the mastery of the technique is challenging enough, and then when confidence is built through repetition, creativity and imagination can be introduced, in terms of changing colors, creating patterns...with the child in the driving seat.

With free creativity, your child might say "I want to make a fire engine". And you say, "OK how can we do that?" And together you think about the shape of the vehicle, its color, how it moves...and you decide you could paint one, or use a milk carton and some lids, or an enormous cardboard box. You discuss what they want it for, what you have and what would work. They might not have a glossy perfect fire engine at the end of it, but they will have what they want, they have applied themselves to creating it and problem solving. At the end they might decide that they want to spend the rest of the day cutting and sticking and painting on tiny details on a two-inch clay model...or they might just want to sit in an unadulterated big cardboard box and role-play firefighter games with the family.

The building blocks of creativity

The remainder of the chapter is full of creative ideas to inspire lots of free creativity in your family, with minimal materials and mess. I have broken the activities down into groupings which I think of as the basic building blocks or skills required for a rich creative spirit: active imagination, play, mark-making, storytelling, finding form, rhythm, finding our centers and celebration.

Active Imagination

Active imagination is one of the bedrocks of creativity. Even if you do not enjoy or have the time or resources to do many creative activities with your children, this is one thing you can do wherever you are: on car journeys, lying on your backs on the lawn, waiting for doctor... Active imagination will feed every aspect of their lives, helping them to be able to reflect, imagine and make enhanced neural connections. This is something that you can do together at first, but which, once they understand, they will be able to do themselves. Activities might include:

- Looking for shapes in the clouds, the stars, tree foliage and trunks, in shadows, patterns in peeling paint or wood-grain.
- Using marbling inks and then drawing over the swirled patterns when they are dry, making images out of what is there.
- Making up crazy new animals with various different heads, bodies and legs – either as part of a story, or by drawing together.
- Combining words together to make completely new words with your own meanings.
- Making up your own stories collaboratively.
- The what if...? game. Take it in turns to suggest what ifs, and then imagine what it would be like: what if we lived on the moon/ had two heads/ were ruler of the world for a day...?
- Doing guided meditations or visualizations.

Play

> *It is in playing and only in playing that the individual child or adult is able to be creative and to use the whole personality, and it is only in being creative that the individual discovers the self.*

Donald Winnicott

It seems too obvious to even list. But too important to leave out. Play – free play, creative play, messy play, tactile play, imaginative play is key to creativity and optimal child development. In play we try on roles, can inhabit imaginary places, we have freedom from the rules of reality. All children need to play. As do adults.

Mark-making

The desire to make marks and express ourselves through images is innate in humans: give a baby a pen and chances are they will be fascinated that they can make color appear on paper through their action of banging or scribbling. Cave paintings attest to the fact that adults and children have adorned surfaces to tell stories, share information and have fun since the dawn of human history.

I love drawing with my children. It is one of the ways that I can really be on the same level as them. We are all creating together, seeing where the colors and our imaginations take us. I make sure that whenever I can I sit and draw with them. Sometimes I color a picture with them, sometimes alongside them, using the same materials but making my own work. Sometimes I help them when they ask.

My favorite times are when my children decide we need to make a family picture. We get a huge roll of paper or stick lots of small sheets together. They set the theme and create it together: we have drawn huge summer and autumn friezes this way, a six-foot-high rocket, a sheet of footprints and labyrinths and mandalas galore. There is no plan, they evolve as they go along and we have ideas, a narrative builds as we draw. It is something I remember doing with my father and loving. Other favorite mark-making ideas include:

- Put a pile of white paper and pencils or crayons on the table and draw alongside each other.
- If you're intimidated by drawing, get yourself a coloring book or find coloring sheets online which are free to download and print off – there are gorgeous ones with Celtic designs, mandalas, cityscapes, fairies, whatever you are into, designed for adults which children love to do too.
- Or if you want an alternative type of coloring book, how about *The Anti Coloring Book* or *The Doodle Book* which give you fascinating starting points for pictures.
- Try using chalks on a pavement outside or on slates.
- Have a pavement art competition.
- How about drawing in the mud? Get some sticks and make some outside art.
- Or the sand – we love using our local beach as our canvas – drawing labyrinths, names, mandalas and faces.
- Talking of canvas, my children's favorite treat is to come on a one-on-one painting session with me to my studio. They get a small canvas to paint on, and use my professional acrylics – they positively glow at this opportunity, and are very proud to hang their very own real painting on their bedroom wall.

Finding form

Don't limit your creativity to just two-dimensions! Children love to work in three-dimensions, and it's really good for building little brains!

- Vary your medium – try playdough, Plasticine, FIMO, clay, sand, plaster of Paris, mud, moonsand… to make three-dimensional forms. Relish how it feels on your fingers, see what marks you can make with various implements, what shapes can be made, how can you connect them?

- Build structures together – dens indoors and out, junk models, Lego, Meccano, straws...let them learn the basics of engineering right at home!
- Stitching, sewing, weaving, crochet, crafting with fabric are a great immersion in color and texture, as well as refining hand-eye co-ordination.
- And don't forget edible creations – modeling figures in marzipan or sugar paste, decorations on cupcakes, gingerbread men and houses...yum!

Storytelling

Stories set the inner life in motion.
Clarissa Pinkola Estes

We humans are by nature storytellers – and listeners! One of the simplest (and tidiest!) ways into getting creative with your child is through the medium of story.

- Light a candle or a fire and tell each other stories.
- Read your favorite storybook aloud, and do all the voices.
- Act it out as a play in costume, through dance or mime, or with puppets.
- Make up a different ending for your favorite story. Or another chapter...
- Tell a story of your own childhood or your parents' childhood. Children love to learn more about the people they love!
- Show photographs and tell the stories connected to them.
- Make up a story together, each person contributes a sentence, then you add a joining word "so...", "and then...", "suddenly...", "however..." before the next person

adds to the narrative.

- Use a torch and use your hands to make shadows as you improvise a story around them together.
- Write and illustrate a book together about your family, a holiday, a tradition or a story you have created together.
- Have journal time each day. Younger children can have more image-based scrapbooks, leading to more language-based entries as they get older.

Rhythm

Rhythm and harmony are woven through our bodies and world – humans of all sizes love to make music, dance, jiggle and jive. Most rhythmic activities are great to raise the energy (and noise level) and wear you out!

- Turn up the music and dance together.
- Improvise new words to a favorite tune.
- Play "Simon Says" using different animals and emotions.
- Sing your favorite songs together.
- Learn a song with different parts and sing it in a round.
- Play clapping games.
- Play percussion together using homemade household instruments.
- Play Follow the Leader with different rhythms.
- Play together on the piano or other instruments.
- Go to a concert or live performance together.

Finding our centers

Sometimes creativity is exuberant, wild, messy, outrageous and fun. Other times it can be contemplative, reflective and calming. These are great activities to help bring the energy down and inwards, good for rainy days, when someone is ill or tired and complaining of boredom. These are great activities for building concentration:

- Color or design mandalas, zentangles or Celtic knotwork together or side by side.
- Throw pots on a wheel – this literally requires you to find your center, as you stop the clay flying round the wheel and bring it under control.
- Listen to gentle, slow music and move expressively to it.
- Watch candles or a fire flicker, share poetry, prayer, stories or songs.
- Cook something slow, relaxing, soothing like kneading bread, baking a cake or a stew.
- Take a walk in nature engaging imaginatively with what you discover.

Celebration

As we discussed earlier, celebration is a key element of creativity. Both celebrating each other's work, but also creating things to celebrate certain events – Christmas, birthdays and other seasonal celebrations.

Many of the mothers I spoke to get immense satisfaction from celebrating the turning of the seasons, the beauty of nature, and the special days in their family through their creativity. They spoke with glowing eyes of decorating their homes, making gifts by hand, creating nature table tableaux and cooking celebratory foods. This is one of the ways our creativity has traditionally united our individual lives with the natural world and our spiritual beliefs, and it is a very effective way of making precious family traditions and memories which will last a life time.

It can also feel like an immense pressure if this is not your sort of thing, if you are adding it to an already bloated to-do list or you are expecting the end result to look like something from Martha Stewart. Be sure to hold your intention at the center of celebratory activities – **how** you do these activities is so much more important than **what** the end result is like.

- Decorate the house together for festivities.
- Make gifts together for the special people in your life.
- Have a seasonal nature table or altar space.
- Use your art work to make greetings cards for family's birthdays and Christmas.
- Create a family blog or a blog for each member of the family according to their interests and share your work on it – and find like-minded people to appreciate it.
- Have a family stall at a local art and craft show or outside your home.
- Display everyone's art work (including your own) and do regular changes of work.
- Keep folders or boxes where all their creative work can be archived.
- Encourage your children to keep scrapbooks to record their passions and creations.
- Get your children to create their own play or dance show.
- Organize a family or community talent show.
- Use your family art work as screen savers on phones and computers.

Making sure that everyone's work is seen and appreciated is great for self-esteem, and helps the artist in us reflect on our own work, what we like and what we will do differently next time. Be sure to be fair if you have more than one child that each child gets fair showing of their work, and each person's work is appreciated according to their developmental abilities.

Tales from the home front
My daughters (ages 10 and 8) and I have a business (Monkey Chi Monkey Do) together where we make things together, and sell them at artisan fairs and online. It's amazing because I get to use my past communication experiences to light our business. Our purpose is to inspire others to be more creative and to disconnect from technology to

create something beautiful, in full presence with someone they love.

*My vision of being a working mother **including** my children, is appearing before my very eyes and I feel deeply blessed and grateful. I created Monkey Chi Monkey Do as a creative outlet to show my children that if we create beauty in the world, we can live a meaningful life by contributing to society and generate money too.*

Although I'd welcome more time for my own artistic expression, right now my personal creativity is channeled through the things we make together which is lots of fun.

*I had to find a way to create with my children, as my husband works in civil service and works very long hours with only a few days off a month. If I'm going to make something or paint, it's going to have to be **with** them, often with my young son on my hip, or it will just never happen. I've had to let go of the idea of "perfect" art, and embrace the beauty in our collaborations, honoring their young talents and abilities.*

My children are my mentors. I used to watch my daughters play when they were really little, and the intensity and belief they activated through their imaginations helped me to reignite my own imagination and creativity. They were 100% fully present and engaged in their play, and this made me realize how important it is for me as a mother to devote times each week to give them my 100% undivided attention — without distraction.

Becky Jaine

Creating about – and for – our children

Many parents find that their children become their muses and inspire them to create all sorts of magic: tree-houses, patchwork quilts, homemade dresses and cute bedroom murals. We begin to see traces of them everywhere in our work, as the things they say or do inspire us. My husband's photography really took off since having our children, and I often find myself choosing to paint or write about my children, trying to capture their incessant changing beings, and find a still point which my mother heart can hold and cherish.

Projects to create about your children include:

- A blog.
- A journal of all the things they say and do that you want to keep and cherish.
- Hand or foot prints in paint, plaster or clay.
- A quilt or rag rug made from their old clothes.
- A recipe book filled with their favorite childhood dishes.
- Photographs – to hang on your walls or fill albums with.
- Paintings and drawings.
- Collages using bits from their favorite drawings.

And finally, there is something very close to our mother hearts in creating something to give to our children. With the cheapness of mass-produced toys and clothing, the time and material cost often make little economic sense. But the sense of truly giving something precious of yourself to your child is priceless, and most things that we make for our children will, regardless of externally judged quality, become treasured objects.

I wish you love, joy, celebration (and not too much mess!) as you grow in creativity together as a family.

Reflections

Before you start thinking "Oh I really ought to do more creative stuff with my kids, I never do any of the things in those lists." Stop. Think over the past week/month/year whatever feels right to you. Write down each of the headings I listed above, and under them list all the things that you have done together as a family that fits under each of them. Really soak up just how much wonder your kids get from you already. You are wonderful. You are enough!

Now, if would you like to incorporate more creativity into your family life, what is it that you'd like to try?

What is it that is stopping you – do you need more ideas, support, to do it outside, or with another mother?

Creative exercise
Self-portrait of myself as heart of the family

Often as mothers we leave ourselves out of the picture, metaphorically and literally. Look through your photos of your family for the past year. Notice your feelings as you see how your children grow and change, or the cute things that they were wearing, the funny faces they made, the places you went to that you would have forgotten otherwise.

Now, look again, how many photographs do *you* appear in? Look at these. What feelings emerge? Are you seeing yourself as you would view another person, in relationship to your children and the event, or are you focusing on your bad hair/double chin/scruffy sweater/bags under your eyes?

Now go and find a picture you treasure from your childhood. Chances are it includes one of your parents or grandparents. We love to see ourselves in relationship to others.

As mothers we tend to keep out of the picture. We have been so programmed by our culture that we do not look good enough, that we lurk in the background, behind the lens rather than star in our family alongside the children that we adore.

So your task for today is to get a picture of yourself with your children – get someone else to take it, hold the camera facing yourselves, or set up the self-timer. Smile. Look with love at your children. Make a funny face. And then print it out, use it as your screen saver, share it on your blog. See yourself, there in the heart of your family. Your kids will treasure it. You will treasure it.

Chapter 26

It All Comes Together

*A woman in harmony with her spirit is like a river flowing.
She goes where she will without pretense and arrives at her desti-
nation prepared to be herself, and only herself.*
Maya Angelou

*It's always our own self we find at the end of the journey. The sooner
we face that self, the better.*
Ella Maillart

There are moments where it all just seems to come together.
These can be isolated moments during creativity, or larger
moments when all the elements in your life suddenly seem to be
working in harmony.

It is as though you are suddenly, after years of searching the
airwaves for a radio channel you would like to listen to, living
your life to third-rate country music and twenty-four-hour news
stations, and lots of static and white noise in between, suddenly
you hit a point on the dial and there you have it: "You FM"! You
had no idea you were so close, and then there it is: all-singing, all-
dancing, totally, perfectly you. And then you come around the
corner, the interference starts, you twiddle the knob, and it's
gone, all you can hear is fizzing and popping. This is how it is on
the Creative Rainbow Mother path! You spend time setting up a
work space, the kids are needing you slightly less, you start
working on a great idea, and then the kids get sick, or you get
busy with other commitments, or you get nervous about how it's
turning out, and you "lose" it.

Right now it has all come together. I feel good in my body, my
kids are getting on, eating and sleeping, my painting is flying, I

have found my style in clothes after what seems like a lifetime of searching, I am writing the book I have always wanted to write. But a week ago the Crazy Woman was with me and the world was a dark inhospitable place where nothing felt right, the children were bickering, I was too fat and my book was really pants.

Bringing up children is full of mundane, repetitive work. We can lose track of the big picture, just as when we are creating we get tired of the seeming repetitions – the layers of oil paint, row upon row of knitting, editing page after page of the book – we cannot see why we started, or what it looks like – we feel lost, despairing, and like we just want to abandon the whole project, or do a half-assed job. Only when it is finished can we stand back and wonder at our work – at its complexity. Even when we were engaged in making it, even though we were there every step of the way, we had no idea really what was being created, we had a vague picture, but no pattern, just a few skills and rules and improvisations...and suddenly, there it is, the finished jumper or patchwork quilt, a symphony, a book, a precious child who has grown into a wonderful fully-fledged adult.

And it is then that we realize that perhaps we weren't so alone after all, and perhaps we knew more than we thought, perhaps we really weren't in control and that other unseen forces were working with, and not against, us all the time. We were weaving magic, though we were barely aware of it at the time, and that every time we were freaked out, every time we tried to control it, we were not letting the creation become itself, but were instead making it in our own small vision, rather than the expansiveness of limitless possibilities and potential.

And I realize as I come to the end of this all-encompassing project, that the key to it all, to health and happiness is as simple as it is hard: maintaining connection. With our bodies, our children, our partners, our creative source. What that connection looks and feels like is up to each of us. This is what we bring ourselves back to again and again as we walk the Rainbow Way: reflecting on our connections, and altering our course so that they are optimized. And often that requires that we cut back and **do** less, and simply **be** more. Or in the exquisite words of Persian poet, **Hafiz**:

> *Just sit there right now*
> *Don't do a thing*
> *Just rest.*
> *For your separation from God,*
> *From love,*
> *Is the hardest work in the world.*

I set out to write a practical book to help women with the challenge of fitting creativity into motherhood. I intended to write a very down-to-earth book. But what emerged was something deeper and more complex than I had ever previously envisaged. And it took me on the journey with it, shaping me every step of the way. It is a powerful path, this Rainbow Way! I had intended to tell you how to find more time for your crochet between the school run and making dinner. I was not anticipating the fact that a woman's soul journey is integral to the creative journey: any woman who embarks wholeheartedly on one, often unwittingly embarks on the other. Our spiritual, creative, erotic and personal development is all deeply interlinked. And from them, the roots of deep healing and social change are born almost unbidden.

It was only on reflection that I realized that the urgency of my need to write, finding the courage to paint, claiming the time to create was much, much more than just doing art: creativity has become my spiritual practice, my healing, and it has a profound effect on the people who come in contact with me too.

This is the crux of being a Creative Rainbow Mama. It is more than how many jumpers you have knitted, or having an exhibition in a fancy gallery, or a bookshelf of your own books. It is about the act of living authentically whilst honoring your mother self and creative self. About saying yes to life, every part of your life, and finding how to weave them all together.

I love what Amanda Oakes says in *Zen and the Art of Being a Work-at-Home Mama*:

> *Sometimes we look at life, our families and friends, self-care, our business, the things on our to-do list…as being a thousand different pieces, a thousand different seeded pots to water and tend to, when in fact, our life is one big garden. Everything we do, no matter what area we hope to be focusing on at the time, is feeding all of it. Any time you spend in the garden, regardless of what area you are in, it feeds everything else. It is nourishing and blessing all other parts of the garden.*

When we have the courage to claim space for ourselves. When we risk creativity. When we relish our sensuality. When we honor our lives and their experiences as valuable. When we create from a female body, expressing ourselves in a woman's voice, using a woman's language. We begin to bloom.

When we see our mothering as providing rich fodder for our creative spirits. When we can translate the experience through words and images. When our creative selves and mothering selves are no longer kept separate, but each nourish the other, rather than compete for our souls. Then we flourish. Then we walk the Rainbow Way.

I am so grateful for our time together here.

Bright blessings on your journey. May you walk beneath rainbows!

In love,

Lucy

The Creative Mama-festo

Here are the lessons that we have learned along the way, our sacred promises that we now make to ourselves and each other.

- Being creative and being a mother are both sacred undertakings.
- It is important to be creative together.
- It is necessary to be creative alone.
- Make time, make space, find your center.
- Make friends with your cycles and womb.
- Find your permission givers and accept invitations
- Listen to your body and your intuition. Follow it.
- Nurture yourself, not just everyone else.
- Recognize your "good enough" – and learn to live it.
- Find what makes your heart sing, and do it.
- Practice daily.
- Relish your sensuality. Honor your experiences.
- Remember that the place where magic happens almost always lies outside your comfort zone.
- Honor the lessons of the Crazy Woman.
- Always be a student to the process...never stop learning or trying new things.
- Know that you are never alone – find allies, accept support and express gratitude to those who support you.
- Share the love – mentor, support others and share your gifts.
- Keep on creating your story.

Reflections

As we come to the end of our time together, think on these questions, and write them in your journal, or in an email to me: **lucy@thehappywomb.com**

Where am I now?

How far have I come since the beginning of the book?
What am I proudest of?
How has my awareness of my creative process developed?
What have I not yet dared to ask for or try?
What am I grateful for?

Contributors

Amber Greene, author, presenter in Creative Parenting, Australia.
www.parentingfuneveryday.com

Amy Vickers Evans, writer and artist, Ireland.
www.mamadynamite.com

Becky Jaine, writer, artist and creative enthusiast, USA.
www.beckyjaine.com

Christiane Northrup, M.D., ob/gyn physician and author of the New York Times bestsellers: *Women's Bodies, Women's Wisdom* and *The Wisdom of Menopause*.
www.drnorthrup.com

Elizabeth MacKenzie, artist and sessional instructor at Emily Carr University (Vancouver), Canada.
www.blogs.eciad.ca/elizabethmackenzie

Elizabeth Palmer, freelance gardener, historical costume and jewelry maker, UK.

Emily Rainsford Ryan, painter, Ireland.
www.thenest.ie

Erin Darcy, writer and watercolor artist, Ireland.
www.starvingartistink.com

Francesca Prior, artist, poet, teacher in creative arts, UK.

Grainne McCloskey, community organizer.
www.thebiglunch.co.uk

Hannah O'Hara, writer. UK.
www.parentingwild.wordpress.com

Heather Stritzke, mother of two, USA.

Indigo Bacal, inspirational mentor of feminine embodiment, intuitive guide, and founder of the WILDE Tribe, USA.
www.indigobacal.com

Isabel Healy, writer and fabric artist, France.

Jennifer Louden, bestselling author of six books on self-care and wisdom, coach, co-founder of Teach Now program, USA.

www.jenniferlouden.com

Joanna O'Sullivan, educator, writer and painter, Ireland.

www.musingsofahostagemother.blogspot.ie

Jools Gilson, broadcaster, writer and choreographer, Ireland.

Julie Daley, teacher, writer, and coach, explorer of the sacred feminine, 5Rhythms dancer and photographer, USA.

www.unabashedlyfemale.com

Karien van Ditzhuijzen, author on food, parenting and stories for children, originally Dutch:

www.kamel-mail.blogspot.sg

Laura Angel, maker of Waldorf dolls, Ireland.

www.nestledunderrainbows.blogspot.com

Laura Parrish, artist and homeschooler, USA.

Leigh Millar, artist and crafter, Ireland.

Leonie Dawson, business and life mentor, artist, entrepreneur, philanthropist and self-help author, Australia.

www.leoniedawson.com

Lisa Dieken, intuitive spiritual guide, author, creativity coach and artist, USA.

www.wildcreativeheart.com

Lisa Healy, writer, Ireland.

www.mama.ie

Lorian Rea, herbalist, nature artist and home-schooler, USA.

www.homeschoolingsteps.com

Lynn V. Andrews, teacher, shaman, member of The Sisterhood of the Shields and international bestselling author the Medicine Woman series of nineteen books.

www.lynnandrews.com

Mary Tighe, aromatherapist, home-schooler and childbirth educator, Ireland.

www.birthingmamas.ie

Mary Trunk filmmaker of *Lost In Living*, a documentary film about four artist mothers, USA.

www.maandpafilms.com/lostinliving

Marybeth Bonfiglio, word alchemist, screen writer and creative mentor, USA.

www.marybethbonfiglio.squarespace.com

Michelle Millichip, technology illuminator, jewelry designer and quilter, New Zealand.

www.artisantopia.com

Monica, writer and photographer, UK.

www.bohemiantwilight.blogspot.com

Pam England, author, midwife and founder of *Birthing from Within*, an innovative, holistic approach to childbirth, USA.

www.birthingfromwithin.com

Paula Cleary, doula, writer, home-schooler and birth blogger, UK.

www.gowiththeflowdoula.co.uk

Rachael, writer and poet, USA.

www.variegatedlife.com

Sally M. Reis, Professor and Teaching Fellow in Educational Psychology at the University of Connecticut. Author of 14 books, USA.

www.education.uconn.edu

Sylda Dwyer, writer, Ireland.

www.mindthebaby.ie

Tessa Rubbra, potter, UK.

Tracy Evans, performance maker, researcher, creative facilitator, Wales.

Wendy Cook, visual artist, founder /facilitator of Mighty Girl Art empowerment camp, USA.

www.mightygirlart.blogspot.com

Permissions

The author has abided by fair use policy in the quotations reproduced in this book. All quotations and ideas have been referenced to the best of the author's ability. Express permission has been given by the original authors to reproduce the extended quotations used in this book. If you feel that your words or work have not been fairly acknowledged, do not hesitate to contact the publishers and this will be rectified in future editions.

Extract, Ch 6, reprinted with permission from Women's Bodies, Women's Wisdom copyright 2010, pages 519-520, by Christiane Northrup, M.D., ob/gyn physician and author of the New York Times bestsellers: **Women's Bodies, Women's Wisdom** *and* **The Wisdom of Menopause***.*

Resources

This is a collection of resources referred to in the text, and others which have inspired and supported me on my journey of creative discovery. I have attempted to classify them, but in truth many of the titles belong in many of the categories. Where possible I have listed them under a category analogous with where they were mentioned in this book.

Books

Creativity

Allen, Pat B. *Art is a Spiritual Path*. Shambhala, 2005.

Allen, Pat B. *Art is a Way of Knowing: A guide to self-knowledge and spiritual fulfillment through creativity*. Shambhala, 1995.

Baym, Nina. *The Norton Anthology of American Literature 1914-* W. W. Norton & Co., 1998.

Bowley, Flora. *Brave Intuitive Painting-Let Go, Be Bold, Unfold!: Techniques for Uncovering Your Own Unique Painting Style*. Quarry Books, 2012.

Cameron, Julia. *The Artist's Way A Course in Discovering and Recovering Your Creative Self*. Pan, 1992.

Csikszentmihaly, Mihaly. *Flow: The Psychology of Optimal Experience*. Rider, 2002.

England, Pam and Rob Horowitz. *Birthing from Within: An Extra-Ordinary Guide to Childbirth Preparation*. Souvenir Press, 2007.

Freeman Zachary, Rice. *Living the Creative Life: Ideas and Inspiration from Working Artists*. North Light Books, 2007.

Goldberg, Natalie. *Writing Down the Bones: Freeing the Writer Within*. Shambhala, 2005.

Johnson, Robert, A. *Inner Work: Using Dreams & Active Imagination for Personal Growth*. HarperSanFrancisco, 2001.

Lammot, Anne. *Bird by Bird: Some Instructions on Writing and Life*. Bantam Doubleday Dell, 2007.

Mason Miller, Christine. *Desire to Inspire: Using Creative Passion to Transform the World*. North Light Books, 2012.

Mountain Dreamer, Oriah. *The Invitation*. Element, 2003.

Mountain Dreamer, Oriah. *What We Ache For: Creativity and the Unfolding of Your Soul*. HarperCollins, 2005.

Phaidon. *The Art Book*. Phaidon Press Ltd, 1997.

Pressfield, Steven and Shawn Coyne. *The War of Art: Break Through the Blocks and Win Your Inner Creative Battles*. Black Irish Entertainment, 2012.

SARK. *Inspiration Sandwich: Stories to Inspire Our Creative Freedom*. Celestial Arts, 1992.

Tan, Amy. *The Opposite of Fate – A Book of Musings*. Harper Perennial, 2004.

Nurturing a Family Culture of Creativity

Baldwin Dancy, Rahima. *You Are Your Child's First Teacher: Encouraging Your Child's Natural Development from Birth to Age Six*. Celestial Arts, 1988.

Blake Soule, Amanda and Stephen Soule. *The Rhythm of Family: Discovering a Sense of Wonder through the Seasons*. Trumpeter, 2011.

Blake Soule, Amanda. *The Creative Family: How to Encourage Imagination and Nurture Family Connections*. Trumpeter, 2008.

Capacchione, Lucia. *The Creative Journal for Parents: A Guide to Unlocking Your Natural Parenting Wisdom*. Shambhala, 2000.

Carey, Diana and Judy Large. *Family, Festivals and Food: guide to seasonal celebration*. Hawthorn Press, 1998.

Danks, Fiona and Jo Schofield. *Make it Wild – 101 things to do outdoors*. Frances Lincoln; 2010.

Fincher, Susanne F. *Coloring Mandalas 1, For Insight, Healing, and Self-Expression*. Shambhala, 2000.

Striker, Susan and Edward Kimmel, *The Anti-Coloring Book: Creative Activities for Ages 6 and Up*. Scholastic, 2007.

Winnicott, D.W. *Home Is Where We Start From: Essays by a*

Psychoanalyst. Penguin, 1990.

Winnicott, D.W. "Transitional Objects and Transitional Phenomena: A Study of the First Not-Me Possession." The International Journal of Psychoanalysis, Vol. 34, 1953.

Archetypes

Frost, Seena B. *SoulCollage Evolving: An Intuitive Collage Process for Self-Discovery and Community.* Hanford Mead Publishing, 2010.

Jung, Carl G. *The Archetypes and The Collective Unconscious.* Routledge, 2001.

Jung, Carl G. and Joseph Campbell (ed.). *The Portable Jung (Portable Library)* Penguin, 1976.

Jung, Carl G. *Psychology of C.G. Jung: The Meaning and Significance of Dreams v. 2.* Sigo Press (USA), 1988.

Jung, Carl G. *Memories, Dreams, Reflections.* Fontana Press, 1995.

Myss, Caroline. *Sacred Contracts: Awakening Your Divine Potential* Bantam 2002.

Myss, Caroline. *Archetypes: Who Are You?* Hay House UK, 2013.

Pinkola Estes, Clarissa. *Women who Run with the Wolves: Contacting the Power of the Wild Woman.* Rider, 2008.

Shinoda Bolen, Jean. *Goddesses in Everywoman: Powerful Archetypes in Women's Lives.* HarperCollins, 2004.

Labyrinths

Christie, Tony. *Labyrinth Wisdom Cards.* 2012.

England, Pam. *Labyrinth of Birth: Creating a Map, Meditations and Rituals for Your Childbearing Year.* Birthing From Within Books, 2010.

Monk Kidd, Sue. *The Dance of the Dissident Daughter: A Woman's Journey from Christian Tradition to the Sacred Feminine.* HarperOne, 2007.

Simpson, Liz. *The Magic of Labyrinths: Following your Path, Finding Your Center.* Element, 2002.

Solnit, Rebecca. *Wanderlust.* Penguin, 2001.

Women's Circles

Baldwin, Christina. *Calling the Circle: The First and Future Culture.* The Windrush Press, 1989.

Deen Carnes, Robin, and Sally Craig. *Sacred Circles: A Guide To Creating Your Own Women's Spirituality Group.* HarperCollins, 1998.

Duerk, Judith. *Circle of Stones: Woman's Journey to Herself.* New World Library; 2004.

Cortlund, Yana, Barb Lucke and Donna Miller Watelet. *Mother Rising: The Blessingway Journey into Motherhood.* Celestial Arts: 2006.

Shinoda Bolen, Jean. *The Millionth Circle: How to Change Ourselves and The World — The Essential Guide to Women's Circles.* Conari Press, 1999.

Womb Wisdom

Aon Prakasha, Padma and Anaiya. *Womb Wisdom: Awakening the Creative and Forgotten Powers of the Feminine.* Inner Traditions International, 2011.

Aon Prakasha, Padma. *The Power of Shakti: 18 Pathways to Ignite the Energy of the Divine Woman.* Destiny Books, 2009.

Gray, Miranda. *Red Moon: Understanding and Using the Creative, Sexual and Spiritual Gifts of the Menstrual Cycle.* Upfront Publishing, 2009.

Gray, Miranda. *The Optimized Woman: Using Your Menstrual Cycle to Achieve Success and Fulfillment.* O Books, 2009.

Northrup, Dr Christiane. *Women's Bodies Women's Wisdom: The Complete Guide To Women's Health And Wellbeing.* Piatkus, 2009.

Pearce, Lucy H. *Moon Time: A Guide to Celebrating Your Menstrual Cycle.* Create Space, 2012.

Shuttle, Penelope and Peter Redgrove. *The Wise Wound.* Marion Boyars Publishers, 2005.

Wolf, Naomi. *Vagina: A New Biography.* Virago, 2012.

Words of Wisdom

Anderson, Sherry Ruth, and Patricia Hopkins. *The Feminine Face of God: The Unfolding of the Sacred in Women*. Bantam USA, 1995.

Andrews, Lynn V. *Jaguar Woman: the Wisdom of the Butterfly Tree*. J.P. Tarcher, 2007.

Andrews, Lynn V. *Medicine Woman*. J.P. Tarcher, 2006.

Andrews, Lynn V. *The Power Deck: Cards of Wisdom*. J.P. Tarcher, 2006.

Dawson, Goddess Leonie. *73 Lessons Every Goddess Must Know*. CreateSpace, 2011.

Duerk, Judith. *I Sit Listening to the Wind: Woman's Encounter Within Herself (Circle of Stones Series, Vol 2)*. Innisfree Press, 1993.

Gore, Ariel. *Bluebird: Women and the New Psychology of Happiness*. Farrar, Straus and Giroux, 2010.

Hafiz, translations by Daniel Ladinsky. *The Gift: Poems by Hafiz, the Great Sufi Master*. Penguin: Compass, 1999.

Johnson, Sonia. *Going out of our Minds: Metaphysics of Liberation*. Crossing Press (U.S.), 1987.

Kent, Tami-Lynn. *Wild Feminine: Finding Power, Spirit & Joy in the Female Body*. Beyond Words Publishing, 2011.

Northrup, Dr Christiane. *Mother-Daughter Wisdom: Understanding the Crucial Link Between Mothers, Daughters, and Health*. Bantam, 2006.

Plath, Sylvia. *Ariel*. Faber and Faber, 1968.

Plath, Sylvia. *The Bell Jar*. Faber and Faber, 2005.

Pope, Alexandra. *The Woman's Quest: Unfolding Women's Path of Power and Wisdom*.WildGenie.com, 2006.

SARK. *Succulent Wild Woman: Dancing with your Wonder-full Self*. Prentice Hall, 1997.

Snow, Kimberley. *Keys to the Open Gate: A Woman's Spirituality Sourcebook* . Conari Press, 1994.

Williamson, Marianne. *A Return to Love Reflections on the Principles of a "Course in Miracles"*. Thorsons, 1996.

Self-Care and Healing

Aron, Elaine N. *The Highly Sensitive Person: How to Thrive When the World Overwhelms You*. Thorsons, 1999.

Brennan, Barbara Ann. *Light Emerging: The Journey of Personal Healing*. Bantam, 1994.

Brown, Brené. *Daring Greatly: How the Courage to Be Vulnerable Transforms the Way We Live, Love, Parent, and Lead*. Penguin Portfolio, 2013.

Brown, Brené. *I Thought It Was Just Me (But It Isn't): Telling The Truth About Perfectionism, Inadequacy And Power*. J P Tarcher/Penguin Putnam, 2008.

DesMaisons, Kathleen. *Potatoes Not Prozac: Solutions for Sugar Sensitivity*. Simon & Schuster, 2008.

Kent, Caron. *Puzzled Body: New Approach to the Unconscious*. Vision Books, 1970.

Hay, Louise. L. *You Can Heal Your Life*. Hay House, 2004.

Jeffers, Susan, *Feel the Fear... and Do It Anyway*. Ballantine Books, 2006.

Judith, Anodea, *Eastern Body, Western Mind: Psychology and the Chakra System as a Path to the Self*. Celestial Arts, 2004.

Gottfried, Dr Sara. *The Hormone Cure: Reclaim Balance, Sleep, Sex Drive and Vitality Naturally with the Gottfried Protocol*. Scribner, 2013.

Louden, Jennifer. *The Woman's Comfort Book: A Self-Nurturing Guide for Restoring Balance in Your Life*. HarperOne, 2005.

Louden, Jennifer. *The Woman's Retreat Book: A Guide to Restoring, Rediscovering and Reawakening Your True Self In a Moment, An Hour or a Weekend*. HarperOne, 2005.

Pennebaker, James. *Opening Up: The Healing Power Of Expressing Emotions*. Guilford Press, 1997.

Pennebaker, James. *Writing to Heal: A guided journal for recovering from trauma & emotional upheaval*. New Harbinger Publications, 2004.

Randolph Pitman, Karly. *Overcoming Sugar Addiction: How I*

Kicked My Sugar Habit and Created a Joyful Sugar Free Life. Kindle, 2010.

Roth, Gabrielle. *Maps to Ecstasy: The Healing Power of Movement*. New World Library, 2003.

SARK. *Transformation Soup: Healing for the Splendidly Imperfect*. Simon & Schuster, 2000.

Uvnas-Moberg, Kerstin. *The Oxytocin Factor: Tapping the Hormone of Calm, Love and Healing*. Pinter and Martin, 2011.

Motherhood

Beaupre Gillespie, Becky and Hollee Schwartz Temple. *Good Enough Is the New Perfect: Finding Happiness and Success in Modern Motherhood*. Harlequin, 2011.

Cusk, Rachel. *A Life's Work: On Becoming a Mother*. Faber and Faber, 2008.

Dawson, Leonie. *Biz & Blog Star Workbook*. (free e-book) LeonieDawson.com, 2012.

Erdrich, Louise. *The Blue Jay's Dance: A Memoir of Early Motherhood*. HarperCollins, 1996.

Gore, Ariel and Bee Lavender (eds.). *Breeder: Real-Life Stories from the New Generation of Mothers*. Seal Press, 2001.

Gore, Ariel and Ellen Forney. *The Mother Trip: Hip Mama's Guide to Staying Sane in the Chaos of Motherhood*. Seal Press, 2000.

Maezen Miller, Karen. *Momma Zen: Walking the Crooked Path of Motherhood*. Trumpeter, 2007.

Oakes, Amanda. *Zen and the Art of Being a Work-at-Home Mama*. (e-book only). KindOverMatter.com, 2012.

Pearce, Lucy H. *Moods of Motherhood*. CreateSpace, 2012.

Rich, Adrienne. *Of Woman Born: Motherhood as Experience and Institution*. W. W. Norton & Co., 1996.

Steinberg, Eden (ed). *Finding Your Inner Mama: Women Reflect on the Challenges and Rewards of Motherhood*. Trumpter, 2007.

Films

Lost in Living, Mary Trunk, Ma and Pa Films, (2013)

Who Does She Think She Is? Pamela Tanner Boll, (2008)

Sylvia, Christine Jeffs, Focus Features, (2003)

Frida, Julie Taymore, Miramax/VentanaRosa, (2002)

Online references for creative mothers

Posts

Andrews, Lynn, V. Creating Bridges: Spirituality and Philosophy: Lynn Andrews and The Path of the Heart: Finding Your Power Center; The Meta Arts.com

www.themetaarts.com/2005May/lynnandrews.html

Changing Minds.org. The Good Enough Mother.

http://changingminds.org/disciplines/psychoanalysis/ concepts/good-enough_mother.htm

Daily Mail, "It's official: Women ARE grumpier than men in the mornings", 3/12/2013,

http://www.dailymail.co.uk/health/article-2292195/Its-official-Women-ARE-grumpier-men-mornings.html

Dawson, Leonie. "Words that Change Me: The Creative Rainbow Mother".

http://leoniedawson.com/words-that-change-me-the-creative-rainbow-mother/

Dawson, Leonie. "Burnout – how to recognise it, how to fix it, how to get better at it".

http://leoniedawson.com/burnout-how-to-recognise-it-how-to-fix-it-how-to-get-better-at-it/

Dawson, Leonie. "You Have Permission" –

http://leoniedawson.com/you-have-permission-the-free-affirmation-mp3-poster/

Desilets, Saida. On Tracy Lee Jones' telesummit, *The Feminine Business Model*, January 2013.

http://www.tracyleejones.com/

Esaak, Shelley. "Where Are All the Famous Women Artists? An

Open Letter to Younger Sisters". **About.com**
**http://arthistory.about.com/od/womenartists/a/where_are_
women.htm**

Ferlic, K. "Sexuality and the creative process". 2008.
http://ryuc.info/creativesexuality/sex_creative_process.htm

Gaiman, Neil. "2012 commencement address to the University of
the Arts" –
http://www.uarts.edu/neil-gaiman-keynote address

Good Enough Caring.com January 2012.
http://www.goodenoughcaring.com/writings/writing185.htm

Gore, Ariel. "Women and happiness", Psychology Today.
**http://www.psychologytoday.com/blog/women-and-
happiness/201004/can-you-be-writer-and-mother**

Halliday, Lisa. "Louise Erdrich, The Art of Fiction No.208." The
Paris Review, Winter 2012.
**http://www.theparisreview.org/interviews/6055/the-art-of-
fiction-no-208-louise-erdrich**

Leipzig, Adam. "Naomi Wolf: On Pleasure and Creativity".
Cultural Weekly, 2012.
**http://www.culturalweekly.com/naomi-wolf-on-pleasure-
and-creativity.html**

MacKenzie, Elizabeth. "Artist mother resources." *Negotiating
Doubt* (blog). 2009.
www.blogs.eciad.ca/elizabethmackenzie

National Endowment for the Arts, "Women Artists: 1990 to
2005". (1996).
http://www.nea.gov/research/Notes/96.pdf

Pearce, Lucy. "Of Earth Mothers and Creative Rainbow
Mothers." Dreaming Aloud.net. 05/2011.
**http://www.dreamingaloud.net/2011/05/of-earth-mothers-
and-creative-rainbow.html**

Pearce, Lucy. "Overcoming Perfectionism in a Culture that
Promotes it." Tiny Buddha.com, 2012.
http://tinybuddha.com/blog/overcoming-perfectionism-in-a-

culture-that-promotes-it/

Pearce, Lucy. "The Confessions of a Domesticated Wild Woman." Dreaming Aloud.net 12/28/2011 http://www.dreamingaloud.net/2011/12/confessions-of-domesticated-wild-woman.html

Perry, Susan K, "Creating in Flow", Psychology Today. 2010. http://www.psychologytoday.com/blog/creating-in-flow/201003/how-creative-flow-is-sex

Quirke, Sheila. "The 'Good Enough' Mother". Huffington Post, 05/18/2012. http://www.huffingtonpost.com/sheila-quirke/mom-enough_b_1528132.html

Randolph, Karly, "Are you Highly Sensitive and Sugar Addicted?" 10/24/2011, First, Ourselves.org http://www.firstourselves.org/highly-sensitive-person-and-sugar-sensitive/

Reis, Sally. "Toward a Theory of Creativity in Diverse Creative Women" www.neiu.edu/~ourgift/Archives/SallyReis/Creativityand Womenarticle2.htm

Shaken Parent Syndrome, "Good-Enough Parenting, Part 2: The Wonderful World of Winnicott". 2012. http://shakenparentsyndrome.com/1/post/2010/12/good-enough-parenting-part-2-the-wonderful-world-of-winnicott.html

Spillman, Robert. "Louise Erdrich: The Creative Instinct." Salon, May 1996. http://www.salon.com/1996/05/06/interview_16/

Blogs/ websites on creativity
www.dreamingaloud.net
www.studiomothers.com
www.kindovermatter.com
www.leoniedawson.com

www.soulemama.com

www.womenandart.wordpress.com

www.keithjennings.typepad.com

www.studiopardes.blogspot.ie

Transformational courses online

Allen, Erin Faith. Creative classes and retreats.
  www.dowhatyoulove.com

Bonfiglio, Marybeth. Word alchemy.
  www.Marybethbonfiglio.squarespace.com

Bowley, Flora. Painting.
  www.bloomtrue.com

Conway, Susannah. Blogging and photography.
  www.susannahconway.com

Dawson, Leonie. Creativity, women's entrepreneurship.
  www.leoniedawson.com

Desilets, Saida. Sensuality and pleasure.
  www.succulencerevolution.com

Friedman Berendt, Mara. Art and classes.
  www.newmoonvisions.com

McCloud, Shiloh Sophia. Painting and creativity.
  www.shilohsophia.com

Plett, Heather. Women's leadership and wisdom.
  www.heatherplett.com

Zydel, Chris. Painting.
  www.creativejuicesarts.com

About the Author

Lucy H. Pearce is a third-generation Creative Rainbow Mother, who has to relearn on a daily basis how to find balance and minimize the visits from her inner Crazy Woman.

She and her husband share the care of their three children, currently aged 7, 5 and 3, and live on the south-coast of Ireland.

Walking the path of the Creative Rainbow Mama is where it's at for her – trying to honor her diverse creative urges (writing, painting, teaching, community-organizing, baking, editing, world-changing...) and her need to be a hands-on, engaged mama to her three young children.

After a liberal arts degree in the UK, she trained as a teacher of English and Drama at Cambridge University, before travelling around the world with her husband-to-be. They settled in Ireland, having their first baby at home aged 25, followed by two more in only four years.

At 29 she was mother of three, with a growing career as a

freelance writer and contributing editor at a natural parenting magazine (JUNO), when she started to blog.

She now writes a number of blogs, including: **Dreaming Aloud.net** for creative mothers, named after her JUNO column; **The Happy Womb.com** – a resource hub for women's empowerment; and a baking blog **The Queen of Puddings.blogspot. com**. Her guestposts can be found on **Tiny Buddha; Rhythm of the Home; Wild Sister Magazine** and **Tree Sisters.org**.

She is the author of a number of woman-craft books: *Moon Time: a guide to celebrating your menstrual cycle; Moods of Motherhood* and *Reaching for the Moon,* which have been lauded as "life-changing" by women around the world. She has also contributed to a number of anthologies:

Note to Self: the Secret to Becoming your own Best Friend – Jo MacDonald (2012)

Musings on Mothering: About Pregnancy, Birth and Breastfeeding: an Anthology of Art, Poetry, and Prose – La Leche League GB. (2012)

Tiny Buddha's Guide to Self-Love: 40 Ways to Transform Your Inner Critic and Your Life. Conari Press (2013)

Roots: Where Food Comes From & Where It Takes Us – BlogHer/Open Road Media. (2013)

Earth Pathways Diary (2011, 2012, 2013 and 2014).

She leads powerful women's and creative workshops and teaches blogging at the prestigious Ballymaloe Cookery School. She exhibits her paintings locally and her work is available to buy as originals and greetings cards.

You can contact her by email at: **lucy@thehappywomb.com**

Index

Soul Rocks is a fresh list that takes the search for soul and spirit mainstream. Chick-lit, young adult, cult, fashionable fiction & non-fiction with a fierce twist